Builders and dreamers

In an increasingly competitive world, it is quality of thinking that gives an edge – an idea that opens new doors, a technique that solves a problem, or an insight that simply helps make sense of it all.

We work with leading authors in the fields of management and finance to bring cutting-edge thinking and best learning practice to a global market.

Under a range of leading imprints, including *Financial Times Prentice Hall*, we create world-class print publications and electronic products giving readers knowledge and understanding which can then be applied, whether studying or at work.

To find out more about our business and professional products, you can visit us at www.business-minds.com

For other Pearson Education publications, visit www.pearsoned-ema.com

# Builders and dreamers

THE MAKING AND MEANING OF MANAGEMENT

Morgen Witzel

*An imprint of* Pearson Education

London • New York • San Francisco • Toronto • Sydney • Tokyo • Singapore
Hong Kong • Cape Town • Madrid • Paris • Milan • Munich • Amsterdam

PEARSON EDUCATION LIMITED

Head Office:
Edinburgh Gate
Harlow CM20 2JE
Tel: +44 (0)1279 623623
Fax: +44 (0)1279 431059

London Office:
128 Long Acre
London WC2E 9AN
Tel: +44 (0)20 7447 2000
Fax: +44 (0)20 7240 5771
Website: www.business-minds.cotn

---

First published in Great Britain in 2002
© Pearson Education Limited 2002

The right of Morgan Witzel to be identified as Author of this Work has been asserted by him in accordance with the Copyright, Designs and Patents Act 1988.

ISBN 0 273 65437 3

*British Library Cataloguing in Publication Data*
A CIP catalogue record for this book can be obtained from the British Library.

All rights reserved; no part of this publication may be reproduced, stored in a retrieval system, or transmitted in any form or by any means, electronic, mechanical, photocopying, recording, or otherwise without either the prior written permission of the Publishers or a licence permitting restricted copying in the United Kingdom issued by the Copyright Licensing Agency Ltd, 90 Tottenham Court Road, London w1p 0lp. This book may not be lent, resold, hired out or otherwise disposed of by way of trade in any form of binding or cover other than that in which it is published, without the prior consent of the Publishers.

10 9 8 7 6 5 4 3 2 1

Typeset by Northern Phototypesetting Co. Ltd, Bolton
Printed and bound in Great Britain by Biddles Ltd
*www.biddles.co.uk*

*The Publishers policy is to use paper manufactured from sustainable forests.*

# About the author

**Morgen Witzel** was born in the USA and educated in Canada, at the University of Victoria in British Columbia. After moving to the UK in 1987 he joined London Business School, where he was first a member of the research faculty, helping to develop and teach courses on doing business in China. He has also worked with Durham University Business School and the Department of Trade and Industry. Since 1991 he has also been running his own business. He is currently the editor in chief of *Corporate Finance Review* and deputy editor of *Mastering Management Online*, a Web journal published by the *Financial Times*. His publications include the *Dictionary of Business and Management*, *How to Get an MBA*, *Doing Business in China* (with Tim Ambler) and the forthcoming *Management in Virtual Organizations*, with Malcolm Warner. He is editor of the *Biographical Dictionary of Management*, a major reference work in management history, to be published in September 2001 by Thoemmes Press. He has contributed more than three hundred articles to management reference works and journals.

# Contents

|   |   |
|---|---|
| Introduction | xi |
| Acknowledgments | xv |

## Part I: MANAGEMENT AND CIVILIZATION

| 1 | **No more heroes any more** | 3 |
|---|---|---|
|   | Why managers don't read history (and why they are wrong not to) | 9 |
|   | The consequences of ignoring the past | 18 |
|   | What is to be done | 22 |
| 2 | **Managers before management** | 24 |
|   | The many faces of management | 25 |
|   | Pyramid power | 27 |
|   | Meanwhile, in another part of the world | 30 |
|   | Two thousand years of bureaucracy | 34 |
|   | Monks and merchants: management in the Middle Ages | 36 |
|   | Management and the *samurai* | 42 |
|   | Science comes to management: the Industrial Revolution and after | 44 |
| 3 | **The management revolution** | 50 |
|   | The man and the system | 51 |
|   | The principles of efficiency | 53 |
|   | Scientific management | 60 |
|   | Bolsheviks and Mensheviks | 66 |
|   | Bring on more science | 69 |
|   | What the management revolution hoped to achieve | 70 |
|   | Is the revolution over? | 74 |

## Part II: THE PRINCIPLES OF MANAGEMENT

| | | |
|---|---|---|
| 4 | **Marketing comes full circle** | 79 |
| | The three ages of marketing | 82 |
| | Marketers before marketing | 86 |
| | Marketing in history | 99 |
| | The early history of brands | 109 |
| | Marketing in the modern age | 111 |
| | As it was in the beginning… | 113 |
| 5 | **Organizations: the building blocks of civilization** | 115 |
| | Families and partners | 118 |
| | Bureaucracies | 125 |
| | Organization and faith: the rise of the monasteries | 129 |
| | Military organization comes of age | 136 |
| | Business: the corporate hybrid form | 143 |
| | New thoughts on an old subject | 146 |
| | Where are we now? | 150 |
| 6 | **Finance: making the world go round** | 152 |
| | The evolution of money | 153 |
| | The unstopable rise of credit | 157 |
| | Commercial paper | 158 |
| | Futures | 161 |
| | Banking: the power behind business | 162 |
| | Accounting and control | 169 |
| 7 | **Roads to victory** | 178 |
| | The late arrival of strategic thinking | 179 |
| | Strategy in the classical world | 182 |
| | Eastern approaches | 184 |
| | From Machiavelli to Moltke | 191 |
| | The influence of Moltke | 199 |
| | Strategic principles reviewed | 201 |
| | Conclusions | 208 |

| | | |
|---|---|---|
| 8 | The quest for the best of all possible worlds | 210 |
| | Managing face to face | 212 |
| | The crisis of output | 220 |
| | Scientific management and labour | 222 |
| | The concern for social justice | 226 |
| | Towards personnel management | 228 |
| | Growing people with the business | 230 |
| | The whole employee | 232 |
| | Alternative approaches | 235 |
| | Conclusions | 246 |

## Part III: THE PHILOSOPHY OF MANAGEMENT

| | | |
|---|---|---|
| 9 | Ethics and identity | 251 |
| | Asking the right questions | 256 |
| | Does it pay to be ethical? | 257 |
| 10 | Leaders and servants | 260 |
| 11 | Risk and reward | 268 |
| | A finite commodity | 272 |
| 12 | The quest for knowledge | 276 |
| | Product innovation: knowledge made tangible | 277 |
| | Process innovation: knowledge in action | 281 |
| | A philosophy of learning | 283 |
| 13 | Personal postscript | 285 |
| | Index | 289 |

# Introduction

> History is the witness that testifies to the passing of time. It illuminates reality, vitalizes memory, provides guidance in daily life, and brings us tidings of antiquity
>
> *Cicero*

'History' and 'management' are not words that normally go together. Few universities or business schools teach the history of management as a subject, and few books are written about it. To most managers, the history of their profession is as unknown and unfamiliar as the dark side of the moon.

Yet the history of management is a vast subject, spanning thousands of years of human civilization, east and west. Down through the centuries, millions of men and women have taken on the tasks of organizing and running business enterprises, for their own profit and for the enrichment of their societies, peoples and nations. The builders of great enterprises have also been the dreamers of great dreams. They have opened up new frontiers, pioneered new trade and transport routes, invented the myriad new technological devices which we now take for granted, and improved the quality of our lives many times over.

Managers ought to be proud of their history. They should also consider using the past as a source of ideas and inspiration for the present and, indeed, the future. Many of today's business problems prove, on examination, not to be new; often in the past, very similar problems have been confronted and solved by a different generation of managers. It is the purpose of this book to show not only how management has evolved as a discipline, but how many of its fundamental aspects and problems are timeless. At the very least, by studying the past more closely, managers may be able to avoid re-inventing the wheel; but the past is also a treasure trove of ideas and knowledge which can be adapted and put to use today.

This book is divided into three parts. In the first part, 'Management and Civilization', Chapter 1 looks at some of the reasons behind the neglect of history in modern management, and suggests ways in which history can be put to better use. Chapter 2 provides an overview of the evolution of management through the ages down to the beginning of the twentieth century. Chapter 3 describes the process we call the 'management revolution', when a combination of Victorian scientific curiosity, an economic drive for efficiency and a genuine desire to improve the lot of working people led to a vast analysis and codification of the activities which make up management. These pioneers of management thinking did not invent management *per se*; rather, they structured it and gave it form and ideals.

In Part II, 'The Principles of Management', we look at several branches of management and show how each has changed and evolved. Marketing, organization behaviour, financial management, strategy and human resources management, functioning under other names but in essence the same, are all as old as business itself; they are fundamental building blocks on which all business activity is based. Comparing across time and across cultures, we show how the ideas of each field developed and were put into practice.

While Part II considers the disciplines of management, Part III, 'The Philosophy of Management', consists of a series of short chapters musing on some of the fundamental questions. What ethical standards are expected of a business? What is leadership? How are entrepreneurship and innovation to be harnessed? What role does culture play in business? Each of these questions, too, is as old as business itself and all have a fundamental bearing not only on the success and failure of individual businesses but also on whether our societies and civilizations stand or fall. We look at the historical lessons for each case.

In the end, history is what you choose to make of it; our only purpose in studying the past is to gather information to satisfy our personal needs. If this book demonstrates to the reader how the history of management can be mined as a source of information, of inspiration, and even of entertainment, then it will have succeeded in its purpose.

# Acknowledgements

The process of thinking, research and experience that led to this book has been a long one, and there are many people whom I should thank, far more than can be listed in this small space. I am particularly indebted to other writers who have begun, in recent years, to introduce historical scholarship into management thinking, and here I would particularly like to mention Karl Moore, David Lewis, Daniel Wren, Sasaki Tsuneo and Malcolm Warner, all of whom have been a considerable influence on me. Especial thanks to Karl Moore and David Lewis for allowing me to 'borrow' from their case-study of Pusu-ken, and similarly to Barbara and Leonard Lesko for allowing me to use their work on Ramose and the workers at Deir el-Medina.

I am grateful too to those who have supported and encouraged me to work on historical aspects of management and business. Rudi Thoemmes, Edward Brech, Tim Ambler and the late Philip Law have all influenced my thinking to some extent. To George Bickerstaffe, James Pickford and Neville Hawcock at FT *Mastering Management* I owe especial thanks for commissioning and editing the series of articles on management history that I wrote for them from 1997–99, which were the genesis of this book; and to Michael Robinson who, looking at these articles, first suggested that they could make the foundation for a book.

Finally, my thanks to everyone at FT Prentice Hall who worked on this book including Neil Maxwell and Linda Dhondy, and to Tim Moore for his title suggestions. Last of all, in the post of honour, I would like to thank Richard Stagg for his commitment to this project and for his patience and support in seeing it through.

# MANAGEMENT AND CIVILIZATION

# No more heroes any more

> We are like pygmies seated on the shoulders of giants. We can see farther than our ancestors could, and to that extent our knowledge is greater than theirs; yet without their accumulated wisdom to guide us, we would be as nothing
>
> *Bernard of Chartres*

Why are there no popular heroes of business and management?

It seems inexplicable. We live (or at least most of us do) in a capitalist society. Free markets and free enterprise have shaped not only our commerce and industry but also to a very great extent our culture. The world is what it is today, in large part because of the efforts of men and women of business. Commerce, trade, industry – call it what you will – has been every bit as important in the history of civilization as war, politics, diplomacy, religion, the arts and science: in fact, business interests have often been behind developments in these other fields. In the Middle Ages, it was businessmen who opened up the age of discovery; in the eighteenth century, it was businessmen who inaugurated the great technological advances of the Industrial Revolution. Without business, there would have been no Renaissance, no Reformation, no Enlightenment, no great Victorian age of science.

Surely it follows, then, that the men and women who led and managed the great businesses of past and present should be household names? In any other field of human activity, this would be the case.

Ask any acquaintance to name some famous explorers, and the names of Columbus and Magellan will probably be recalled without effort; those of Drake, Cabot, Vasco da Gama or Captain James Cook might also be given. Stop a passer-by in the street and ask for the names of three famous musicians, and they will usually respond with Bach, Beethoven and Mozart (or, depending on the age of the person questioned, perhaps Robbie Williams, Madonna and Elton John); many will even be able to hum a few bars of their work. Ask your fellow guests at a dinner party to name three great scientists, and Einstein, Newton and Galileo will probably be heard immediately; ask them for three famous artists, and they may name Rembrandt, Monet and Michelangelo. And so it goes on. Philosophy, literature, mathematics, sport, warfare: all our great endeavours have their heroes.

Ask the same question about great business leaders and managers, though, and blank faces are likely to be the result. Bill Gates has probably the highest profile of any business leader today, though few people know much about him and his name is usually in the news for reasons which have little to do with his real achievements. (Poor Bill: half the world sees him as some sort of techno-nerd – well, he does things with computers, doesn't he? QED – and the other half sees him as a threat to our entire society and way of life. In fact, like him or not, it is hard to deny that he is one of the most successful business leaders of our age.)

**Most people could probably name Henry Ford, partly because the brand he founded remains omnipresent**

Most people could probably name Henry Ford, partly because the brand he founded remains omnipresent (although Walter Chrysler, André Citroen and Louis Renault have slid into oblivion). A few contemporaries like Percy Barnevik and Jack Welch are admired by the *cognoscenti*, but they are not exactly household names. A few other names like Carnegie and Rockefeller survive in popular memory, largely because their charitable work did buy them a kind of immortality, but they are hardly thought of as heroes. And many other great figures of management have faded into the shadows. How many now, even in business circles, talk with admiration and respect of Richard Arkwright, Charles Schwab, William Pirrie, William Knudsen, Warren

Hastings, Robert Owen, Cosimo dei Medici, Fukuzawa Yukichi, Iwasaki Yataro, Ibuka Masaru, Henry Heinz, Li Hongzhang, Matsushita Konosuke, Shibusawa Eiichi, Arch W. Shaw, Toyoda Kichiro, Alfred P. Sloan... The list could go on and on.

Uniquely, it seems, business has no heroes, no folklore, no great myths about its past. There is no wellspring of inspiration from which today's managers can draw; no sense of tradition to help bond business people together, to give them a common culture and common basis from which to work. The economist Philip Sargant Florence once commented that capitalist societies operate in a state of near anarchy: in nearly all business sectors, there is no formal organization larger than the individual company. By the same token, there is no overall managerial culture: there are only the (often partial and incomplete, sometimes downright negative) microcultures that businesses have been able to cobble together within their own organizations.

This is an important point. Most people would agree that management is a profession; it was generally recognized as such early in the last century. But it is a singularly rootless one. Compare it with another profession, one which has some similarities with management – the practice of law. Lawyers, no matter what branch of the law they work in, have a common heritage. In the West, they can trace their codes and practices back to the Emperor Justinian's *Corpus Iuris Civilis*, to the beginnings of English common law and its interpretation by men like Sir William Blackstone, and to more recent great figures such as Oliver Wendell Holmes and Jeremy Bentham, whose practice and thought has shaped the legal world. Lawyers (mostly) are aware of and close to the processes that created today's legal environment, and they draw regularly upon the legal past in their present work.

Managers do not. Indeed, many managers are positively anti-history. I have been talking to managers and business academics about history for more than a decade now, and in my experience very few see themselves as part of an historical tradition. Some are actively prejudiced against the past and anything connected with it. (Many years ago, attempting to stave off imminent redundancy, I explained to my own manager that I needed to keep my job in order to pay my way through an MA in history. 'History?' he snorted. 'Bloody useless subject.' I was off the premises by the end of the day.) Many others feel instinctively that the past has value, but do not know how to go about extracting that value. Most managers spend their time either working in the present or trying to guess the future; they spend little if any time interpreting the past.

## TRADITION! TRADITION!

**TEVYE, IN *FIDDLER ON THE ROOF*,** is in no doubt about the importance of tradition, particularly when it means that he, the master of the house, has the final word at home. The problem is that tradition, if accepted uncritically, results in stagnation and rigidity. For this reason it has become a dirty word in management circles.

But there are two kinds of traditions, dead ones and living ones. Living traditions are ones which grow and adapt with the passage of time, nourishing and sustaining organizations and people. The livery companies of the City of London are a good example; the oldest of these companies are many centuries old, yet in the past decade new livery companies have been founded in fields such as marketing, public relations and IT services, proving that the tradition is still a living force. The challenge of keeping traditions alive is not an easy one, but the resulting value is usually more than worth the effort.

If anything, the situation is getting worse. A century ago, when management was still young in terms of its recognition as a profession (though not in its practices; see Chapter 2), the thinkers and writers on management were busily borrowing from other disciplines in order to construct their own fledgling codes. Economics, psychology, warfare, engineering and the physical sciences were all studied and their traditions in part adopted. If management did not have many heroes of its own, it could bask in the reflected radiance of those in other fields.

A hundred years on, few in the profession of management would see themselves as having much in common with psychologists, scientists or engineers, and perhaps only a very little with economists or generals. The relationship between these fields in management is rather like that between management and history; most know there is value to be gained from the study of these other fields, but few know how to go about unlocking that value. Yes, psychology continues to inform practices in marketing and human resources management, and science is important in research and development; but their impact is limited to a few functions, and there is little if any impact on the fundamentals of management, especially general management.

Of all the disciplines which influenced management in its early days as a profession, only economics regularly appears on business school curricula. Only a tiny handful of business schools teach any history (the recently launched management history programme at the UK's Open University Management School is an honourable exception). Teaching military science or physics to MBA students is unheard of. And what would today's business school deans make of the three fields cited by scientific management guru Harrington Emerson as being most influential on his work: classical music, racehorse breeding and railway surveying?

**Only a tiny handful of business schools teach any history**

Our sources of learning and knowledge are growing ever narrower; yet our need for broad learning has never been greater. In business today, we are faced with a multitude of challenges. Globalization seems all-embracing. New technology is like a tornado, rushing towards us at impossible speeds and seeming to sweep everything from its path. New models of doing business, like e-commerce, are suddenly emerging out of nowhere, forcing us to think again about how we deal with our customers, our suppliers, each other. Businesses are like wrestlers in the dark, grappling with these and other half-unseen forces, shifting their stances and changing their positions in hopes of getting a firm grip on the opposition.

But are these forces the real danger? In fact, as this book will show, great management challenges have been met before, and overcome. New markets, new technology and new business models have happened at other times and places. Instability and uncertainty have always been present wherever businesses have operated in a free market. Paul Cherington, one of the founder teachers of marketing at Harvard Business School, once argued that businesses should deliberately seek out instability and challenge, because stability can (like tradition) lead to stagnation. The greater the chaos, the greater the opportunity. So is our case today really so special?

The real challenges, it seems, are those we pose ourselves; our real foes are inside us. One of the great paradoxes of business is that an organization's people are its greatest asset, but they are also potentially its greatest liability. Lack of the necessary human qualities and knowledge is the most common cause of business failure. Our own lack of knowledge and inspiration leads to uncertainty, insecurity and fear, which in turn kill off our enthusiasm and cripple our judgement. We should be viewing today's business environment as a brave new world; instead, too often, we see it as a landscape peopled with monsters.

Great Business Challenges 1
## THE ROAD TO THE INDIES

FEW MORE CATACLYSMIC EVENTS have occurred in the history of business than the news which reached Europe in 1501, that Portuguese ships commanded by Vasco da Gama had succeeded in opening the sea road to India, giving Europe direct access to the Oriental spice trade at its source. There was utter panic in the European bourses; the price of pepper in Venice fell dramatically, and leading merchants predicted the ruin of their economy and their city.

Did it happen? No. The markets shifted, but the increasing ease of transport served to grow the overall market rather than depress prices; not only did the prices of spices remain buoyant but in succeeding decades new commodities such as tea and porcelain began increasing overall trade. The Venetian and Genoese businessmen who had dominated the trade as middlemen shifted their focus and instead became its capitalists and financiers; their banks financed many of the Portuguese, Spanish and early Dutch expeditions to the Far East. Global trade increased, and great global trading houses like the British and Dutch East India companies emerged. In the end, the resourcefulness of the leaders of business was more than a match for the change in environment.

History does not have all the answers. Heroes have their limitations and their failings. Tradition, if accepted uncritically, can choke the life out of a corporation. But the key word is *uncritically*. Study the past like any other source of knowledge, and you will find it can be a launchpad, not an anchor. The question should not be, does the past have any value, but rather, can you afford to neglect *any* source of knowledge and inspiration that might help you to compete and win?

> **Study the past like any other source of knowledge, and you will find it can be a launchpad, not an anchor**

## Why managers don't read history (and why they are wrong not to)

Although the foregoing comments can be applied to history generally, our interest here is in the history of management, and the relevance of that history to management today. Before going any further, it might be useful to look at some of the reasons why managers do not study their own history. Here are some of the most common:

- history is bunk: history is inherently valueless and no one should waste their time studying it
- everything is new: we live in a time of revolutionary change, and all the old values and traditions are being swept away, so studying history is fruitless
- if history could be used to predict the future, then it would be useful; but it cannot, and is not
- the history of management is full of immoral and unethical things, like slavery and child labour, and these are not fit subjects of study for the modern manager
- history may be of value, but managers do not have sufficient time or resources to study it properly.

## History is bunk

This phrase is famously attributed to Henry Ford. But did Ford actually believe that history has no value? In fact, Ford's argument was not with history *per se*, but with the abuses of history. Historicism, the belief that events happen inevitably according to so-called 'laws of history', is one such. Using historical precedent to justify inaction or failure to change – 'we do it this way because we've always done it this way' – is another. Ford, an engineer, designer and entrepreneur, was like many Americans of his generation a man who valued freedom and free will – essential qualities in a good manager – and regarded restrictions based solely on past precedent as anathema.

That Ford respected history is apparent from the attention he gave to his own history. Few business leaders have been so conscious of their own place in history, or done so much to secure that place. In a great American tradition of self-publicity going back to P.T. Barnum and the gun-maker 'Colonel' Sam Colt, Ford worked hard at cultivating his own image, delivering speeches and writing articles and books (helped along by a professional writer, Samuel Crowther), all attempting to sell himself as one of the greatest industrialists in history. (Aldous Huxley's satirical novel *Brave New World* promoted Ford to the status of deity, with people praying to 'Our Ford' rather than 'Our Lord'.)

The problem with 'history is bunk' is that it is an opinion, not an argument. Ask anyone to prove this statement, and they cannot. Yet the pompous statement, 'history has no relevance to the modern business', seems to greet almost every attempt to make businesspeople more aware of the past. In 1999 the *Financial Times* began a series on classic business books with a two-part serialization of Sun Tzu's *The Art of War*. A correspondent promptly denounced the 2,500-year-old work as 'patronizing and irrelevant', and concluded that he could see no use or application to his own business. How does one respond to this? In the words of Lily Tomlin, 'Information cannot argue with a closed mind.' But there are plenty of ways in which history *does* have value, as we shall see in this book.

## Great Business Challenges 2
## THE FACTORY SYSTEM

IN 1775, RICHARD ARKWRIGHT put the finishing touches to his greatest achievement, a continuous mechanical process, driven by water power, for spinning cotton yarn. Within two decades, the Arkwright factory system had been copied (legally or illegally) by dozens of manufacturers across Britain, and a former Arkwright employee had introduced the factory system into the United States. The Industrial Revolution had begun.

As a technological breakthrough, this easily rivalled the information technology revolution of the late twentieth century. As in the latter case, the consequences went far beyond mere production issues. The factory system also made for improvements in quality and lower prices to the end consumer. It led to a vast increase in trade (cotton imports into the UK from India increased tenfold in just thirty years). Famously, it also changed the social fabric of England and other countries where the system was introduced.

But the factory system was not universally adopted, even within the textile industry. Important though the system was, it did not squeeze out the smaller businesses, many of whom simply adapted their own business to suit the new environment. The literature of the period does not show that the factory system was thought of as a 'challenge' that needed to be 'overcome'; rather, it was an opportunity that was there for those who cared to use it. The factory system was a means, not an end.

## Everything is new

This is a commonly heard view, often expressed by people who are old enough to know better.

Change has become the modern business mantra. Everyone is under pressure to change, which of course leads to change for change's sake; no manager ever became a hero by leaving things as they are. So, the view that some principles of management are timeless finds little favour with managers and academics who believe that change, not continuity, is the most important aspect of modern business. The idea that they are managing processes or using modes of thinking that were invented in the Middle Ages fills them with horror: what a blow to their self-esteem, to know that they are behaving like primitive medievals! The modern business is progressive, forward think-

> **Change has become the modern business mantra**

ing, on the move! To paraphrase George Orwell, 'forward good, backward bad'!

This tendency is reinforced in management literature. Most management textbooks try to soothe the *amour-propre* (and wallets) of their readers by reassuring them that by reading this book, they are at the cutting edge of change. These books regularly begin with phrases like, 'Today, the speed of change/processes of globalization/impact of IT/importance of knowledge/quality of boardroom sandwiches is greater than ever.' Big business is new, globalization is new, technology is new, innovation is new; business is the last great frontier. Take this quote, the opening paragraph from Patrick Young and Thomas Theys's *Capital Market Revolution*:

> There is nowhere to hide from capital markets. Nobody is safe from the Capital Market Revolution. The Capital Market Revolution presents the greatest upheaval ever seen in the fabric of financial markets, and is born of, and driven by, new technology which will ultimately change the lives of every individual on the globe.[1]

This may be true; certainly the authors seem to believe it. But two points need to be made. First, the capital market revolution will change *some* things, perhaps *many* things, but it will not change *everything*. In the aftermath of the capital market revolution, the world will still be round, the sky will still be blue, and human beings will still be born, make love (and money) and die. Continuity and change nearly always go hand in hand.

And second, change itself is not new. Businesses and their managers and leaders have been confronting change since the dawn of civilization. It could even be argued that the only constant in the history of human civilization has been the omnipresence of change. The onslaught of the new is not, in itself, particularly new: change and continuity are two sides of the same coin, and cannot be separated.

## Great Business Challenges 3
## MEIJI JAPAN

IN 1878, THE MEIJI EMPEROR OF JAPAN, realizing that his country had to modernize or risk becoming a colony of the aggressive Western nation-states, overthrew the old regime of the Tokugawa shogunate and established direct personal rule. His first priority was to learn from the West and to achieve rapid modernization. There followed one of the most phenomenal periods of managerial change in history.

The leading thinkers of this movement, like the banker Shibusawa Eiichi and the academic Fukuzawa Yukichi, did not achieve their goal by scrapping Japanese culture and adopting Western methods wholesale. Instead, they searched for a fusion, seeking to adapt Western techniques and technology to a Japanese context. At businesses like Mitsubishi, Sumitomo and Mitsui, managers sought to shift their existing business organizations into a modern context, adapting rather than rebuilding. Their success was outstanding: by 1900, most Japanese firms were fully modernized, using the best of Western technology, competing in international markets and innovating new products, yet still part of the Japanese cultural heritage.

### History and prediction

In the 1970s, science fiction writer Isaac Asimov's novel *Foundation* posited a future universe in which the keys to history had been unlocked. Asimov's hero, the scientist Dr Hari Seldon, claimed to have discovered a system for calculating with mathematical precision how the future would unfold. In Seldon's system, past events and future events existed on a continuum; all that was necessary was to analyze the past fully and completely, and then the future would unfold itself like a road map.

> If the future *could* be predicted in this way, of course, then life for managers might become a lot easier

If the future *could* be predicted in this way, of course, then life for managers might become a lot easier. Unfortunately, despite the best efforts of futurists and historians for many centuries, no such system of prediction has been found. All attempts, such as those of the German philosopher Hegel in the nineteenth century, to prove that historical events were 'inevitable' or in some way predictable have failed miserably.

Why? The reason, once again, lies in ourselves. As human beings, we have free wills and are capable of making free choices; and this includes the freedom to make wrong decisions. If we all behaved rationally all the time, then it might be possible to devise some sort of calculus that would show how we would behave in any given situation. Such systems can show how we *ought* to behave, but they cannot predict with any confidence how we *will* behave because, at any given moment, we are quite capable of having a rush of blood to the head and doing something that is illogical, ill-considered or just plain wrong. And we do not yet have a system for predicting illogical action. (To do so would require an illogical system, which, by definition, would not work.) So, human agency creates a discontinuity between past and future. Asimov knew this, too: *Foundation* and its sequels are in fact nicely ambivalent, with human beings acting illogically so as to break the chain of predicted events.

This problem affects most attempts at mathematical or linear forecasting. Economic forecasters, for example, can usually predict with some certainty how the economy *ought* to behave. But they cannot predict how it will behave, because they cannot predict how we, as individuals and *en masse*, will spend or earn our money at any given point in time. The best they can do is provide approximations, usually with suitable margins for error; and even these go wrong when, for example, we all rush out and buy dotcom shares.

So the question is actually quite logical: 'if the past cannot be used to predict the future, then what good is it?'

This is where it gets complicated. Yes, it is impossible to *predict* the future by reference to the past, as every good historian knows; but equally, a knowledge of the past is essential if we are to *understand* the future. History's inability to predict the past is now widely accepted. Futurists no longer aim for hard predictions of what will happen; rather, they build on past experience to construct alternative versions of what might happen.

Let us take a simple example of the relationship between past and future. I am driving my car down a highway when I see a 'dangerous bend' sign ahead. That sign gives me some information, but not much. How dangerous is the bend? Is it dangerous because it is very sharp, or because I might meet oncoming traffic in the middle of the road? Do I need to slow down, and if so by how much? If I have never driven the road before, I will not know the answers to these questions. But if I am familiar with the road, the chances are that I will know the answers to most or even all of them; I know that I have to slow down to about 40 mph, as the bend is quite sharp. I cannot predict with certainty that I will not have an accident, but I know that if I rely on my own experience and behave appropriately, I should be able to avoid it.

Now let us take a somewhat more complex example. Twice in recent years, financial markets have boomed and then busted. First, the Asia crisis saw Far Eastern stock markets rise to giddy heights, then crash through the floor and into the basement. Three years later, high-tech stocks in Europe and America did something fairly similar. In both cases, observers commented on how financial panics and crashes seem to have a wearying inevitability about them; financial markets do not seem to learn from experience, and repeat the same mistakes over and over again. Stephen Adamson, a partner in Ernst & Young who was closely involved in the restructuring of the Thai banking industry after the crash, believes a repeat performance is inevitable: 'Will it happen again? Yes. Not in Thailand, hopefully, but wherever the intoxicating and explosive cocktail of ingredients is mixed and drunk again by others.'[2]

Past experience tells us that financial bubbles will happen. It does not tell us where or when they will happen, not with certainty. The Asian crisis and the dotcom bubble were not inevitable, any more than were the South Sea Bubble in the eighteenth century or the Dutch tulip craze in the seventeenth. At any point in time, alternatives were open to the main players in the game; different decisions could have resulted in different events. Reference to past experience – their own and others – might have helped them to do so. We know this, because some players *did* avoid disaster, mainly because their experience and knowledge led them to suspect that the situation was inherently more risky

> **Past experience tells us that financial bubbles will happen. It does not tell us where or when they will happen, not with certainty**

than the rest of the market seemed to believe. Thomas Martin of the Grasshopper bank did not buy South Sea shares and likewise advised his clients not to; those who listened steered clear of the disaster. Samuel Courtauld refused to allow his firm to go into debt in the 1920s, when everyone else was gearing up to the skies, and came through the crash of 1929 relatively unscathed. Canny investors who refused to buy Tiger economy shares or dotcom stock in the late 1990s found themselves in sound positions once the dust had settled.

## The ethical view

Oddly enough, many managers are slightly ashamed of what they do. To take pride in one's accomplishments as a manager is to somehow admit complicity in all the sins which are laid at the door of business by neo-Marxist intellectuals, political economists and anti-globalization theorists. Hide yourself away in the shadows, or anti-capitalist activists will come along and spray red paint on you, or worse, Naomi Klein will come and write a book about you.

Western society has an enduring liberal guilt complex, and the fact that business has in the past been involved in evils like slavery and child labour repels many from further examination of the past: what other skeletons might be hiding in the closet? And, too, criticizing business and management has become an enduring tradition in its own right, and those who attempt an ethical defence, like the economist Milton Friedman in the 1970s, are likely to be intellectually mugged by their peers.

It is an odd sort of world, in which the things responsible for the greatest part of our prosperity are also the targets of the greatest scorn. The paradox is most obvious when one looks at the career of Karl Marx's friend, colleague and supporter, Friedrich Engels. Engels was one of the godfathers of communism; he co-wrote *The Communist Manifesto*. He was also a highly successful capitalist, a Manchester mill-owner and pillar of society. While calling for the end of capitalism, he nonetheless used its profits to support the indigent Marx and to fund his own far from simple lifestyle, which included riding to hounds with his local fox hunt and keeping two mistresses (the girls were sisters, as it happens).

You can call Engels a hypocrite: a lot of people have. Or you can respect him as a pragmatist. He had strong beliefs, and fervently hoped his dreams would be realized. In the meantime, he came to terms with the reality of living in a capitalist society and made the best of it (which in his case was quite good). Running his own business badly would not have made the capitalist system decline any more quickly. So, Engels was a good businessman and manager even while advocating the end of the system that supported him.

The point we are trying to make here is that even if the capitalist system is far from perfect, even if some of its sins have been very black indeed, it still exists. We are part of it. Not studying the system we are part of is like not reading the owner's manual of a car before driving it. Our business systems and organization also have an 'owner's manual' which we as managers should read. Understanding our history will help us to understand how these systems work.

## Lack of time and resources

I have some sympathy with this view, as managers already have quite enough to do trying to make sense of the present without having to struggle with the past. The problem is that there are no easy resources for managers to turn to. Very few people are writing management history these days, and most business schools do not teach it.

The problem needs to be addressed at an organizational level, and study of the past needs to be built into organizational knowledge management systems. Two kinds of history need to be provided. The first is general background history that will be of use in the study of markets, cultures and so on. Ask anyone who is an expert on business in China, for example, and they will tell you that a grounding in Chinese history is an essential prerequisite to entering the market. Second, companies need to pay more attention to their own history. Many companies do produce corporate histories, of course, but in general these range from pedestrian sequences of events to self-glorifying puff pieces,

**Very few people are writing management history these days, and most business schools do not teach it**

uninformative and unreliable. Few companies produce any kind of history of how the firm was managed in the past; fewer still analyze that history and provide lessons for the future.

I wait on the day when I open a corporate history and read, 'In 1956, CEO John Smith committed the company to spending $40 million on an expansion into the widget market. This was a disaster from which the company almost did not recover. There follows an examination of this problem, some reasons why it went wrong, and the lessons to be borne in mind for the future'. I may be waiting for a long time.

## The consequences of ignoring the past

The above are some of the reasons why managers fail to study history as they should. The reasons are of mixed value; some, such as lack of time and resources, are in many individual cases quite valid in their own right. But before simply accepting these reasons and shrugging our shoulders – yes, it would be nice to study history, but we can't, so there it is – we should realize the potential consequences of our failure. Divorcing ourselves from our historical context and our heritage raises in its turn a whole series of constraints and barriers. Some examples of these are as follows:

THE RE-INVENTION OF THE WHEEL

This is the most obvious consequence, and the one that is most commonly encountered; as we shall see later in this book, it has tended to be one of management's worst sins. Time and again when new problems are encountered, we waste time working out solutions from scratch, when we could have gone back and looked at how our predecessors managed in similar circumstances. To take an obvious example, today's e-commerce firms, especially the retailers, are busily developing 'new' systems in the belief that what they are doing is 'new' and unlike anything else ever done in retailing. In fact, very many of e-commerce's most perplexing problems were faced by mail-order retailers in the late nineteenth century when they first burst onto the scene; and many of the solutions developed then will apply now. By focusing so heavily on the genuinely new aspect of their operations – the technology – e-tailers have missed the chance to learn from their own heritage as retailers. Some have paid for this failure with their corporate lives, lined up against the wall of their local stock exchange and shot by angry shareholders.

## NARROWNESS OF FOCUS

As we discussed above, management is becoming increasingly divorced from the disciplines which once exerted a great influence over it, especially psychology, economics, engineering and military science. No other comparable influences have emerged and become broadly accepted. Individual writers have attempted to introduce subjects such as political science (see Antony Jay's *Management and Machiavelli*) and philosophy (see the works of Charles Handy), but with limited success; these books were and are admired, but there is little evidence that they have had much impact on the day-to-day practices of management. The loss of contact with history provides a further narrowing of focus; not only has management lost touch with its sister disciplines, but it has also lost touch with its own past. Tunnel vision – managers who focus on nothing but managing here and now – is becoming increasingly common.

## DEVIATION FROM FUNDAMENTALS

And at the same time as managers become more focused on the here and now, they are also losing touch with the fundamentals of their craft. Already in business schools, subjects such as leadership, innovation and entrepreneurship are becoming distant from the core curriculum; leadership is often not taught until managers have reached positions of seniority, as only then are they 'ready' for it, and innovation and entrepreneurship are becoming virtual ghettos, taught only in specialized elective courses. Businesses spend billions every year sending their managers away to teach them how to be creative.

So why in the name of all that is holy did these firms hire these managers in the first place, if they were not already creative? What else have managers to do *but* be creative (apart from drawing salaries and massaging the egos of their superiors, of course)? What is management about, if it is not about being innovative, entrepreneurial and a leader? Again, go back to the early twentieth century when management was first being recognized as a profession, and you will find these three features built into the core of the management concept. They are at the heart of the principles of management laid down by men like Harrington Emerson and Herbert Casson;[3] they are concepts implicit in almost everything Peter Drucker has written. For the American Henry Dennison as for the Briton Walter Puckey, managers are nothing if not leaders and guides of organizations.[4]

> **What else have managers to do *but* be creative (apart from drawing salaries and massaging the egos of their superiors, of course)?**

## ROOTLESSNESS

So what kind of organizations have we? How do we build strong and permanent businesses with no foundations? How, as Herbert Casson says we must, do we breathe life into an organization, giving it not only a heart and a brain but also a soul;[5] how do we do this if our organizations have no past?

By giving up on the past, we become intellectual refugees. Our organizations are not castles and palaces but transit camps, temporary shelters as we roam from management fad to management fad. We have no permanence; worse still, we are giving none to our employees, our suppliers or our customers. Relationships, say the gurus of today, are the key to future success; but relationships take time to develop; relationships must have a past. We need some ground on which to build.

## ISOLATION

Worst of all, perhaps, by giving up on our past we increase the distance between managers and the broad sweep of society. We are in danger of becoming like Socrates in Aristophanes's play *The Clouds*, so wrapped up in our own business that we lose touch with the world:

I have to suspend my brain and mingle the subtle essence of my mind with that air, which is of the like nature, in order to clearly penetrate the things of heaven. I should have discovered nothing, had I remained on the ground to consider from below the things that are above, for the earth by its force attracts the sap of the mind to itself. It's just the same with the watercress.

Management stands accused by many, with varying degrees of validity, of elitism; businesses are said to care only about their own profits, not about society as a whole. Many managers are starting to believe this as well: the only things that matter are the quarterly results and the share price. But this trend, if carried forward, will have terrible consequences. It is not just that this renders businesses more vulnerable to attack by those who would like to see the entire capitalist free market structure taken down; these are not the real threat. The *real* threat is that described by Tom Wolfe in his novel *Bonfire of the Vanities*, where an elite class develops which thinks it stands apart from society, the 'masters of the universe'. But society is everything; businesses are part of society, they get their customers there, they hire their employees there. Thinkers ranging from St Thomas Aquinas in the Middle Ages to Fiat's Gianni Agnelli in the 1990s have known this and made it explicit in their own thought and practice. (Perhaps not just by coincidence, both are Italians; in Italy, the relationship between business and society has always been seen as important.)

The past teaches us many things. One of them is humility. Who cannot stand before the grand sweep of history and feel small? Who cannot contemplate the career of the former telegraph operator Andrew Carnegie as he built his titanic steel corporation, or that of the barber and wigmaker Richard Arkwright as he devised the factory system that would revolutionize the Western world, or even that of more minor figures like William Ellison, the freed slave who set up as a cotton gin-maker and rose to become one of the most prominent businessmen in South Carolina *before* the American Civil War; who can read about these and other men and women and not feel dwarfed by their accomplishments? Read a few of these stories, and I guarantee the reader will come away with a proper sense of his or her own worth and place, and of how he or she fits into society. An unlooked-for consequence of studying history, this sense of proper worth is also a valuable one.

## What is to be done

Managers need to study their past. They need to respect it and be aware of the lessons it has to teach them. They must be under no illusions; the past cannot predict the future, and it is essential to understand the discontinuity that human action provides. Instead, they need to treat the past as a form of collective experience. The managerial know-how, inspiration and dreams of millions who have held managerial positions – even if they did not hold the title of manager – are locked up in the records of the past.

As in any knowledge-gathering system, priorities need to be established. The history of management is too vast for any one person to master without a lifetime's dedicated work and study. But the history of management can, like any other knowledge, be broken down into smaller fields. There is the history of one's own organization: the real history, that is, not the glossy documents emanating from the PR department. There is the history of one's industry or market: what has happened in the past, what factors caused change, what elements of continuity remain? There is the history of one's specialist function or discipline: how did marketing emerge and from where? Why did strategy become an issue for businesses? And finally, there are issues of business and society. Concepts such as business ethics, globalization and culture are not new; they have been around for many hundreds of years. How did managers deal with these before, and what lessons can be learned?

> **The history of management is too vast for any one person to master without a lifetime's dedicated work and study**

This book is a journey into management's past. We turn now to the earliest origins. Long before management was fully recognized as a profession, there were managers in business, government and religious organizations. Where these earliest heroes of management came from and how they developed is the subject of the next chapter.

*Notes to chapter 1*

1  Young, Patrick and Theys, Thomas (1999) *Capital Market Revolution*, London: Financial Times Prentice Hall.
2  Adamson, Stephen (2000) 'Thailand's party and the hangover', *Corporate Finance Review* 4(4): 13–17.
3  Emerson, Harrington (1913) *The Twelve Principles of Efficiency*, New York: The Engineering Magazine Co.; Casson, Herbert N. (1917) *Lectures on Efficiency*, Manchester: Mather & Platt.
4  Dennison, Henry (1931) *Organization Engineering*, New York: McGraw-Hill; Puckey, Walter (1945) *What is This Management?*, London: Chapman and Hall.
5  Casson, *Lectures on Efficiency*.

# 2

# Managers before management

> History may not repeat itself, but it sure does rhyme.
> *Mark Twain*

On the dusty plain to the south of Cairo stands one of the greatest structures ever erected by human hands. Built four and a half thousand years ago to serve as the tomb of the second pharaoh of the Fourth Dynasty, the great pyramid of Khufu (or Cheops) stands 146 metres high on a base 230 metres square. A marvel of engineering and design, the pyramid was built with a technology just coming out of the stone age. Copper saws and chisels were used for finishing work on site, but each of the 2.3 million limestone blocks that make up the structure was quarried using dolorite hammers and cutting tools. Each block then had to be moved from the quarry to the building site by hand, using wooden levers and rollers and with nothing for motive force beyond manual labour. The economics of the project were equally primitive: money had not yet been invented, and labour, tools and materials had to be paid for in goods.

Think about it: the pyramid-builders had stone age tools, no money economy and only their own bodies for use as power. How could they possibly have achieved this task?

Despite what they lacked, what they *did* have was an administrative hierarchy with seventeen grades of management.

## The many faces of management

We all know what a manager looks like. The distinguishing features are few but obvious: suit, laptop, mobile phone, company credit card, MBA diploma in a drawer somewhere, and enough frequent flyer points to travel to Jupiter and back (Neptune if you fly economy) but no chance of a holiday to use them up. More seriously, there are many different definitions of what or who a 'manager' is – I personally am aware of more than thirty – but for the sake of argument let us use a fairly simple one: a manager is a member of a corporation, who is tasked with planning and directing the efforts of other members of that same corporation. You can tinker with this definition if you want; the exact words matter less than the thrust of the argument. Managers are those who manage the work of other people within a corporation.

**Most people think of the corporation as it exists now: a large, usually publicly-owned private-sector business**

But what is a corporation? Again, most people think of the corporation as it exists now: a large, usually publicly-owned private-sector business enterprise trading at a profit. Most corporations are composed of a number of divisions or departments, divided functionally, geographically, by product type or by whatever principle the board of directors deems to be most efficient. This is what a corporation looks like *now*: but it was not always thus, and history suggests that it will not always be so, either.

The many faces of the corporation were first explored nearly a century ago by the American lawyer and economic historian, John Davis. By 1900, the American economy was starting to flex its muscles, and corporations were emerging as a powerful economic and social force. Many Americans, like the muck-raking journalist Ida Tarbell who wrote an influential history of Standard Oil in 1904, treated large corporations as an entirely new phenomenon and saw them as a threat to both economic competitiveness and society more generally. Davis was not so sure. He took the view that while corporations are *economic* entities in terms of how they function, the forces that create them are *social*. Indeed, he refers to corporations as 'social forms'; the appearance of the corporation is an evolutionary response to a social need. The large industrial corporation was a social response to the needs of the rapidly growing economy and society of nineteenth-century America. The country needed railroads to link its scattered settlements together and provide a sense of nationhood: Vanderbilt, James J. Hill, Jay Gould and others provided them. The railroads needed steel to build tracks and bridges: Andrew Carnegie provided it. The new internal combustion engines needed fuel: John D. Rockefeller provided it.

Did other ages with other social needs develop corporations in the same way? Davis believed they did. In the Middle Ages of Europe, religious belief was an important social need; the response of the Catholic church was to generate corporations like the great monastic orders. When new technology such as gunpowder began to make warfare more expensive and complex in the seventeenth century, military leaders like Wallenstein, Gustavus Adolphus, Maurice of Nassau and Montecuccoli began applying corporate forms to the organization of war. When the European powers began to expand overseas, the colonial corporations like the British and Dutch East India companies, the Hudson's Bay Company and the African Lakes Company, supplied a corporate form which encompassed both the governance of business and, in many cases, civil administration in newly acquired territories. Even in the modern world, says Davis, we use corporations for a variety of needs: universities, fraternities and the Loyal Order of Masons are all 'social forms' which we use to meet common needs and seek common goals.

Davis's 600-page master-work, *Corporations*, was written in the foothills of Idaho while its author was in the last stages of terminal cancer, and was published the year after his death. The book contains many gaps which have never entirely been filled in, and it was possible to argue that some of the things Davis described as corporations had no relationship to modern business corporations; perhaps the argument was not relevant after all. Then, almost a century later, Karl Moore and David Lewis produced their book *Foundations of Corporate Empire*, which not only goes much further back in time than Davis but also compares early business forms to modern corporate models. Their findings –

for example, the similarity between the business structures used in the Phoenician city of Ugarit around 1500 BC and the modern Japanese *keiretsu* – leave little room for doubt about the universality of the corporate form.

And if we accept the universality of corporations, we must also accept the universality of management. We need to look beyond the face of management that we know and recognize. Managers will have many faces; they will come in many shapes and sizes. In the past they have been scribes, priests, soldiers, slaves and freed slaves, monks, merchants and scientists. Wherever men and women have had responsibility for planning and directing the efforts of others, there has been management.

## Pyramid power

It was long thought that the pyramids were built using slave labour, with a workforce made up of criminals or captives taken by the pharaoh's armies in battle. (There is also a small school of thought which believes that the pyramids were built by little green people from outer space, but this argument can be safely set aside for the moment.[1])

But more recent evidence from the workers' camp at Giza, and even more detailed knowledge of later builders and their lives from Deir el-Medina, further south near Thebes, shows that even the 'warm bodies', the unskilled labourers who dragged the blocks of stone from the quarries and heaved them into place, were paid workers. There was also a core of skilled professionals: surveyors, draughtsmen, engineers, carpenters, quarrymen and the like, as well as the sculptors and painters who decorated the tomb chambers inside the pyramids.

All these workers had to be housed, fed and paid; more importantly, all their efforts had to be directed so that the pyramids were built correctly and to specification (or else they would fall down). All the efforts of all the workers had to have a guiding hand, to ensure that the goals set for them by the pharaoh (whose tomb, after all, this was going to be) were met. That is where the managers came in. They were not called

**If, as is sometimes said, civilization was born in the valley of the Nile, then management was born along with it**

managers then, of course – the generic term was 'scribes' – but they were managers in fact if not name. They were trained, paid professionals of high status, whose job was to oversee the workers, the materials and the production process, to undertake plans and see those plans executed, and to solve problems when things went wrong.

If, as is sometimes said, civilization was born in the valley of the Nile, then management was born along with it.

## RAMOSE

RAMOSE, SON OF AMENEMHEB, was born in the Egyptian city of Thebes near the end of the 18th Dynasty. He was educated and trained as a scribe, probably at one of the temples on the west bank of the Nile near Thebes. His competence at scribal work brought him to the attention of Paser, the vizier of Upper Egypt and head of the Egyptian civil service in the region. In the fifth year of the reign of pharaoh Ramesses II, Ramose was appointed scribe of the royal necropolis, and moved with his wife Mutemwia to the village of the tomb-workers (now known as Deir el-Medina). He spent the rest of his career at the necropolis. His role was the supervision of the workers on the tomb sites: his duties included keeping records of work completed, collecting blunt tools for recasting and weighing, and distribution of supplies, pay and rations to the workers.

The technical aspects of the work were left to foremen; Ramose had the job of controlling and reporting the project as a whole. In addition to his supervisory duties, he also reported to superiors further up the hierarchy; one of his tasks was to keep a running diary of events, making notes on stone chips and then drawing up formal reports on papyrus scrolls. A well-paid skilled professional, Ramose was a conscientious manager who put his employer's interests first.[2]

---

The Egypt of the pharaohs had a very highly-developed administrative system. The structure of this system was, unsurprisingly, pyramidal. At its head, in a position not unlike the chairman of a modern board, sat the pharaoh, who was the civil ruler, the commander of the army and the chief priest all in one. Below him came the *t3ty* (don't ask how it is pronounced), or vizier, the chief executive who interpreted the pharaoh's policy decisions and translated them into action. Below the vizier were the various departments of the administration. Egyptian administration was divided along two lines: (1) functionally, with different departments tasked with looking after the treasury, agriculture, commerce, religious affairs, mines, monument building and so on, and (2) regionally, with Egypt being split into geographic units known as nomes, each under the control of a nomarch. Each nomarch had his own staff of functional specialists, so the departmental structure was partly replicated at the regional level. The vizier also had his own department, the *h3 n t3ty* or headquarters staff, who assisted him and served as his links between the departments and the nomes.

We know all this partly from archaeological evidence but also from some texts which have survived. The earliest of these, usually known as *Duties of the Vizier*, dates probably from about 1520 BC, during the reign of the pharaoh Ahmose. The first copy was discovered some time in the nineteenth century, and its exact nature was unknown for some time; the French translator who prepared the first modern edition did not understand how hieroglyphs work, and managed the quite incredible feat of translating the entire text backwards. (The reader will be aware of many modern management textbooks which read as though they have had the same treatment.)

**By now a thousand years had passed since the Great Pyramids were built, and the administration had if anything become even more complex**

When the confusion was finally resolved, it was discovered that the document was a concise but quite detailed manual showing not only the duties of Egypt's chief executive officer, but also giving a rough outline of how the bureaucracy worked. By now a thousand years had passed since the Great Pyramids were built, and the administration had if anything become even more complex, with the temples, the army and the civil administration becoming to some extent separate administrative structures. Interestingly, too, the moving force behind the writing was probably a woman, Queen Ahhotep, the mother of the pharaoh. Ahmose was often in the field with his armies fighting against rebels and foreign invaders, and it was Ahhotep who stayed behind and did most of the work of running the country. *Duties of the Vizier* is probably her attempt to codify and set out the duties of her important executive officers. Several copies have been found, showing that it must have been a reasonably popular manual of administration.

It is important to stress that these administrators, or scribes, or managers, were not simply civil servants. Pharaoh's Egypt recognized little distinction between the private and public spheres. Virtually all commerce, agriculture, mining and manufacturing of finished goods was carried out by the government, using paid labourers. So the Egyptian department of commerce, or its equivalent, did not just oversee commerce; it actually made the commercial decisions and managed trade within Egypt and with foreign lands. The department of agriculture planned agricultural production, gave orders for the harvest and sale of finished produce, and even checked the gauge called the Nilometer, which measured the rise and fall of the river and indicated when crops should be planted and harvested.

## Meanwhile, in another part of the world

East of Egypt, across the intervening wasteland of Sinai and the Syrian desert, other civilizations were growing up. Mesopotamia, the fertile crescent of land between the Tigris and Euphrates rivers, held some of the world's richest farmlands. Its farmers could grow far more food than the population could eat, generating sizeable surpluses that could be used for trade. At the same time, the people lacked the metal they needed for tools and weapons. By 3000 BC if not earlier, the city-state of Sumeria was sending merchants as far as modern Afghanistan, trading foodstuffs and cloth for tin; and competing for trade with other merchants coming up from the south, from the valleys of the Ganges and Indus rivers where yet another civilization was springing up. As Babylon succeeded Sumer and Assyria succeeded Babylon, the trade became more far-reaching and complex. At first the trade was simple in structure; merchants went out to foreign markets, bought goods, conveyed them home and sold them in their own markets, then used the profits to buy more goods. The traders were travellers who accompanied their goods to and from the markets. But by 2000 BC, men like Pusu-ken of Ashur and his wife Lamassi were establishing international trading partnerships on a more complex scale, with permanent depots in Ashur and in Kanesh, their chief market in Anatolia.³

## PUSU-KEN

**PUSU-KEN, SON OF SUEJJA**, was a businessman based in the Assyrian city of Ashur around 1900 BC. He was primarily a trader, dealing in wheat, copper and textiles between Ashur and Kanesh. The business was a family concern, involving his wife Lamassi and their four sons. Women played a full role in business in Assyria, and Lamassi was often in charge of the Ashur business while her husband travelled to and from Kanesh; the sons managed the Kanesh business, which seems to have had a considerable number of employees. The family also developed partnerships – *naruqqum* – with other Assyrian businessmen who contributed finance to ventures managed by Pusu-ken and Lamassi. In managing a relatively large-scale business over distance with limited technology, Pusu-ken was confronted with one of the central problems of management: how to manage remotely the activities of those whose work you cannot directly supervise or control.⁴

The importance of business – and not just farmers selling their produce in the market, but large-scale business involving international trade by water and land – in the ancient Near East cannot be overestimated. By now these cultures had developed most of the apparatus of civilization, including cities, codes of law, writing and monetary economies. Complex economic structures were required to keep these empires running, feed their peoples and fight their wars. The great Code of Hammurabi, widely regarded as the first known set of laws, devotes around 20 per cent of its articles to the regulation of business. Corporate forms emerged to support these economies and meet their needs. The corporations prospered, and grew. With increasing size and complexity came the beginnings of management; business-owning families like that of Pusu-ken could not be everywhere at once, and they began entrusting their affairs to paid employees. Along with the scribes of ancient Egypt, these employees can be counted as some of the first known managers.

By 1000 BC, the centre of commercial gravity had moved west. Phoenician cities such as Tyre and Sidon, with access to the sea, set up trading networks that spanned the Mediterranean and reached out into the Atlantic. Phoenician traders bought tin from Cornwall and spices from India. The kings of Tyre and Sidon were also high priests, and their temples became mighty corporations, overseeing and regulating trade where they were not actually directly involved. As Karl Moore and David Lewis point out, these were the first multinationals, and their priests and scribes were the managerial agents of corporate empires. And, as well as goods, the Phoenicians also exported their business methods. By 500 BC, the age of Socrates and Plato, Athens was beginning to emerge as a commercial power, using business methods learned from the Phoenicians; three hundred years later, the Romans looked to Athens as a model in establishing their own commercial empires. As Moore and Lewis show, the corporate form kept evolving, from Phoenicia to Greece to Rome, but one common factor shows up along the way. Whatever the *form* of business enterprise favoured by each society, once those enterprises grew beyond a certain size, the owners needed assistance to run the business effectively. And when that need arose, they hired professionals to help them manage.[5]

> Along with the scribes of ancient Egypt, these employees can be counted as some of the first known managers

One of the great breeding grounds for international commerce has always been the spice trade. Pepper, ginger, nutmeg and other Oriental spices, as well as other products like drugs, porcelain and textiles, were being shipped from the Far East to the West in Phoenician days. The trade boomed during the Roman Empire, as economic prosperity drove demand to new heights. It boomed again in the Middle Ages as Western European governments and entrepreneurs competed with each other to control the trade. Sitting handily astride the trade routes were the Indian businessmen and shipowners who became the trade's middlemen. Ships, sometimes Chinese but more often of Indian origin, carried cargoes from the East to the ports of eastern India. Middlemen unloaded the cargoes and transhipped them across the sub-continent to avoid the long sea journey around Cape Comorin. More ships, usually of Arabic origin, carried the goods from the ports of western India to the head of the Red Sea, where they were again shipped by land the short distance to the Mediterranean ports. Alexandria, the greatest trading entrepot of the Middle East for more than a millennium, had an entire street called *Sharih al-filih*, Pepper Street, given over to the trade in this one spice.

The size and complexity of this trade – especially given the distances involved and the technology available – were astonishing, and India's middlemen grew rich. There is a dearth of evidence on business practices in India before about 300 BC, but later records show that large-scale business must have been developed in India before this. The management of the spice trade called for complex structures and, especially, considerable capital investment. By 1500 AD, India had probably the world's largest banks; the Bengali banking house of Jagat Seth, which rose to prominence in the eighteenth century, was estimated by the British politician Edmund Burke to be more powerful than the Bank of England. These great banking houses had wide-flung networks of agencies and branches; and once again, while control at the top rested in the hands of the Jagat Seth and his immediate family, the lower supervisory and administrative posts were delegated to paid managers.

## JAGAT SETH

FATEH CHAND WAS BORN AROUND 1680 IN MURSHIDABAD, BENGAL. His family were Jains, an Indian religious sect whose members often had (and still have) an involvement in banking and finance. Taking over the business of an uncle who had died childless, Fateh Chand built up a good business relationship with both the Nawab of Bengal and the Moghul emperor in Delhi. His services to the emperors were rewarded in 1723 with an emerald seal and the hereditary title of Jagat Seth (Banker to the World). Growing his business rapidly, Fateh Chand extended his network of banking branches (*kothis*) all across North India to Delhi, the imperial capital. He cultivated relationships with banking houses in other parts of India, such as the Chellabys of Surat and the Chettys of Coromandel, helping to establish a financial structure which covered all of India. In Bengal he became the pre-eminent financial power, taking control of the state's finances, mints and taxation and managing these for the government. He also developed networks with the East India Company through the latter's post at Calcutta. His son and heir later supported the East India Company against the Nawab of Bengal, and was murdered as a result; the fortunes of the house declined thereafter, and the last Jagat Seth died a pensioner of the British government in Calcutta in 1912.[6]

## Two thousand years of bureaucracy

The case of China is different again. Once more early records are patchy, though new archaeological finds are constantly adding to our store of knowledge. The age of Confucius was succeeded by the turmoil of the Warring States period, but in 221 BC Qin Shi Huangdi unified the quarreling kingdoms of China by force and proclaimed himself first emperor of China. He built the Great Wall and the Grand Canal, two of the country's enduring monuments. A harsh and despotic ruler who has sometimes been compared to Mao Zedong, he also attempted to consolidate his rule by eliminating not only political opponents but opposing philosophies and systems of thought, and in the resulting orgy of book-burning and destruction of monuments perished much of our knowledge of China before his time. But Qin's consolidation of power also had one positive element: he organized and structured the country's civil service administration.

The thinking behind this organization was provided by Qin's ideologue Han Feizi, who was the political and philosophical force behind the Qin empire. Han Feizi's conception of administration was legalistic and hierarchical. Each man in the bureaucracy had a defined set of tasks and duties; he was clearly aware of his own rank, the names and stations of those who reported to him, and the name and station of his own superior, to whom he would report. Although the senior members of the administration tended to come from the upper classes, the lower ranks were appointed on merit and paid a salary. When the Qin empire collapsed and was

**Han Feizi's conception of administration was legalistic and hierarchical**

replaced by the more tolerant Han dynasty, many of Qin's 'reforms' were swept away, but his major monuments remained: the Great Wall, the Grand Canal and the civil service.

## HAN FEIZI

HAN FEIZI WAS BORN IN NORTH CHINA AROUND 280 BC, and died in 233 BC. He was a great influence over Qin Shi Huangdi and may have been Qin's tutor. He was also the foremost exponent of the Legalist school of Chinese philosophy, and his principles exercised great influence over subsequent Chinese concepts of bureaucracy. Han developed three important principles:

- *fa*, meaning roughly 'prescriptive standards', but also with connotations of law and punishment. People should comply with *fa* so that their behaviour conforms with the public good, or be punished as a result
- *shi*, meaning 'authority' or 'power'. The exercise of *shi* is necessary to ensure compliance with *fa*; but conversely, *shi* should also be governed by the dictates of *fa* to prevent abuses of power
- *shu*, the technique of controlling bureaucracy, by comparing 'word' with 'deed' (or more generally, potential performance with the actuality)

Taken together, the three principles of *fa, shi* and *shu* provide a system of management which was the guiding force for Chinese administration for the next two millennia.

Over successive centuries the practice and structure of Chinese bureaucracy were honed and refined. Competitive examinations were introduced, reinforcing the merit system; now any peasant's boy could, in theory, rise to the highest levels of the civil service. Administrators acquired great social stature and prestige. Even Chinese religion acquired an administrative tinge; among the numerous gods of the classical Chinese pantheon can be found the gods of examinations and of payrolls. Eventually the system ossified and became ineffective; but it lasted for two thousand years, right to the end of the Manchu dynasty and the overthrow of the last emperor in 1911, and Westerners who do business in China today sometimes grumble that the system has still not changed that much, after all.

# Monks and merchants: management in the Middle Ages

Thus far, the many faces of management have been only dimly glimpsed. Lack of sources, or uncertainty over how to interpret those sources that do exist, means our knowledge tends to be patchy. We have seen individuals here and there – Ramose, Pusu-ken, Han Feizi – who we can recognize as managers, but we have only limited knowledge as to how management developed.

By the European Middle Ages, though, the situation changes. There are more and better records now, and we can see more clearly what management is becoming and who is doing it. Two new corporate forms emerged during this time which dominated management and continue to influence how we do it today. These were the large international diversified trading companies which arose chiefly in Italy in the thirteenth century, and the monastic orders, especially the Benedictines and the Cistercians.

## God's entrepreneurs

The first great corporation of the Middle Ages came about almost by accident. Somewhere around 510 AD, not far from Rome, a hermit named Benedict of Nursia who had a reputation for holiness was asked by a group of monks if he would become their abbot, the leader of their community. Benedict accepted, but found the job to be a not particularly easy one. In order to become a monk in the early sixth century, all one had to do was join a monastic community; there were no rules to speak of and no authority to obey. Benedict had an idea that one thing an abbot should do was instil discipline in his community to ensure that monks behaved appropriately and pulled together to work for their community; but when he took steps in this direction the monks, who had other ideas, attempted to poison him.

> **The first great corporation of the Middle Ages came about almost by accident**

Though he survived, the experience left him – unsurprisingly – with the conviction that monastic life needed order, structure and discipline. In 525 he set up an experimental monastic community at Monte Cassino in central Italy. To be accepted into this community, the monks had to agree to abide by the Rule of the abbey, which Benedict had written himself. The Rule of St Benedict was divided into 73 precepts, which laid out the duties of the monks. It begins with a statement of goals: monks are to dedicate their work to the glory of God. The remainder of the precepts specify how those goals should be achieved, setting not only times of work, meals, prayer and rest but also the hierarchy and chain of command within each monastery. Supreme over all was the abbot, who directed the affairs of each monastery; below him were subordinate officers such as the treasurer, and then came the general chapter of monks. The monks were to obey the orders of the abbot, but those orders had to be explained in chapter, and monks could voice their own views of the abbot's decisions.

## BENEDICT OF NURSIA

BORN IN THE TOWN OF NURSIA, CENTRAL ITALY, around 480 to a middle-class family, just a few years after the Western Roman Empire finally capitulated to its barbarian invaders, Benedict was educated in Nursia and Rome. He found his religious calling early in life, and would probably have remained a contented hermit had he not been persuaded to take over the abbacy of a nearby monastery. However, his new vocation as an administrator suited him equally well. Hard-working, tireless and above all an accomplished organizer, he made his abbey at Monte Cassino a model community in terms of both religious belief and community organization. By the time of his death around 547, he had the satisfaction of knowing that his model was fast becoming universally adopted in the Catholic world.

Benedict's monasteries did not just provide spiritual comfort. By the time of his death Italy was once more being wracked by war, as Byzantine armies led by Belisarius tried to 'liberate' Rome from its Ostrogothic overlords. Italy was devasted by conflict and famine, and local government collapsed; the monasteries were often the only social institutions left that could fill the void, providing safety and security in time of crisis. Thus in yet another way, this corporate form filled a social need. Benedict's monastery at Monte Cassino stood as a monument to him until 1944, when it was blown to rubble by the US Army Air Force.

Earlier sets of rules had been written, but none had been widely accepted. Benedict's rule, which was simple and easy to follow, was immediately successful and was promptly adopted by other monastic communities. By the time of Benedict's death there were more than thirty monasteries following his rule. By 600 AD there were hundreds across Europe, and the Benedictines had been organized into a monastic order with all monks reporting to an abbot and chapter. One weakness of the system was the lack of central control; the abbots were only nominally responsible to the head of the order, and if abuses did occur it was hard to check them. This was partly remedied by reforms based at the monastery at Cluny in central France in the eleventh century, which greatly centralized and tightened controls. In the twelfth century a rival monastic organization, the Cistercians, sprang up to rival the Benedictines (see Chapter 5), and by about 1300 the two orders, along with smaller orders of monks, canons and friars, had thousands of houses all across Europe, the Middle East and beyond; in 1300 there were monks and friars in the Mongol capital Karakorum and as far east as Peking.

The great monastic orders were corporations in all but name. As well as their religious duties, they were vast corporate enterprises; it has been estimated that by the time of the Reformation in the sixteenth century the monasteries controlled from one-quarter to one-third of all productive land in Europe. They were also involved in manufacturing and trade on a large scale. Individual houses were expected to be self-sufficient; those that ran into debt were closed down by the order's leaders as ruthlessly as any modern corporation would shut down a loss-making subsidiary. The abbots and their management teams, the treasurer, steward and so on, spent a large portion of their time making commercial decisions. In some larger monasteries, owning thousands of acres of land worked by tenants and paid employees, nearly every monk had some managerial function. Furthermore, most of the large orders including the Benedictines and Cistercians had associated women's orders as well; some nunneries rivalled their male counterparts in size and wealth, and the managerial responsibilities laid on their abbesses and officers were no less.

**The great monastic orders were corporations in all but name**

The Benedictines and Cistercians were the largest enterprises of their day, and their models of administration were widely copied. Royal courts, viewing the orders as a pool of experience into which they could tap, often appointed senior members of the orders to their own fledgling administrations, and monastic practices informed much of the development of civil administration, especially in England and France. For a few centuries, the monks and abbots of these two great corporations were the supreme exponents of management in Europe, and possibly in the world.

## For God – and profit

For the next great innovators, we once again have to thank the eastern spice trade. The western terminus of this, as already noted, was Alexandria and other ports of the Middle East. A new set of middlemen began to appear around the year 1000 in the port cities of Italy, engaged in the trade of transporting silks, spices, dyes, medicines and other eastern products to northern and western Europe. The profits made in this trade were staggering: one Venetian merchant reckoned that he could afford to lose four ships and their cargoes at sea, yet if the fifth made port safely he would still turn a profit. The canny merchants of Venice, Genoa, Ancona and Pisa ploughed their profits back into their businesses. To spread risk, they diversified into other forms of trade, such as commodities (wheat, salt), arms and armour, religious artefacts and, especially, cloth. Before long, more surplus profits were invested in mining and manufacturing, and in banking.

We know about these men – and occasionally women – from their own accounts, their diaries and letters and records of transactions they left behind. One man alone, Francesco di Marco Datini, who ran a middle-sized business with branches in Florence, Genoa, Barcelona and Avignon, left behind 150,000 letters, 500 account books, 300 deeds of partnership, 400 insurance policies and several thousand other documents including bills of lading, bills of exchange and cheques. This archive and others like it show how medieval business corporations grew and diversified; through these centuries-old pieces of parchment, we not only see how businesses were structured and managed, but we can even dimly begin to see the faces and understand the minds of these our business ancestors.

The apogee of the medieval corporate enterprise came in the middle of the fifteenth century. For several generations the Medici, a minor family of Florence, had had a prosperous trading and banking business. Now, under Cosimo dei Medici, the firm grew to be one of the largest corporate entities yet seen. Its business interests included major textile manufacturing businesses, producing both silk and woollen cloth; interests in mines, especially alum mines (alum was a scarce commodity used in the dyeing of cloth); overseas trading interests with permanent branch offices in Milan, Rome, Pisa, Venice, Avignon, Bruges, Geneva and London, and agency relationships all over Western Europe, the Middle East and North Africa; and the largest and most powerful financial services operation west of India, dealing in large-scale lending, insurance and even venture capital. At the height of their power, the Medici had business interests as far afield as Iceland and China.

At the head of this vast diversified organization stood the head of the family, Cosimo dei Medici. Cosimo was senior partner in the 'holding company', the Medici Bank, which controlled the other enterprises. At his right hand was Giovanni d'Amerigo Benci, his salaried general manager. Nearly every other division of the Medici enterprises was in the hands of a management professional. We know the names of most of them, and something about their backgrounds too. Francesco Sassetti, Simone Nori, Giovanni Ingherami and Jacapo Tanaglia, for example, were hired employees who were promoted through the ranks to management positions on the basis of their own merits. Tomasso Portinari, who ran the Bruges office, was a slightly different case in that he had some family connections with the Medici, but even he was accepted only on merit.

**At the height of their power, the Medici had business interests as far afield as Iceland and China**

## GIOVANNI D'AMERIGO BENCI

**BORN IN FLORENCE IN 1396**, Benci joined the Medici business at the age of fifteen as an office boy in the Rome branch, and worked his way up through the ranks. He became the branch's chief book-keeper around 1420; by now a trusted junior manager, he was sent to Geneva with responsibility for setting up a new branch there. Again he was a success; the Geneva branch prospered, as did a temporary branch set up in Basel during the church council there in 1433. In the following year the Medici's banking operations in Florence ran into difficulties, and Cosimo dei Medici looked around for a troubleshooter. Benci was recommended, returned to Florence and re-established the bank on a sound footing. Cosimo liked Benci's style and appointed him his general manager, a post he held for the next twenty years until his death in 1455. Described by the historian Raymond de Roover as 'a very efficient businessman with an orderly and systematic design', Benci managed the Medici companies through their greatest years of expansion and prosperity. Cosimo dei Medici was a gifted strategist with an almost uncanny sense of how the market was turning; but it is doubtful if he could have succeeded half so well without the backing of this tough professional.[7]

---

The Medici ushered in the age of the professional managers. Training and skills acquisition was now a major part of a management career, and even the younger members of the Medici family had to do apprenticeships in the business and study at one of the many *scola d'abacco* (accounting schools) which had sprung up, where they learned double-entry book-keeping and probably also some rudiments of corporate law, organization and marketing. They had to study handbooks for merchants like Francesco Balducci Pegolotti's *Practica della Mercatura*, written in the previous century, which gave guidance on how businessmen should work and operate in different cultures, and they had to learn how to use and be a part of the Medici Bank's fabulous information system, which used a system of mounted couriers and coded messages to pass market-sensitive information from all over Europe and the Mediterranean back to headquarters in Florence in a matter of days. (Information gathering and speed of response were just as important in Medici times as they are now; 'speed' of course being a relative term.)[8]

## Management and the *samurai*

In 1600, the warlord Tokugawa Ieyasu crushed his rivals at the bloody battle of Sekigahara and became *shogun*, or commander-in-chief, of the armies of Japan. Although the emperor still ruled in name, under Tokugawa and his successors, all political power centred on the *shogun*. The succeeding period, known to Japanese historians as the Tokugawa Era, lasted from 1600 to 1868 when the Meiji Emperor overthrew the last shogun and established his own cabinet government.

Those two and a half centuries were for Japan a time of great peace and prosperity. They brought to an end the era known as Sengoku Jidai, literally the 'Age of the Country at War', a century of bloodshed when marching armies tracked across the country and tens of thousands died fighting in the service of the rival warlords, or *daimyo*. In this age of violence, the most honoured figure in society was the sword-wielding warrior, the *samurai*; peasants and merchants were seen as subservient to the warrior caste.

Tokugawa suppressed the powers of the *daimyo* and their clans of followers. He allowed the *samurai* to preserve their mystique and their sense of honour: only *samurai* were allowed to wear swords, for instance, and much honour and reverence was paid to the memory of figures like Miyamoto Musashi, the legendary sword-fighter and duellist, and to the famous band known as the 'Forty-Seven Ronin', whose lives were said to embody the philosophy of *bushido*, the way of the sword. Miyamoto's *Book of Five Rings* and the *Hagakure* (Behind the Leaves) of Yamamoto Tsunetomo were texts which embodied the spirit of the age.

In reality, though, the country was at peace, and the *daimyo* and their *samurai* were without occupation. Some returned to their provinces and lived in feudal isolation off the profits of agriculture. Others, however, decided it was time to make money. Sometime in the early sixteenth century Sumitomo Rizaemon, a minor member of the Sumitomo clan, developed a new technique for refining copper and also established a profitable copper mine at Besshi, near Osaka. He received backing and funding from his clan chief, Shibata Masatomo (his son married Shibata's daughter), and the Sumitomos went on to own the Besshi mine and its associated copper business for the next two and a half centuries.

Sumitomo was perhaps the best known and most successful clan business in pre-Meiji Japan, but it was far from being the only one. *Samurai* were technically a social elite above the class of merchants, so to preserve the fiction that the former were not involved in business, agents (managers) were employed, usually junior members of the clan or others of lower social status. Servants and adopted children were commonly employed in this manner. The great Sumitomo manager Hirose Saihei, who turned the family's fortunes around in the 1860s and led it through the Meiji period to become a vast diversified company (which it remains today), was of middle-ranking status, orginally employed as a junior accountant at Besshi and promoted to the post of general manager of all the Sumitomo businesses on merit.

> ***Samurai* were technically a social elite above the class of merchants**

The role of the businessman in Japan also received a boost in the early eighteenth century when the philosopher Ishida Baigan, himself a former apprentice with the business house of Kuroyanagi in Kyoto, developed the ethical system known as *sekimon shingaku*. A synthesis of Shinto, Buddhist and Confucian ethics, Ishida's system had at its heart an appreciation of the role of the merchant and businessman as a creator of wealth and of articles of value which improve people's everyday lives. Although Ishida did not overturn the view that businesspeople were subordinate to the warrior class, he maintained that they had an honoured place in society and were part of the heavenly order of things. Ishida's philosophy became widespread, among the *samurai* as well as among the middle classes, and from thenceforth trade and industry were increasingly seen as powers for social good.

## Science comes to management: the Industrial Revolution and after

In 1767, a Lancashire barber and wigmaker, Richard Arkwright, sat down with a clockmaker named John Kay and worked out a device called a spinning frame, a powered machine that would spin cotton.[9] Moving to Nottingham, Arkwright found partners to back him and built the first successful cotton-spinning mill. But Arkwright's real inspiration was still to come. Like any good process engineer, he broke down the tasks required to produce cotton cloth into their component parts. Then, using a variety of mechanical means, some based on ideas he patented himself and others 'borrowed' from other inventors, he put together a complete mechanized system for cotton yarn production, the entire apparatus to be driven by water power. In 1775 at Cromford in Derbyshire, Arkwright built the world's first mechanized factory, and stood the world of business on its head.

The most immediate consequence was for Arkwright himself. Of only modest mechanical abilities, few other figures in history can match his skill at exploiting technology. He patented his complete factory system, which gave him a lock on the technology for six or seven years until his commercial rivals persuaded a court to declare the patent null and void; but those years gave Arkwright all the competitive advantage he needed, and thereafter by refining and improving his system he always managed to produce cloth more cheaply and efficiently than his rivals. He built his own mills, either using his own capital or bringing in partners; he also licensed the technology to others. Still others, anxious to keep up with the competition, either stole Arkwright's technology or developed their own.

> **Others, anxious to keep up with the competition, either stole Arkwright's technology or developed their own**

RICHARD ARKWRIGHT ..................................................................

RICHARD ARKWRIGHT WAS BORN IN PRESTON, LANCASHIRE, the youngest of thirteen children of a tailor. He demonstrated his entrepreneurial spirit early on, developing a prosperous barbering business and then, with less success, taking over and running a tavern. None of these occupations promised to make him rich, however, and like plenty of other ambitious young men of the time, he turned to new discoveries in science to see if something could be exploited. His success must have been beyond his wildest dreams; by the time of his death of heart disease at the age of sixty, he was one of the wealthiest men in Britain. And he had made a lot of other people rich as well.

Arkwright was an inventor and an entrepreneur. He was also an extraordinarily skilful manager. He knew how to build networks to acquire capital and tap into key markets. He had a clear understanding of how the raw cotton and textiles markets functioned. Most of all, he seems to have realized that the new factory technology gave him a priceless asset in terms of managing quality. Formerly, textiles production was managed through a putting-out system with work being done by cottage contractors; the manager could only assess quality at the end of the process and accept or reject goods as seen. The factory gave him control over the process and allowed him to quite literally 'build in' quality. It took another two centuries for Deming and Juran, two great twentieth-century quality gurus, to work out how to express this in so many words; but the concept was plainly there. The gap between practice and description of practice can take a long time to close.

........................................................................................................

The factory system was based on the division of labour, which had been recently described and analyzed in detail by Adam Smith, the professor of moral philosophy at the University of Glasgow. It required, in fact, two kinds of labour: unskilled manual labour to work the machinery, and skilled administrative labour to oversee the entire plant. (Andrew Ure, who wrote on factory management in the 1830s, thought the idea of division of labour was a red herring; what was important about the factory system, he thought, was the *combination* of labour under one roof as part of one system.) The number of administrators required for each plant was fairly small, and usually consisted of one superintendent, a varying number of deputies depending on the size of the plant, and foremen to manage smaller groups of workers employed in individual functions and processes. Unlike the Medici, who had associated trading businesses which sold their manufactured goods, Arkwright and the other mill-owners tended to contract out their sales and marketing to wholesalers and agents. The system was simple to manage, and the number of managers required was low.

Those managers, however, were a technical elite. They had to know how to manage machinery, which meant a close familiarity with all the machines and plant, and also how to manage people. Only a few men had the necessary skills to serve as a plant superintendent, and these men could usually command high wages. We see now the beginnings of a mobile group of skilled professionals who went where the best jobs were offered; one year a plant superintendent might work for Arkwright at one of his mills, the next year might see him working for Samuel Oldknow, the year after that he might join Robert Owen. As they moved around, these men diffused the skills they had learned, not only into textiles manufacturing but into different industries; by 1800, the techniques of factory management were beginning to appear in other industries.

Around this time, too, an ex-Arkwright manager emigrated to the newly-born United States of America, where he set up the first textiles factory in New England. More factories followed. In the 1840s, when Samuel Colt established his firearms factory in Connecticut, he learned from, among other sources, the mass production techniques in use in the textile business. When in the 1860s Cyrus Hall McCormick built a factory outside Chicago to make combine harvesters, Colt's operation was one of those he used for a model. When Henry Ford began making automobiles on a mass production basis, he had the experience of McCormick's business and its skilled employees to draw on. And so on, and so on.

Even more than the diffusion of mass production techniques and their management, though, Arkwright's achievement did something else: it demonstrated the practical application of science to business and management. The eighteenth-century Age of Englightenment was the great age of natural philosophy; educated men and women took a keen interest in scientific discoveries, and Britain in particular was full of more or less amateur scientists working in mechanics, chemistry, physics, optics, medicine and a variety of other fields. A belief arose that science could change the world and make it a better place. The application of science to all walks of life, including business, was argued; and after Arkwright, the proponents of science in business had an example to which they could point.[10]

> **A belief arose that science could change the world and make it a better place**

From there it was a short step to urging the adoption of science not just in terms of technology but in terms of management practice. Scientific innovation, some began to believe, could be applied not just to products but also to organizations and processes. Andrew Ure, mentioned above, sketches the outline of this idea in the introduction to his *The Philosophy of Manufactures* (1835). But the first clear statement of the possibility of management as a science was made five years later by one of Victorian Britain's most remarkable men: Charles Babbage.

## CHARLES BABBAGE

MATHEMATICIAN, UNIVERSITY PROFESSOR, INVENTOR OF THE COMPUTER, political economist, racecourse gambler and author of a long-running campaign to abolish street musicians: there were many facets to Charles Babbage. Born in Devonshire on Boxing Day 1792, he was a self-taught mathematical genius who believed that calculation and analysis could, properly applied, solve most if not all of the world's problems. His ideas for calculating machines were at first no more than advanced versions of machines which had been built and marketed as early as the sixteenth century, but his mathematical abilities soon took him into another realm. The analytical engine, which he developed in partnership with Ada, Countess of Lovelace, the daughter of Lord Byron, was a programmable computer based on mechanical rather than electric power; it could input instructions by means of punched cards, print out data, and store data in memory. Sadly, the principle was far in advance of the technical capabilities of the day, and no working model was built in Babbage's lifetime. His work was widely scorned, and he fell out of favour and died in neglect. In 1940, the British scientist Alan Turing, developing code-breaking machines to crack the German Enigma code, referred to Babbage's work and discovered that the Victorian had to all intents and purposes invented the computer. Without Babbage, the world of management today might have been a very different place.

Today, Babbage is best known as the inventor of the computer. His design for an analytical engine, though never successfully completed, anticipated the modern computer in many respects. But, like most intellectuals of his day, Babbage was a broad thinker. Functional specialisms had not really been invented then, and when inventors and scientists had a new idea they generally tended to think of the widest possible range of applications. Babbage believed that the kind of technology which went into his calculating machines was on the verge of revolutionizing the economy and society (sound familiar?). In his book *The Economy of Machinery and Manufactures*, published in 1835, he broke ground on paths that would later come to be well-trodden. Technology could be used to improve production, to sell better quality goods to consumers; improvements in quality would in turn stimulate demand. Technology could also be used to improve the lives of workers, leading to a transition from unskilled to skilled labour; Babbage foresaw that better relations between managers and workers would be required as a result.

The dominant theme of Babbage's work, however, is the need for business management – and indeed all human activities – to be carried out according to scientific principles. His calculating engines were intended to assist in the implementation of those principles; technology was not an end in itself, but a means to a higher end of greater prosperity, better incomes and living conditions for workers, and a more ordered and rational society. Like most men of his time, Babbage saw no distinction between business and society; the two were interdependent parts of a whole.

*The Economy of Machinery and Manufactures*, like Babbage's protocomputers, was far ahead of its time. Several decades were to elapse before anyone would work out how to put his ideas into practice. When they did, the result would be a revolution.

*Notes to chapter 2*
1   And besides, even if they were, who says little green people from outer space don't have a system of management?
2   Taken from Barbara Lesko, 'Rank, roles and rights', in Lesko, Leonard H.

(ed.), (1994) *Pharaoh's Workers: The Villagers of Deir el-Medina*, Ithaca, NY: Cornell University Press, 15–39. My thanks to Barbara Lesko for permission to draw on this work.

3   Karl Moore and David Lewis in their excellent *Foundations of Corporate Empire* (London: FT Prentice Hall, 2000) go into the roots of the corporation in the ancient Near East in detail, and most of this section is drawn from their work.

4   Taken from Moore and Lewis, *Foundations of Corporate Empire*, 32–33. My thanks to the authors for permission to draw on their work.

5   Moore and Lewis, *Foundations of Corporate Empire*.

6   The history of the house of Jagath Seth has yet to be comprehensively treated in English. See Morgen Witzel, 'Chand, Fateh' in Witzel, Morgen (ed.), (2001), *Biographical Dictionary of Management*, Bristol: Thoemmes Press.

7   Benci's career is described in more detail in de Roover, Raymond (1963) *The Rise and Decline of the Medici Bank*, Cambridge, MA: Harvard University Press.

8   The outstanding work on the organization of the Medici businesses remains de Roover's *The Rise and Decline of the Medici Bank*.

9   The phrase 'worked out' is used advisedly; another inventor, Thomas Highs, claimed Kay and Arkwright had stolen his design, and the legal battles and mudslinging over this continued after all three parties were dead. Wrangles over intellectual property, like so much else in management, are not new.

10  The role of innovation in the development of management thought and practice will be discussed more fully.

# 3

# The management revolution

> We have not put our trust in kings; let us not put it in natural resources, but grasp the truth that exhaustless wealth lies in the latent and as yet undeveloped capacities of individuals, of corporations, of states. Instead of oppression from the top, engendering antagonisms and strife, ambitious pressure should come from the bottom, guidance and assistance from the top
>
> *Harrington Emerson*

yOn 4 August 1870, the armies of Prussia disembarked from their trains along the river Rhine, formed into marching columns, and moved swiftly across the border into France. Brushing aside the French forces along the frontier in a series of battles, they quickly occupied the eastern provinces of Alsace and Lorraine and bottled up the main French field army in the fortress of Metz, where it was later forced to surrender. Marching west into Champagne, the Prussians encountered the French reserve army led by Emperor Napoleon III in person. This army was defeated in two days of fighting at the Battle of Gravelotte and driven northward; at Sedan, it too surrendered and the Emperor of France was led away into captivity. With few French troops left in the field to oppose them, the victorious Prussians turned southwest, marching in their long blue columns down into the valley of the river Seine to surround Paris with a ring of steel.

In just four weeks, the finest army in the world had been destroyed and France had been driven to her knees; Prussian uhlans watered their horses in the fountains at Versailles. The management revolution had begun.

## The man and the system

The architect of the Prussian victory, Field Marshal Count Helmuth von Moltke, is an unlikely hero of management. A career officer in the Prussian army, he had spent most of his career with the general staff; incredibly, apart from a short spell of service seconded to the Turkish army as a young officer, he had never commanded troops in battle until the Seven Weeks War with Austria in 1866, just a few years earlier. Nor was he the classic Prussian *junker*, jackbooted and militaristic; rather, he was a sensitive man who admired the English poets (he also married an Englishwoman, Marie Burt), enjoyed translating Byron into German, liked discussing philosophy and music, and once wrote a novel; possibly the only field marshal in history to have done so.

How did this mild-mannered officer bring down the world's foremost military power? The Prussian army was in no way superior to the French. Thanks to Alfred Krupp's factory at Essen they had good artillery, but the Prussian infantry was hopelessly outclassed by the French, armed as they were with Dreyse needle guns which had only half the range of the French Chassepot rifle. The Prussian army had almost no experience of battle, whereas the French troops and generals had been toughened in wars in Italy, North Africa and Mexico. In the end, the observers decided, Moltke had only one competitive advantage: he had a system. Superior Prussian military organization had won the day, and the armies of Europe, the French included, scrambled to imitate the victors.

> How did this mild-mannered officer bring down the world's foremost military power?

One of the observers of the conflict was a seventeen-year-old American student, Harrington Emerson. He saw both sides of the conflict – intriguingly, he does not tell us how he managed this – and later commented that he admired the Germans for their efficiency and the French for their character in equal proportions. In later years, working as consulting engineer for American railways, Emerson looked back on his experience and considered the roots of the Prussian success. Moltke, Emerson believed, had been successful because he had managed to fully integrate the 'line' – the fighting units in the field – with the 'staff' – the controlling and coordinating body immediately around the leader. The 'line and staff principle' used by Moltke to control armies could, said Emerson, be used to control business organizations as well.

It is worth looking more closely at the line and staff principle, which remained a standard topic in organization textbooks until the 1950s and was discussed in depth by authorities as eminent as Emerson, Herbert Casson and Lyndall Urwick. The idea of a functional line and an executive staff had been around for at least a century; the Prussian king Frederick the Great had been one of the first to appreciate how a staff could be used to control and direct the movements of the fighting units in the line, and he had laid the foundations for the Prussian, later German, general staff. Unfortunately, the staff along with the rest of the Prussian army became fossilized and ineffective. Staff officers had little or no training or sense of their own function, beyond a vague sense of superiority over officers of the line. Narrow, rigid thinking characterized the staff work of the day.

Poet, humanist and philosopher, Helmuth von Moltke's thinking was the opposite of narrow. As a member of the general staff, he had long been aware of that body's limitations, and when he took over as chief of the staff in 1858, he radically revamped it. Moltke did not believe wars were fought according to rigid principles. No matter what plans one develops, he said, there will always occur 'friction', a concatenation of unforeseen events that will throw that strategy off track; as he once said, 'No plan survives contact with the enemy.' The first requirement from a military organization, then, was that it had to be flexible and able to respond rapidly and effectively to change. For an army, this meant the ability to change strategies or deployment rapidly without impairing its fighting function. To achieve this required two things: (1) the line units had to be well drilled and disciplined to respond to orders, so that when orders were changed they would respond rapidly and effectively; and (2) the staff had to become a genuine coordinating body, capable of coordinating and directing the line units towards a common goal. Training for staff officers emphasized flexibility, integrated thinking and creative responses to threats and problems. Though there were few systems, there were important commonly held doctrines. The staff worked always to these common principles, with the result that officers could and did take independent action which harmonized with, rather than jeopardized, the overall plan. It is this professionalism and focus at the top level which allowed the inexperienced Prussian army to mobilize rapidly and defeat quickly the tough and experienced French army.

## HARRINGTON EMERSON

THE SON OF A PROFESSOR OF POLITICAL ECONOMY who taught at a number of European universities, Emerson grew up in Germany and Italy and took his degree in engineering from the Royal Polytechnic in Munich. After a spell teaching languages at the State University of Nebraska, he went into business as an engineer and surveyor. As a contractor for the US government, he undertook a number of important surveys, notably of submarine cable routes to Alaska and Asia for the War Department, and later of West Coast coalfields, and also prospected for gold in the Yukon. In the 1890s Emerson began a series of private consultancies with railway firms, particularly in the field of systematizing management in railway shops. He made his name with a project that reorganized the maintenance shop of the Santa Fe Railroad, which saved the railway some $1.25 million over the course of three years. Emerson's services as a consultant were in great demand for the next ten years, and he became one of consultancy's most respected figures. In 1921 he served as a member of Herbert Hoover's Commission on the Elimination of Waste in Industry, and published his final book, *The Science of Human Engineering*, a home-study course for managers which combined the features of efficiency with those of psychology. He retired in the mid-1920s.

## The principles of efficiency

In this combination of effective line units and flexible staff, Emerson thought he saw the answer to a dilemma. In the four decades following the end of the American Civil War in 1865, the United States put on one of the most astonishing spurts of growth seen in human history. Population, fed by a steady stream of immigrants from Europe, multiplied several-fold. Some of the new arrivals settled in cities, leading to rapid urban growth; others moved out to colonize the American West, leading to geographical dispersal. All these 'teeming millions', as one writer of the time put it, had to be fed and their material and social needs attended to.

The response in America was the rapid growth of large corporations, first in railways and transportation, then in steel and raw materials, and finally in machinery and manufactured goods. But American business was not used to large-scale operations, particularly not ones that were dispersed over a wide geographical area; before the Civil War, most US businesses had been small in scale and scope, easily controlled by an owner-manager. With rapid growth came serious problems of control and management. If corporations were to meet the social needs for which they had been formed, they had to be capable of delivering products of adequate quality at the time and place where they were needed. They had, in other words, to be *efficient*.

It was this problem of coordination and control in large organizations that Emerson sought to solve. He saw the achievement of efficiency as being reached through a circular process involving both the line and the staff. First and foremost, there was a requirement for information. In his own work as a management consultant, Emerson spent hundreds of hours on the shopfloor gathering data, and he advised all managers to do likewise. Once in possession of all the facts about the operation, management, could analyze these facts and look for ways of achieving efficiency. Could wastages be eliminated? Could work be rescheduled so as to cut down times? Were the right tools being used and did workers have the right skills? Were workers happy and motivated, and could they be encouraged to produce better results? When these questions had been answered and improvements to work routines decided upon, these could be communicated back through the staff to foremen and workers, who would make the necessary adjustments.

**With rapid growth came serious problems of control and management**

It sounds fairly simple, and it was intended to be. Emerson, like most men and women of his age, was looking to science for answers. Science was governed by a set of principles or natural laws; it was possible to treat management, like any other human activity, in a scientific way; and so *ipso facto* there must be scientific principles by which management could be governed. Emerson boiled these down to his famous 12 principles of efficiency, summarized below.

1. Clearly defined ideals: the organization must know what its goals are, what it stands for, and its relationship with society.
2. Common sense: the organization must be practical in its methods and outlook.
3. Competent counsel: the organization should seek wise advice, turning to external experts if it lacks the necessary staff expertise.
4. Discipline: not so much top-down discipline as internal discipline and self-discipline, with workers conforming willingly and readily to the systems in place.
5. The fair deal: workers should be treated fairly at all times, to encourage their participation in the efficiency movement.
6. Reliable, immediate and adequate records: measurement over time is important in determining if efficiency has been achieved.
7. Despatching: workflow must be scheduled in such a way that processes move smoothly.
8. Standards and schedules: the establishment of these is, as discussed above, fundamental to the achievement of efficiency.
9. Standardized conditions: workplace conditions should be standardized according to natural scientific precepts, and should evolve as new knowledge becomes available.
10. Standardized operations: likewise, operations should follow scientific principles, particularly in terms of planning and work methods.
11. Written instructions: all standards should be recorded in the form of written instructions to workers and foremen, which

detail not only the standards themselves but the methods of compliance.

12. Efficiency reward: if workers achieve efficiency, then they should be duly rewarded.[1]

This, as will be seen at a glance, is not a prescriptive recipe for how to *do* management; rather, it is more of a philosophy of how to *approach* the tasks of management. Like Moltke, Emerson understood the concept of friction and believed in flexibility. Like many management writers since, he believed there was no one best way to do management: the exact recipe would depend on circumstances, including the nature of the firm, its products and its environment. This is particularly noticeable when he comes to discuss standards. Although his 12 principles stress the need for standards, he believes that the exact nature of what those standards should be cannot be pre-determined:

**Like Moltke, Emerson understood the concept of friction and believed in flexibility**

> Staff standards are not theoretical abstractions but scientific approximations, and are evolved for the use of the line, the sole justification of standards being that they will make line work more efficient.[2]

This philosophical approach to management was widely popular. Emerson, a persuasive speaker and writer, did much to publicize the ideas of efficiency through his books and through articles in journals such as *Engineering Magazine*. He believed that efficiency was not just a good business policy but a social ideal. Like Charles Babbage (see previous chapter), whom he admired, Emerson believed that the scientific approach could change society. This view was echoed by his friend and fellow proselytizer of efficiency, Herbert N. Casson.

By anyone's standards, Casson had a bizarre career (see inset). Like Emerson, he had been exposed to a wide variety of influences and took a broad view of culture and institutions. His academic background in philosophy and theology plus his stint as a socialist had predisposed him to a search for deeper meaning. Picking up Emerson's principles, he applied them in areas such as advertising where even Emerson himself thought that the prospects for efficiency were limited. But Casson showed not only that a philosophy of management was possible, but that practical management adhering to philosophical principles could lead to commercial and competitive success, something which he demonstrated over and over in his career as a businessman and consultant.

Ideals, said Casson, were the foundation of good management. To be *efficient*, a business needed three parts: it must have hands, a brain and a soul. The hands were required to do the work, to carry out the tasks needed to reach the goal. The brain was there to provide direction, to gather information and to formulate that information into effective task management. The soul was there to provide the *raison d'etre*, the motivation, the systems of beliefs, desires and wishes that kept both brain and hands functioning. Without a motivating soul, said Casson, the company would fail; and it was one of the tasks of management to keep that soul alive.

## HERBERT N. CASSON

**B**ORN ON THE CANADIAN FRONTIER, Herbert Casson grew up among the Indians and Métis in Manitoba. After taking a degree at the University of Toronto he became a Methodist minister, but within a year had been tried and convicted of heresy and forced to leave the church. Moving to Boston to take up a job in publishing, he was so affected by the poverty he saw in the city's slums that he took up socialism, and was soon one of the country's most prominent agitators. Ten years later, the scales fell from his eyes after a short stay in a utopian commune, and he decided, in his own words, 'to see what capitalism could offer instead'. Moving to New York, he took a job as a journalist working for Joseph Pulitzer and soon became one of New York journalism's star columnists, interviewing the rich and famous, the confidant of President Grover Cleveland and hob-nobbing with the Rockefellers, Morgans and Carnegies. Turning his attention to what it was that made great men successful, he wrote *The Romance of Steel*, a highly popular book which explored the careers and lives of the great steel barons and analyzed the secrets of their managerial success.

Becoming popular now as a writer on management, he joined forces for a time with Harrington Emerson as a management consultant, but then left to join a venture attempting to apply the principles of efficiency to advertising. The venture, which established the advertising agency now known as McCann-Erickson, was a considerable success, and Casson sold his share a few years later at a price which made him a wealthy man. He moved to England just before the First

World War, intending to retire, but found that (horror!) the efficiency movement was little known in the UK. He quickly founded a publishing company and a journal, *Efficiency*, which he edited, set up a consultancy business and began writing more books. By the time of his death at 81, he had written more than 170 books which had sold half a million copies around the world.

........................................................................................................................

Casson later settled in the UK and many of his most influential books were published there. Influenced heavily by Emerson, he in turn influenced the two best British management writers before the Second World War, Oliver Sheldon and Lyndall Urwick. Sheldon was a senior manager with the chocolate makers Rowntree & Co. in York, and was involved in many of the radical management changes there under the direction of Benjamin Seebohm Rowntree. Inspired in part by Casson's concept of the soul of an organization and in part by the Rowntree approach to social responsibility, Sheldon devised an explicitly philosophical approach to management which sought to integrate the social and the technical. American trends such as the efficiency movement and scientific management (see below) were widely regarded in Britain as being incompatible with British management and work cultures. Sheldon did not believe this; what was necessary, he said, was to adapt these new and progressive ideas to the ethics of social and workplace responsibility. His aim was to create not a technical approach that embraced ethics, as Emerson and some others had done, but an ethical-philosophical approach that helped frame and determine management practice.[3]

> **American trends such as the efficiency movement and scientific management were widely regarded in Britain as being incompatible with British management and work cultures**

More influential and more prolific than Sheldon, Lyndall Urwick was also more pragmatic. He admired Frederick W. Taylor and the scientific management movement, but his writings and his consultancy work betrayed strong influences of Emerson and Sheldon. He does not speak of souls, but he does speak of vision. For Urwick, writing in 1933, the ideal organization should have three components. He follows Casson on the need for a strong organization or 'body' and an effective management team or 'brain' (an ex-army officer, Urwick was a strong promoter of the 'line and staff' principle in management), but his third element was what he described as 'vision'. This was a move to a pull factor rather than a push factor; rather than a 'soul' to motivate the organization, Urwick stressed the importance of a vision or goal that would act almost like a magnet to draw the organization towards it. More than any other management writer of his day, he stressed that one of top management's key tasks was to formulate a clear vision of what lay ahead, and then to communicate that vision to all levels of the organization.[4]

## LYNDALL FOWNES URWICK

As an army officer in the First World War, Lyndall Urwick won the Military Cross for gallantry on the battlefield and later the Order of the British Empire (OBE) for his staff work. Few others were in quite the position that he was to appreciate the realities of the line and staff system, and how it could lead to disaster if not properly administered. Despite this, he was a strong promoter of the system, but added to the efficiency movement an element lacking in the earlier work of Emerson; an emphasis on vision and strong leadership. After working with Rowntree in the 1920s, where he met Oliver Sheldon, and then with the International Management Institute in Geneva, in 1934 he set up his own consultancy business, Urwick Orr and Partners. He continued to write and practise until the early 1960s, before retiring to Australia where he died in 1985.

The need for vision and focus on goals is a strong chord running through all Urwick's work as both a writer and a consultant. He urged the study of great men and women of the past – management heroes – because like Casson he believed that the study of the methods of those who had been successful could inspire others. He was a strong believer in biography as a tool for management learning, and he and his colleague Edward Brech argued that by getting to know management thinkers and practitioners of the past as people, we could get closer to understanding their ideas and their genius.

So, the British management writers of the 1920s and 1930s – and practitioners too – took the efficiency movement and ran with it. Efficiency was also popular in France, where the mining engineer and writer Henri Fayol appears to have at least some knowledge of Emerson's works. Fayol's classic work *General and Industrial Administration* shares the same broad focus and emphasis on a philosophical and systemic approach. By then, another current of the management revolution had appeared and was now dominating management thinking: scientific management.

## Scientific management

The astounding industrial growth achieved in the USA during the period between the Civil War and the First World War was not achieved without a cost in pain, blood and death. Workplace violence rose to unprecedented heights. Strikes and lockouts were always bitter, and frequently violent. At the Pullman plant near Chicago, at the Carnegie steel works at Homestead and at a hundred other places, strikers fought armed security guards and police with pistols and rifles; when the police brought up machine guns, the strikers broke into military arsenals and wheeled out cannon. When the industrialists called on the government and the army, the workers organized into unions. Marxism, syndicalism and anarchism became popular movements with followings in the thousands. Even where outright violence did not rule, relations between workers and employers were strained and fearful. 'Goldbricking' and slacking were – or were perceived to be – endemic. Workplace productivity was poor, and output and quality suffered. The harm being done to America, said observers, was not just economic, it was also social and moral. Pressure for industry to make changes came from three directions.

> **The astounding industrial growth achieved in the USA during the period between the Civil War and the First World War was not achieved without a cost in pain, blood and death**

1. If workplace relations could be improved, then output and quality would be improved and companies would earn higher profits. Managers should begin treating workers as they would treat their machinery, a valuable investment that needed to be kept in the best possible condition for optimum performance.

2. If workplace relations could be improved, the damaging strikes could be avoided, and so too could the wider threat of social unrest. Managers should pay more attention to cooperating with their workers, and build harmonious relationships with them.
3. Employers have a moral and ethical duty to treat their workers well. All are partners together in the human enterprise of business, and it is unjust that workers should be treated unfairly.

Many of the same views, it should be noted, were being uttered in Britain and in continental Europe, and some innovative solutions were developed here. But it was the American response which was to have the real impact.

The key to the problem, it was felt, must lie in the relationships between employers and workers, and in particular in how the latter were motivated and paid. It was theoretically possible to motivate workers to produce more by paying them according to output. There were several theories as to how this could best be done:

1. Profit-sharing; giving employees a share in the total profits.
2. Payment based on piecework; paying employees bonuses according to the quantity of work they were able to achieve in a given time.
3. Payment based on rate of work; paying employees bonuses according to the speed with which they could perform particular tasks.

Profit-sharing was the most popular and common response in Britain, and was often instituted in conjunction with workplace welfare systems such as medical care and housing for employees. Notable profit-sharing schemes included those developed by the chocolate–maker George Cadbury and the department store owner John Lewis (in the latter case, the system is still going strong). Profit-sharing was also introduced on the Continent, most notably by Ernst Abbé at the Carl Zeiss optical works in Jena, Germany, around 1885. Profit-sharing worked best, however, in cultures where there was a strong tradition of collective behaviour and action. Individualistic America was less willing. A common objection there to profit-sharing was that it was unjust; an equal share-out of profits meant that employees were not rewarded directly for their efforts. The top hand got the same money as the goldbrick. Profit-sharing, or gain-sharing, was advocated by the manufacturer Henry Towne in 1886; Towne and a few others tried the system and reported it to be successful enough, but it never had mass appeal.

Piecework was beset by different problems. Employees working under this system could, and frequently did, become sufficiently skilled to earn good wages by completing large volumes of work in a short space of time. By doing so, however, they dangled temptation before the employers. Over and over again, factory owners watched productivity and worker wages rise together, and realized that they could get the same productivity by cutting the piece-rate. This effectively trapped the worker into working harder for the same money, a spiral that could only go one way. Workers, sensing this, tended to have little motivation to increase production under piece-rate systems. In 1891, the engineer Frederick Halsey proposed what he described as the 'premium plan', which combined a basic day rate – itself capable of supporting the worker and his family – with graduated bonuses based on piecework output. This was a considerable improvement, but there were still difficulties; in particular, no one knew what was a reasonable rate of output on which to base the bonus system, and many mistakes were made in setting rates. Too high and the employer lost out; too low and the worker was demotivated. The Halsey system and variants on it were employed successfully in both the USA and Britain, but it never really caught on (in part, perhaps, because its progenitor did not show much interest in promoting it, devoting himself instead to a lifelong crusade against the metric system).

**The work-rate system was easily the most difficult to manage, as once again, no one really knew how to set rates**

The work-rate system was easily the most difficult to manage, as once again, no one really knew how to set rates. How fast could a worker be reasonably expected to complete a task? To answer this question, there appears on the stage one of the great figures of the management revolution, a man who has been lionized and demonized in almost equal measure: Frederick Winslow Taylor.

## The Taylor system

In 1895 Taylor, then a foreman with the Midvale Steel Works in Philadelphia, stood before the American Society of Mechanical Engineers and presented a paper entitled simply 'A Piece-Rate System'. In this paper, Taylor launched a vigorous attack on employers who, as described above, cut piece-rates once they reached a certain level. This practice could be eliminated, he said, by focusing on the *rate* at which tasks were completed, not the quantity of work completed. He advocated a rate of pay based on the speed at which workers could be reasonably expected to complete their tasks. The system was an equitable one, as it perceived that all workers would be rewarded equally; the system would cut out slacking by showing at once if a worker was failing to meet his targets, but it would also ensure that every worker capable of doing the job received a fair day's pay. According to Taylor, it was up to the employers to ensure that the rates of pay were fair. To do him justice, throughout his life he urged that high wages would always be rewarded with greater employee loyalty and productivity, and he never ceased to remind employers of the need for equity and fair treatment.

### FREDERICK WINSLOW TAYLOR

Born into a family of Pennsylvania Quakers, F.W. Taylor is both the best-known and most controversial figure in the history of management. An austere and at times difficult man, his only known passions were for scientific management and sport (he and his brother-in-law won the US Lawn Tennis Association doubles championship in 1881). He has often been portrayed as a cold and unfeeling man who cared nothing for the rights of workers, and in his own writings he often displays a considerable cynicism about the men who worked for him; he believed the average workman to be incapable of independent thought and requiring constant guidance and supervision. Personally austere, he also believed that paying excessively high wages to workers would stimulate greed. But at heart he was a humane man who constantly urged managers to have a care for their employees and to treat them as, at very least, valuable assets to the organization; in later life he grew increasingly frustrated with employers' efforts to abuse his system so as to sweat more work from their staff. His temper often got him into trouble, and he quarrelled with many of his associates, including Frank Gilbreth and Henry Gantt. By 1912 he had all but given up work, devoting himself to the care of his wife, who was seriously Ill. Worn out by strain, he died of pneumonia in 1915 at the age of 59.

........................................................................................................................

The fundamental element of Taylor's system was the effective measurement of the optimum time required for a given task. To find this, Taylor took the division of labour to its ultimate limits. Within each factory that he studied, he broke down the work required into tasks, then sub-tasks, then sub-sub-tasks, until the elements of the job could logically no longer be divided. Then, using stopwatches, he and his team timed a series of workers performing each subordinate task, analyzing the data to work out an optimum time. Then the times were gradually recombined, giving an overall optimum time for each job. The adjective 'scientific' refers here to the approach, which combined measurement and analysis with control. It was entirely in keeping with the scientific spirit of the time that all activity should begin with measurement, and what could be effectively measured could then be effectively controlled.

**It was entirely in keeping with the scientific spirit of the time that all activity should begin with measurement, and what could be effectively measured could then be effectively controlled**

To develop his system fully, Taylor brought in colleagues like the Norwegian-born mathematician Carl Barth, who invented an advanced form of slide rule to assist in measurement, and the engineer Sanford Thompson, who developed new and more sophisticated ways of managing the time study. He also developed a relationship with the husband-and-wife team of Frank and Lillian Gilbreth who, independently of Taylor, had developed the technique of motion study. The Gilbreths, who worked initially in the construction industry, had the idea that much of the motion being undertaken on building sites and in workshops was wasted effort. By repositioning equipment, changing the heights of controls and a myriad other adjustments to the working environment, the Gilbreths showed how work could be performed faster and more efficiently but without the worker having to expend more effort.

## FRANK AND LILLIAN GILBRETH

**THE FIRST EVER HUSBAND-AND-WIFE MANAGEMENT CONSULTANCY TEAM,** Frank and Lillian Gilbreth were married in 1904. He was from Maine, chief superintendent of a construction company, who had already begun working out the rudiments of motion study and how to use it to save labour and improve working efficiency; she was from California, and had just completed a master's degree in literature, studying the works of Ben Jonson. They went on to have twelve children (two of whom later chronicled home life in the Gilbreth household in the amusing books, *Cheaper by the Dozen* and *Belles on their Toes*). Their professional collaboration included nine books, and Lillian Gilbreth also produced several important works of her own, including *The Psychology of Management* (1914), an early and important introduction of psychological theory into management thinking. The Gilbreth philosophy was centred not just on making labour more productive, but also on reducing stress and fatigue for the labourers to improve the quality of their lives. The term 'labour-saving device' was first used by them.

By now, the system was taking on the proportions of a true science: intricate, detailed, complex, with its own body of theory and practice and its own codes of learning and understanding. Few outsiders could master the intricacies of scientific management, which meant that the inner circle around Taylor were able to earn fortunes as consultants helping firms implement the system. Workers often hated it; resistance to Taylorism was particularly strong in Britain, where workers often colluded deliberately to distort the data being gathered by the experts and render the whole system useless. The system reached its zenith or its nadir, depending on your point of view, in the late 1920s when Charles Bedaux developed an even more sophisticated system of time measurement which purported to build in time lost through worker fatigue, and offered a generalized system of measurement of task times which involved breaking jobs down into 'B units' or 'B seconds'. A fine salesman, Bedaux persuaded many companies around the world to adopt his system, with predictable results; he became a multi-millionaire, and the plants where his system was employed were rocked by strikes.

## CHARLES BEDAUX

THE QUESTION OF WHETHER CHARLES BEDAUX WAS A GENIUS or a charlatan has never been satisfactorily answered. After growing up in Paris, where he may have been involved in running a brothel, Bedaux emigrated to America at the age of 20; here jobs included digging tunnels for the New York City subway and selling toothpaste. Eventually he fetched up in Grand Rapids, Michigan, where he went to work for a furniture-maker; it was here that he worked out his Bedaux system for improved time measurement. He quickly set up a consultancy system to help sell the system to companies, and was highly successful; more than 1,000 companies worldwide adopted the Bedaux system, more than ever took up Taylor's system. Bedaux became a wealthy man and returned to France in 1927. In 1934 he attempted to pioneer an overland route from Edmonton, Alberta to Telegraph Creek, British Columbia and thence to Alaska, and set off with an expedition that included himself, his wife, his mistress, his chef, several surveyors and a Hollywood film-maker; supplies included profuse quantities of caviare and champagne and a supply of ball gowns for the ladies. The expedition's equipment broke down half way to its goal and had to be abandoned.

Returning to France, Bedaux rubbed shoulders with the wealthy and powerful; the Duke of Windsor, the former Edward VIII, married Mrs Wallis Simpson at Bedaux's chateau shortly after his abdication. After the defeat of France in 1940, Bedaux became a consultant to the Vichy government and later to the Nazis. Sent to North Africa to build a peanut-oil pipeline across the Sahara desert, he was captured by Allied troops in 1942 and sent to the USA, where he was charged with treason; he committed suicide before he could be brought to trial. Conspiracy theorists still believe he was murdered by the FBI.

## Bolsheviks and Mensheviks

No revolutionary movement is ever entirely unified, and the management revolution was no different. It is customary today to speak of the entire movement as 'scientific management', but that is a considerable misconception. The efficiency movement pioneered by Emerson and the scientific management movement developed by Taylor had different origins and indeed developed in isolation from each other at first; Taylor and Emerson did not meet until around 1903, and when they did, seem not to have got along. Efficiency was effectively a philosophy, which Emerson and Casson saw as starting from the top and spreading down through the organization. Scientific management began on the shop floor, with measurement and control, and what happened in the shop drove policy.

> Even among the scientific management movement there was considerable infighting

Even among the scientific management movement there was considerable infighting. The relationship between Taylor and the Gilbreths was positively poisonous, with the latter accusing Taylor of theft of their ideas. Henry Gantt, a loyal Taylor lieutenant for many years, fell out with him in the end and developed a friendship with the Gilbreths. Sanford Thompson was also accused of stealing other people's ideas and using them for his own profit. Morris Cooke, one of the younger members of the Taylor team, spent much of his time pouring oil on troubled waters.

The death of Taylor in 1915 led to a reduction in tension all around. There was considerable cross-fertilization in later years; and, as the efficiency movement began to wane, its protagonists began to identify themselves more closely with the more successful and high-profile scientific management movement. As in the contemporary Communist Party, the Bolsheviks of scientific management eventually overcame the more liberal Mensheviks of the efficiency movement, and it is the formers' ideas that went forward.

But already a reaction was beginning, not only to the overly harsh ways in which scientific management was implemented, but to the principles behind it. While no one disputed the need for more accurate information and analysis, the idea that the human components of the organization could be treated like machines came under attack as early as 1918 by the engineer and consultant Charles Knoeppel, who conceived of organizations not as mechanical systems but as biological organisms (see Chapter 5). In 1924, the gifted sociologist and political scientist Mary Parker Follett launched a vigorous attack on the cult of the expert which accompanied scientific management. Experts, she said, were not necessarily revealers of truth; indeed, they could be quite the opposite, even if unwittingly. Instead of reliance on experts, in business as in any walk of life, we need to develop our own clarity of purpose and creative thinking. We need to take a holistic vision of any enterprise, not just focus on the minutiae of technicalities. Follett's book *Creative Experience* was in effect a clarion call for businesses to begin to (a) stand on their own two feet and do their thinking for themselves and (b) pay more attention to the human issues involved in business rather than just the machine aspects.

Scores of business owners (no doubt relieved at having an excuse to sack their expensive consultants) took up Follett's ideas. So too did academia, where sciences like psychology were having an impact on thinking about management. Within a few years, the Australian George Elton Mayo had published *The Human Problems of an Industrial Civilization*, supporting much of Follett's thinking. In the 1930s a ground-breaking series of studies at Western Electric's plant at Hawthorne, Illinois, led to new insights into the psychology and motivation of the worker, and to the founding of the 'human relations' school of management (see Chapter 5).

## MARY PARKER FOLLETT

L**YNDALL URWICK, WHO KNEW HER WELL,** once described Mary Follett as 'a political and social philosopher of the first rank'. Certainly her ability to master the social sciences and apply them in practical terms has rarely been bettered. A brilliant scholar, she graduated *summa cum laude* from Radcliffe College in 1898, and went on to become a prominent figure in Boston intellectual circles. Her keen, incisive mind and considerable wit won her respect in a male-dominated milieu. *Creative Experience*, her master work, was published in 1924 and resonated around the world of business and management; in New York, Henry Metcalf, director of the Bureau of Personnel Administration, regularly invited her to give lectures, and Luther Gulick, presiding genius of the Institute of Public Administration, included her work in the landmark *Papers on the Science of Administration*. In the UK, Urwick and Benjamin Rowntree both regularly invited her to speak at conferences. Right until her retirement, Mary Follett never ceased to urge the importance of individual, independent, critical thinking in management.

## Bring on more science

Scientific management did not disappear. By 1920 its influence had spread around the world. Japanese businesses adopted many of the principles of scientific management, and proved more able than most at separating out those principles which emphasized technical precision from those that emphasized worker motivation. It is a curious fact that while many American firms saw scientific management as providing a way to control their workforce, Japanese businesses saw it as a way of improving production management and making better products.

But engineering could not provide solutions to all the problems of management. Academics and managers alike turned to other realms of ideas, including biology, sociology, psychology and political science, studying and analyzing these for their relevance to management. The most important impact was probably that made by psychology. By around 1910, awareness of the work of Sigmund Freud, Carl Jung and their followers was beginning to penetrate management thinking; the first references to psychology in management writing appear around this time. The strongest impact was on marketing, where from about 1918 to 1925 marketers began moving from a consideration of their subject primarily as a distribution problem to one which focused on customer needs and behaviour (see Chapter 4). Writers on organization like Charles Knoeppel and Dexter Kimball were moving in this direction as well (see Chapter 5), and then in the mid-1920s Follett and Mayo began to swing the focus of management thought towards a consideration of human nature. Psychology, with its emphasis on human beings in all their uniqueness and fragility, posed a direct challenge to the mechanistic views espoused by scientific management. At the same time, nascent sociological theory began examining how human beings behave in groups and what stresses and strains group activity imposes on them, and posed the question of whether efficiency and control might be achieved through less rigidity, rather than more.

> **By around 1910, awareness of the work of Sigmund Freud, Carl Jung and their followers was beginning to penetrate management thinking**

Political science also had an impact, as observers began considering the business organization in terms of its power relationships. In the 1930s, Adolph Berle and Gardiner Means considered the nature of power within businesses and analyzed the growing separation between ownership and control. The same question preoccupied James Burnham in the 1940s; the first to use the term 'revolution' with reference to the recent changes in management, Burnham was fiercely critical of the tendency towards technocracy which he saw inherent in scientific management. Political economists, too, especially those of a leftist bent (which meant most of them) rounded on scientific management as deskilling and degrading of labour. Even biology, most notably through the works of Thorstein Veblen, asked whether organizations should not be considered as organic entities rather than mechanical ones.

## What the management revolution hoped to achieve

The goals the management revolution had set for itself were ambitious. Nothing less than a complete change in approach to the management of corporate enterprises was sought. Emerson, Casson, Taylor, Urwick and even Mary Follett were united in one thing: they saw a new age coming, with new economic threats and challenges, and tried to rouse managers and business leaders out of their torpor and focus them on what lay ahead. To compete successfully in the future, they argued, management had to do several things:

- it had to become more efficient at managing operations, curtailing waste, ensuring productivity and focusing on profitability
- it had to develop effective methods of man-management to preserve industrial peace and promote productivity
- it had to recognize its own responsibilities to society and the ethical standards required of it
- it had to develop a sense of identity and become fully professional in attitude and outlook.

Did businesses become more efficient? The answer is generally, yes; but how far the scientific management movement can claim credit for this is debatable. Those firms which called in Taylor, Bedaux and their associates to implement scientific management systems show a mixed record of success and failure. Scientific management was by no means the panacea some of its proponents claimed it to be. But the basic principles – attention to detail, gathering of information, measuring productivity and so on – still hold good, and most successful companies and managers pay attention to these issues today. Can this be claimed, then, as an achievement of scientific management? Well, yes and no. Successful businesses have *always* paid attention to detail, gathered information and measured productivity; the correspondence of Francesco Datini in fifteenth-century Florence, for example, shows that he placed a high premium on all three of these activities. But what scientific management *did* do was make the world of management generally more aware of these necessities. In the wider diffusion of best practice, then, the management revolution did have an important impact. That diffusion took place not only in America and Europe, of course, but circled the globe.

**Successful businesses have *always* paid attention to detail, gathered information and measured productivity**

## ARAKI TOICHIRO

ONE OF THE FIRST PROFESSIONAL MANAGEMENT CONSULTANTS IN JAPAN, Araki studied chemistry in Tokyo and then in Akron, Ohio. It was during his sojourn in the USA that he first encountered the management revolution, and he met and was influenced by both Harrington Emerson and Lillian Gilbreth. Determined to promote these new ideas in Japan, he returned home and set up the Araki Efficiency Centre in 1923. He spent the next forty years tirelessly promoting the virtues of the efficiency movement in Japan, one of many such consultants who worked to diffuse new management practices throughout the world.

## KAREL ADAMIECKI

**A** POLISH MINING ENGINEER WHO ALSO WORKED IN RUSSIA, Adamiecki developed in the 1890s what he called a 'theory of harmonization' which showed how production should be planned and controlled using an organized series of teams. His 'harmonograms' were graphic devices – in effect, process maps or flow charts – showing how the various stages of production should be managed by different teams working under the same direction. In 1903, Adamiecki presented the results of his experiments with harmonograms to the Society of Russian Engineers in Ekaterinoslav. He and Frederick W. Taylor were not aware of each other's work, but their theories bore striking similarities. The harmonization system was widely adopted in Russia and Poland, with significant results, production increasing by as much as 400 per cent in some cases. Following the First World War, Adamiecki became involved in teaching and also in establishing links with scientific management movements in other countries. He died in 1933.

## ROBERTO SIMONSEN

**A**FTER TAKING AN ENGINEERING DEGREE AT SÃO PAULO POLYTECHNIC, Simonsen founded his own construction business, the Cia. Constructora dos Santos, in 1909. The company was involved in a wide variety of civil engineering projects in southern Brazil and quickly built a reputation for efficiency and high-quality work. Simonsen became one of the leading industrial figures in Brazil and was involved in a number of other business concerns in Santos and São Paulo. Unlike Adamiecki, he did not develop his own theory of management, but played a leading role in adapting the techniques of scientific management to conditions in Brazil. Simonsen was particularly influenced by Taylor's colleague Henry Gantt and the latter's views on fairness in the workplace. He believed that scientific management held the key to both greater efficiency and improving the lot of the worker, and held that both these goals were interrelated.

In terms of promoting better labour relations and industrial peace, scientific management is usually judged to have failed. Even when outright worker resistance was absent, excessive specialization and deskilling are generally believed to have done great harm to the capabilities and competences of many of the firms that employed these methods. Assembly-line production is only now, and at great cost, being abandoned by many firms, and suitable models to replace it are still hard to find. In defence, it should be said that even the most mechanistic approaches such as that of Taylor placed a premium on good workplace relations. Taylor repeatedly stated that his system could *only* work if it had the full cooperation of the workers, and that only highly skilled, trained and motivated workers could make the system work. That managers and firms ignored this advice is not Taylor's fault. And yet, is a system that is so complex that only the most highly-skilled workers can make it work really a good system? It is a question we are still asking today, of course, only in different contexts.

It may seem strange to us, but scientific management and the efficiency movement were at heart ethical systems. They were designed not only to correct iniquities and injustices in the ways workers were rewarded for their work, but also to ensure that business met its responsibilities to society. By this I do not mean social responsibility, as conceptualized at British firms like Cadbury and Rowntree, but something deeper. If, as John Davis suggested, corporations are social forms brought about to meet social needs, then it follows that the corporations must work to meet those needs effectively, or be replaced by something that will. In the 1880s and 1890s, that problem confronted big business in America squarely; meet society's needs for growth, for better transport, for food, for more consumer goods squarely, or be replaced by socialism. In order to do this, business had to become more efficient. At this level, by and large it succeeded. Scientific management, then, was a necessary step in the development and consolidation of the modern corporation as a social form, just as the rule of St Benedict consolidated the monasteries as a social form. Maybe, then, with each new type of organization that emerges, we should look for a similar rationalization and consolidation of ideas that will both define the organization and set out its relationship with society.

> **It may seem strange to us, but scientific management and the efficiency movement were at heart ethical systems**

Did management become more professional? The jury is out on this one; in part, the answer depends on what is meant by a profession. In the 1920s and 1930s it was argued, especially by Lyndall Urwick, that management needed to be set on the same professional basis as the practices of law, medicine, accounting and so on. There needed to be regular and systematized training, based on scientific principles; there needed to be self-governing professional associations in each country that would govern the conduct and behaviour of members; and managers themselves needed to adopt a professional identity that enabled them to think of themselves as *managers* first and foremost. Their primary loyalty, like that of doctors and lawyers, should be to their profession and its ideals, not to their employer.

Clearly this has not happened. Great steps forward have been made in terms of training, but those professional associations that have appeared have no authority, and managerial class awareness has been vague at best. Ultimately, managers remain more tribal than professional; like the managers of a hundred or a thousand years ago, they identify primarily with their organization, not with their peers in other organizations. The drive towards full professionalism has stalled, and while it can be argued that this is a good thing (Burnham, in *The Managerial Revolution* in 1942, suggested that class-aware managers were on their way to setting up a technocratic society based on total world domination), it has certainly inhibited growth and development in the concept of management.

## Is the revolution over?

Scarcely a year goes past without some new 'revolution' being proclaimed in management. Re-engineering was one such in the early 1990s; at time of writing, e-commerce is being discussed in revolutionary terms. In fact, close examination usually blows such myths away. Re-engineering was nothing more than a more sophisticated form of the process engineering undertaken by the Taylorists, and traces of this approach are older still. The arrival of the internet and the world wide web was a jolt to the managerial system, and has certainly changed approaches in many fields, most importantly the manner in which we gather and employ knowledge and information. But e-commerce, on closer inspection, looks suspiciously like many of the advances in marketing made in the early twentieth century, and firms are now starting to realize this; the bloom is already fading from that particular rose.

What none of the recent developments in management thought and practice has done is provide a paradigmatic shift, an idea which would totally change our thinking about and our approach to management. Not even the information revolution has done that; it has given us a powerful new set of tools for use in many disciplines, *but the core tasks we face remain exactly the same as they were twenty years ago*. We are still preoccupied with how to produce goods at a profit, how to get and keep customers, how to manage labour effectively; and how to manage our own careers for a satisfying life.

**We are still preoccupied with how to produce goods at a profit, how to get and keep customers, how to manage labour effectively**

The same twenty years ago; and the same two hundred years ago, or two thousand? By and large, as the previous chapter showed, yes. The *fundamentals* of management have not greatly changed, as we will see in Part II. What the management revolution really achieved was to show us what these fundamentals were and how they were changing and evolving over time. The management revolution did not create management, nor did the people involved in it believe they were doing so; almost without exception, they looked to the past for inspiration and examples of best practice. What it did do – and for this we should be everlastingly grateful – was codify and describe best practice and diffuse those practices so that they were more widely available. That, indeed, is the truest and best goal of all management science.

*Notes for chapter 3*

1  From Emerson, Harrington (1913) *The Twelve Principles of Efficiency*, New York: The Engineering Magazine Co.

2 Emerson, Harrington (1909) *Efficiency as a Basis for Operations and Wages*, New York: The Engineering Magazine Co., p. 98.
3 Sheldon, Oliver (1923) *The Philosophy of Management*, London: Pitman.
4 Urwick, Lyndall (1933) *Management for Tomorrow*, London: Nisbet.

# PART 2

# THE PRINCIPLES OF MANAGEMENT

# 4

# Marketing comes full circle

> The business world is sparkling with romance and adventure. There is nothing wonderful in the fairy-tales of Arabia that cannot be equalled by any department store
>
> *Herbert N. Casson*

Philip Kotler, professor of marketing at Northwestern University in Chicago and the man who has perhaps done more than any other to shape modern thinking about marketing, classifies corporate and managerial approaches to marketing into five levels of increasing sophistication. First of all, says Kotler, there is the *production concept*, in which managers believe their main aim is to produce and distribute products as cheaply and efficiently as possible. Next comes the *product concept*, in which managers believe that consumers will always be attracted to products of the highest quality and most useful features. Next is the *selling concept*; recognizing (implicitly at least) the Marxist concept of overproduction, the selling concept argues that in cases where supply begins to exceed demand, sales and revenue can still be stimulated by actively selling goods to consumers through 'hard selling' methods which focus on the sale itself and not on the needs of the consumer. Then comes the *marketing concept*, which reverses the picture: the company must first understand and analyze the needs of consumers and then develop products which meet those needs. Last of all comes the concept that Kotler himself invented, *societal marketing* (also sometimes known as social marketing). Here, the company not only works to serve the needs of consumers but does so in a manner which is consistent with the latter's best interests; products should not only not be harmful to consumers, but they should actively promote the well-being of individuals and society.

Seven centuries before Kotler, St Thomas Aquinas mused on the nature and function of markets in his two great works, *Summa theologia* and *Summa contra gentiles*. Markets, said Aquinas, exist to serve the needs of the people; their primary function is a social one, in that they allow people to buy goods (food, clothing, tools, etc) which help them to live better, more rewarding lives. Aquinas promoted the concept of the 'just price' or 'fair price' for goods in the marketplace. Breaking with centuries of Catholic theological tradition, Aquinas argued that the fair price of a product depends not on its intrinsic worth, but on the value of the product to the purchaser. It is the needs, wants and desires of consumers, said Aquinas, that determines value. He offered an example: take the relative values of a pearl and a mouse. If value were measured intrinsically, the mouse, a living creature, should surely be of much more value than the inanimate pearl. Yet the opposite is the case. Why? Because value is in the eye, and the mind, of the purchaser.

> **Aquinas argued that the fair price of a product depends not on its intrinsic worth, but on the value of the product to the purchaser**

It is the customer's idea of value, says Aquinas, that determines market price. And, if the seller knows what is in the mind of the customer, the former can create value (what we would call 'value added' today) by influencing the nature and quality of the goods. In other words, the seller – or marketer, if you like – by understanding the *needs* and demands of customers, and by knowing what products will satisfy those needs and demands, can then influence the *availability* of those products and provide them to customers.

Reading Aquinas's views on markets poses a fascinating question: have Kotler and his many colleagues in marketing departments around the world invented something new? Or have they returned marketing to its roots, going back to a concept of marketing that is both economic and social and that sees marketing not as an isolated activity of 'selling' but as a stage in a process by which human needs are met and civilization is built?

## PHILIP KOTLER

**PHILIP KOTLER WAS BORN IN CHICAGO IN 1931.** He initially trained as an economist, studying under such luminaries of the field as Milton Friedman and Paul Samuelson, but on joining the faculty of Northwestern University chose to teach marketing instead. Northwestern has a long tradition of high-quality teaching and research in marketing, and Philip Kotler has carried on that tradition. At the time he began teaching, marketing was regarded as a narrow, specialist discipline, quite separate from the production and other functions of the business; further, it was regarded as being applicable only to the sale of manufactured industrial and consumer goods, and there was grave doubt as to whether services, for example, could be marketed.

In the late 1960s and early 1970s Kotler caused uproar within the academic marketing community by showing how the marketing concept could be 'broadened'. Marketing, he insisted, was not just about commercial transactions, but was about social values. Every product performs some sort of social function; every transaction has a social aspect and social values are part of all exchanges. Thus marketing is a social function. It is thus possible, he went on, to apply the value principles of marketing to primarily social services such as education and health care; to non-profit goods and services such as those provided by welfare agencies and charities; and to situations where no formal transaction takes place at all, such as elections of political candidates. Kotler's ideas, though revolutionary, were widely accepted, and marketing became increasingly to be seen not as a 'bolt-on' business function but as a core concept within management; which, of course, it had been all along.

## ST THOMAS AQUINAS

**BORN AROUND 1225 NEAR NAPLES,** Thomas Aquinas was educated at Monte Cassino and the University of Naples. After joining the Dominican Order of friars in 1244, he continued his education in Paris and Köln. Internationalist in outlook, he spent the rest of his life in teaching and administrative positions with the Dominicans, working in Naples, Rome and Orvieto and twice serving as professor of theology at Paris. He died in 1274 and was canonized in 1323. Aquinas towered over the people around him, both intellectually and physically (he stood well over six feet tall). His philosophical works became the basis for virtually all subsequent philosophical writing for the next century and a half. He remains a pivotal thinker in the western, especially Catholic, intellectual world. In particular, his views on ethics remain at the heart of modern ideas of ethical behaviour (see Chapter 9). It is from an ethical standpoint that Thomas considers economics and markets: what are their purposes, whom do they serve, what value do they create? It is this focus on broader purpose, over and above the immediate generation of sales and profits, that is beginning once more to affect thinking on marketing in our own time.

## The three ages of marketing

It is perceived wisdom among modern marketers, and particularly among many marketing academics, that marketing as an academic discipline began in the early twentieth century. Writers like Arch Shaw, Walter D. Scott, L.D.H. Weld and Paul Cherington have each in turn been hailed as the 'father of modern marketing'.[1] When modern marketing practices became widespread in business is more debatable: Kotler dates the general acceptance of marketing to the 1950s, while Bill Donaldson, writing in the *International Encyclopedia of Business and Management*, traces the development back to the 1930s.

What then came before marketing? How did businesses find customers and how did they sell goods to them? Most writers on marketing (or at least, those who pause to consider the history of marketing at all) take the view that marketing as we know it today did not exist in the past because there was no need for it. They classify business activity into three stages of development, rather in the same way that Lewis Mumford and Marshall McLuhan wrote of the 'three ages' of technological development. For marketers, there was first the pre-industrial period. For many centuries, from antiquity through at least to the end of the Reformation in Europe – and later in India and the Far East – economies were largely agrarian and production was localized and craft-based. Markets, in this view, existed as places where producers and consumers came together and exchanged goods face to face, first on a barter basis and then later for cash. Exchanges were simple and lacked sophistication, it is claimed, and so there was no need for specific marketing practices and techniques.

Then came the Industrial Revolution, beginning in the textile industries in Britain in the 1770s and expanding to other sectors and then other countries: France and Germany by the 1830s, Russia and the USA by the 1870s, Japan in the 1880s, India and China by the early twentieth century. As Donaldson describes it, the Industrial Revolution was:

> ... characterized by the systematic, regular and progressive application of science and technology to the production of goods and services. The volume of production rose rapidly, while prices continued in relative terms to decline... Consumers were satisfied because the availability of goods was greatly increased, and producers enjoyed increased sales and profit.[2]

However, the Industrial Revolution was not just a matter of increasing production. Side by side with the factory system came new developments in transportation, first the canals and then, more importantly, the rapid development and expansion of the railway system. The Industrial Revolution not only increased production capacity manyfold, it also increased the power and reach of distribution channels. During this time, according to many modern writers, demand always outstripped supply; markets were hungry for new consumer goods, and industrial producers were able to sell their goods almost automatically. Marketing, and even selling, were barely needed; or so the theory goes.

As the variety and choice of merchandise grew, companies found they could gain advantage by differentiating their offerings from those of rivals. Increasing competition in many sectors, particularly after the First World War, provided further stimulus: in tougher economic times, those companies which were best at attracting customers were more likely to survive. Mass production, in the view of many, led in turn to mass consumption, with increasing quantities and diversity of goods, and this in turn was responsible for the appearance of marketing.

Most writers from the 1920s onward took this view, but others were not so sure. Paul Cherington of Harvard Business School, one of the most important and thoughtful marketing writers of all time, believed that the physical separation between producers and consumers was the single most important factor behind the rise of marketing. Improved transportation, said Cherington, meant that companies no longer had to rely on customers in their immediate neighbourhood; the railways and steamships meant that producers could reach out to customers across the continent or across the seas. But with physical distance came many problems, chief of which was how to find customers, how to understand their wants and needs, and how to develop suitable products, in situations where producer and customer were not in close physical contact. It was these problems, Cherington believed, that marketing was designed to solve.

## PAUL CHERINGTON

**BORN IN OTTAWA, KANSAS IN 1876**, Cherington was educated at Ohio Wesleyan University and the University of Pennsylvania, going on to become a journalist and then managing the publications department of the Philadelphia Commercial Museum. In 1908, Edwin Gay recruited him as a founding faculty member of Harvard Business School. Here he was responsible for the development of courses in marketing, and also founded the School's Bureau of Business Research, one of the functions of which was to gather information which could be used in teaching and developing case studies. Leaving Harvard in 1919, he was for many years director of research for the J. Walter Thompson advertising agency, and in the 1930s worked with Elmo Roper to develop methods of opinion-polling which are still in use today. After Philip Kotler (above), Cherington was probably the most important writer and thinker on marketing in the twentieth century.

---

A contemporary of Cherington, the American professor Lewis Haney considered these developments in a broader historical context, from antiquity up to 1900. Like many of the early marketing academics, Haney had trained as an economist, and he believed that markets evolved as an economic response to social needs. As society grew and developed, needs changed and became more diverse; markets, in turn, became more sophisticated, and the activities associated with markets became correspondingly more complex. For example, the increasing urbanization and prosperity of late nineteenth-century America led to consumers demanding both more and different goods to improve their standard of living. But, says Haney, these are differences of degree, not of kind. At its heart, marketing is as old as business itself. Though much had changed by Haney's day – as indeed much has changed since – the fundamentals of marketing have been practised by successful business men and women for centuries.

**At its heart, marketing is as old as business itself**

Another view on the subject was offered by the noted British management consultant Lyndall Urwick. As in all his work, when writing on marketing Urwick stressed the continuity between past and current practices. In the 1930s he observed that much of what we now call marketing could be observed in the practices and methods of English market-traders going as far back as the seventeenth century:

> The functions of the original market were fourfold. The first thing a producer had to know was where he could find a group of persons who would be willing to purchase his goods or services. Having discovered this market, he would transport his product to it. On arrival, he would display his wares to attract the attention of possible customers. Finally, having gained their interest, he would carry out the actual transaction of sale, centring round the question of price. All the complexities of our modern distributive system are merely new combinations and re-arrangements of these four basic processes. They constitute the four main activities carried on under the general heading of distribution.[3]

He goes on to comment: 'Most of the modern methods of marketing, both here and in the United States, owe their origin to these pioneer traders of the seventeenth century. At that date, marketing problems appear to have been as pressing as those of production. The foundations of commercial supremacy were apparently laid then, because Englishmen knew how to sell better than their neighbours, rather than because of any extraordinary merit in English products.'

The development of modern marketing is in reality the development of *mass marketing*: the sale of mass-produced goods and services to large numbers of consumers spread over a wide region. And while mass marketing was the dominant paradigm, as it was for much of the twentieth century, the marketing practices of earlier times could be to some extent ignored. But today, things are changing. The trend is increasingly towards relationship marketing, with producers getting to know their customers and personalizing their approach and their offerings. Even large companies, especially in areas like financial services, are now talking about having one-to-one relationships with customers. E-commerce and other advances in information technology are now making individual customer relationships easier, if not face to face then in virtual space. Services marketers are increasingly realizing that the customer is part of the service process and are encouraging direct, proactive customer involvement in the business.

The small-scale, highly personalized marketing of earlier times is becoming relevant once again, and this is calling into question the nature and specialist role of marketing professionals and marketing departments. In today's new one-to-one marketing environment, who has responsibility for marketing? To paraphrase the former French President Clemenceau, marketing may be too important to be left to the marketers. The idea that marketing is everyone's job is not a new one; it has just taken us a while to remember it.

## Marketers before marketing

One of the most noticeable features of marketing before the modern era – let us say, for convenience's sake, before the First World War – is how responsibility for marketing was assumed by those at the very top of the company hierarchy: the chairman, managing director or president, who was also often the owner or senior partner. This is especially noticeable in business-to-business marketing, where the leaders were often personally involved in the selling effort. But in retailing, too, responsibility for and direction of the marketing effort was often one of the leader's primary roles.

Among business-to-business marketers, two approaches can be distinguished. In one, what we might call the *full product approach*, the leader is closely concerned with both product design on the one hand and marketing and selling on the other.

> **In retailing, too, responsibility for and direction of the marketing effort was often one of the leader's primary roles**

These two activities are seen as complementary and of equal importance: in close personal contact with customers, the leader evaluates their needs and feeds this knowledge back into the design process. The other approach, the *relationship-building approach*, sees the leader devote the bulk of his or her time and effort to maintaining customer relationships; although he or she provides information on product needs to the design team, actual responsibility for design is delegated.

A good example of the full product approach can be found in the person of William Pirrie, who led the shipbuilders Harland & Wolff through their glory days from the mid-1880s until after the First World War. During Pirrie's tenure, Harland & Wolff dominated the passenger liner market: nearly every major shipping company in the world came to Harland with orders for luxury passenger liners. Pirrie's ships were a byword for luxury, speed and comfort.

Before taking over from the company's founder, Edward Harland, Pirrie had been in charge of marketing. He built up a network of personal contacts with the major shipowners in Europe, and spent the bulk of his time travelling, visiting his contacts and selling ships through a mixture of persuasion, Belfast charm and irresistible deals. It was Pirrie who put together the first 'customer club', offering regular buyers first access to building stocks and repair facilities and a substantial price discount based on cost-plus pricing, in exchange for cash up front. He was legendary for his persistence and selling ability. A Liverpool shipowner once saw a colleague looking glum. 'Why the long face?' he asked. 'That fellow Pirrie has just sold me a ship,' came the answer, 'and I don't know what the deuce I'll do with it.'

When Pirrie took control of the firm, he continued to lead the marketing effort. Assessing the information he gleaned from his contacts with customers, he understood that the paramount needs of the latter were for speed, comfort and safety. Trans-oceanic travel had long been dangerous and full of hardships; if the market were to grow, passengers needed to be assured that they could travel quickly, safely and in comfort. Pirrie gave both shipowners and the travelling public what they wanted. His naval architects were instructed to use the latest technology in ship construction and propulsion, no matter what the cost. Pirrie himself designed many of the interiors of his liners, adapting designs from grand continental hotels and turning sea-going passenger ships into floating palaces. From this simple process of translating knowledge of customer needs into products that would give customer satisfaction, Pirrie built up the world's most powerful and successful shipbuilding company. Today, Harland & Wolff is a shadow of its former self, but the principles of speed, safety and comfort developed by Pirrie continue to influence passenger liner construction around the world today.

## WILLIAM PIRRIE

**BORN IN QUEBEC CITY IN 1847**, the son of a shipowner, William Pirrie was educated at the Royal Belfast Academical Institution and, at age fifteen, became a 'gentleman apprentice' at the Belfast shipyard of Harland & Wolff. Gentleman apprentices were in effect management trainees; they spent anything up to six or seven years in various departments of the business learning the ropes, and were then promoted into management positions. A methodical worker who paid great attention to detail, Pirrie was soon noticed by the senior partners, Edward Harland and G.C. Wolff, and was promoted rapidly, becoming a partner himself at the age of twenty-seven. He proved to be a first-class salesman, and took over much of the firm's marketing activities; Edward Harland's wife Rosa once commented that 'my husband builds the ships, but Mr Pirrie gets the orders for them'. Pirrie gradually took over the management of the firm as Harland and

Wolff moved into retirement. As well as managing the shipyard, he was Lord Mayor of Belfast from 1896–98, and was made a viscount in 1903. The loss of the *Titanic* and the death of his nephew Thomas Andrews, the ship's chief designer, shook Pirrie deeply, and he never fully recovered his vigour, although the firm's reputation for first-class building and design was little harmed. He died on board a liner passing through the Panama Canal in 1924.

---

Among relationship-builders, Richard Arkwright (whose career was described in detail in Chapter 2) is notable for his personal attention to his clients, the manufacturers of finished textile goods. Although Arkwright's early success came from his design and implementation of the first factory system, in later years his management style was notably hands-off; management of individual factories devolved to superintendents and partners, while Arkwright himself planned strategy and networked with customers. But perhaps an even better example of this approach is the German steel-maker Alfred Krupp. Famous, or infamous, as the 'Cannon King', the builder of heavy artillery for the Prussian army and later many other armies around the world, Krupp in fact owed the bulk of his success to the manufacture of railway rails (the Union Pacific trans-continental line was largely built of Krupp steel rails) and heavy steel components for railway rolling stock. Originally an autocratic manager who insisted on personally controlling every aspect of his business, Krupp worked himself into a nervous breakdown in the late 1860s and thereafter (reluctantly) delegated much of his authority. He did, however, remain closely involved in the marketing of his main product lines, artillery and railway components. Like Pirrie, Krupp had built up a relationship network with key clients. Rather than charm (he had none), Krupp employed an unshakeable faith in his own products combined with a dour persistence; he laid siege to the Prussian government for more than twenty years before the latter finally caved in and agreed to test his new designs for cannon.

> **Rather than charm (he had none), Krupp employed an unshakeable faith in his own products combined with a dour persistence**

## ALFRED KRUPP

**B**ORN IN ESSEN IN 1812, ALFRED KRUPP inherited a bankrupt steel business from his father at the age of fourteen. He spent the next three decades turning the business round and building it up slowly; money was so short that the Krupp family often had to melt down their table silver to pay the wages bill. What money did come was invested in high-technology production such as the newly invented Bessemer process for steel-making. Krupp's qualities of persistence and determination became legendary, and they paid off when, in the 1860s, railway building began to become widespread and Krupp's steel rails and components were in great demand. Around the same time Otto von Bismarck, the new chancellor of the state of Prussia, reversed the policy of his predecessors and tested, then adopted, Krupp's cannon for the expanding German army.

In 1886, Krupp guns went into action with the Prussian army against Austria at the Battle of Königgratz. Several of the guns exploded. Krupp, who had built his entire reputation on the quality of his products, had a nervous breakdown. His health never fully recovered, and he spent increasing amounts of time at health resorts. In 1871 he spent some months at Torquay in Devon, recovering his health after yet another collapse, during which time he drafted a document later known as the *General Instructions* which provided regulations for the management of the Krupp works and set out his own philosophy of business. A paternalist who provided housing, shops, recreation facilities and churches for his employees, Krupp became increasingly bitter and reclusive in his old age, separated from his wife and tyrannizing his only son. He died alone in his great house outside Essen, known as The Hill, at the age of seventy-five.

## Living the brand

In consumer marketing, some of the best-known marketing successes of the past occurred when the leader of the business involved himself so closely with the business and its products that he actually became part of the offering. Today, 'living the brand' is talked about more than it is practised. In the past, when marketing conditions were often even more uncertain than they are today and risks were constant and real, business leaders did not need reminding that reputation is everything. Merchants of the Italian Renaissance like the diarist Marino Sanudo often spoke of their own 'credit': they meant not so much their own financial credit, important though this was, as their reputation in the community. A good 'credit', a good reputation, could be worth millions, as in the case of the Augsburg banker Jakob Fugger in the sixteenth century. Fugger's bank, the largest financial services house in Europe for much of the century, was founded on his own personal reputation for financial acumen and probity. Much the same was true of the banking side, at least, of the Medici business empire in the previous century; the day-to-day management of the bank was handled by professionals like Benci and the Ingherami brothers (see Chapter 2), but the brand was Medici and the prime responsibility for networking with major clients rested with the head of the business, Cosimo dei Medici.

> A good 'credit', a good reputation, could be worth millions, as in the case of the Augsburg banker Jakob Fugger in the sixteenth century

The greatest exponent of living the brand, however, comes from the USA. Phineas Taylor Barnum, circus impresario, music promoter and museum owner, went through a series of business ventures of a conventional nature, all of which failed. Eventually, he realized that in order to draw crowds he needed publicity. He proved to have a natural flair. He noted in his memoirs, 'I often seized upon an opportunity by instinct, even before I had a very definite conception as to how it should be used, and it seemed, somehow, to mature itself and serve my purpose.' Although Barnum used advertising, he realized that publicity was cheaper, and cultivated newspaper editors like Horace Greeley in hopes of placing favourable stories. Gradually, he found that he himself was becoming part of the attraction: 'what Barnum would do next' was becoming the subject not only of newspaper articles but street-corner gossip. Barnum played to this, cultivating a near legendary status for himself which has won him a permanent place in American culture. In his later years, as Barnum and Bailey's circus toured America, farmers would bring their families twenty miles by horse and wagon to the fairground, not so much to see the circus but to see the legendary Barnum himself.

Many of Barnum's methods were adopted by a young Connecticut mechanic, Samuel Colt. Colt had designed and patented a simple and easy to manufacture design for a revolver, but found both the public and the army uninterested in his products. Like Barnum, Colt established several unsuccessful ventures before his breakthrough came. An officer in the Texas Rangers, who had purchased some of Colt's early revolvers, wrote to thank Colt; in a skirmish with hostile Indians in west Texas, the superior firepower of the revolvers had driven off the attackers and saved the lives of a number of Rangers. Colt seized on this as a heaven-sent publicity opportunity. Establishing a new business in Connecticut, he began marketing his guns using a theme that set the pattern for nearly all later advertising in the gun market, associating his products with the frontier, the opening up of the West, and such American virtues as independence and courage. The final flourish was to re-create his own image: he became 'Colonel' Sam Colt, superb marksman and rider, the embodiment of the virtues of the frontier. Whether Colt himself ever went west of Kentucky is not known, and is not relevant: the myth was created, the image stuck and the Colt brand became forever associated with the 'frontier virtues' Colt himself had created.

## SAMUEL COLT

**COLT WAS BORN IN 1814 IN HARTFORD, CONNECTICUT,** the son of a textile merchant who later went bankrupt. A schoolboy experimenter with chemistry and explosives, Colt's formal education ended when he designed a fireworks display which malfunctioned and burned his school to the ground. According to legend, while working as deckhand on a passage to India, he came up with the idea of a firearm with a revolving cylinder (in fact, other revolvers had been patented in both the USA and the UK before Colt).

Back in the USA, he worked as a travelling salesman selling nitrous oxide (laughing gas) around the towns of New England, calling himself 'Dr Colt'. Raising a little capital, he set up his first workshop in Paterson, New Jersey, and made fewer than a thousand guns before going bankrupt. The contact with Captain Walker of the Texas Rangers provided him with a lifeline, and soon after he was back in New England, setting up a new factory and designing new guns. Thereafter he never looked back.

Colt died comparatively young, in 1862. Successful though the company had been during his lifetime, it reached its apogee during the next two decades when, under the management of his widow, Elizabeth Colt, it designed and sold such famous guns as the .45 Single Action Army, later immortalized as the 'Peacemaker'. Colt's name and the brand he created were powerful forces that lived on long after him.

...........................................................................................................

Not every great marketer of the nineteenth century had the personal flamboyance of a Colt or a Barnum. Although the showmanship of the latter continues to influence advertising and promotional techniques, the development of direct sales management methods has probably been more important in the long run. Sales management is one of those fields of management that has seen fashions come and go through the ages, particularly in relation to whether sales staff should be employed directly or whether sales should be contracted to outside agencies. The slow speed and high risks associated with transportation in the Middle Ages meant that distribution chains were often highly complex, with a variety of middlemen and a considerable distance between retailer and producer.

The Italian textiles manufacturers of the fourteenth and fifteenth centuries tried to close this gap by developing partnerships with sales agents in other countries, giving themselves more control, and super-large firms like the Medici could even afford to have full-time sales forces; some of these businesses also maintained retail premises, but these were usually close to home and could be directly supervised by the owner and senior managers. The debate about whether sales should be conducted by paid employees or contracted agents on commission can be seen in the correspondence of the time. The former were expensive but gave the business greater control; the latter were less expensive and easier to maintain over distance, but the control of agents and dealing with problems such as incompetence and dishonesty on the part of the latter was a constant concern.

In the late nineteenth century in America, the contracting out of sales to external agents, often freelances, was common practice. The system was widely acknowledged to be imperfect; travelling salesmen were known for their venality, incompetence, dishonest methods and occasional outrages perpetrated on female members of the community (all those travelling-salesman-and-farmer's-daughter jokes didn't come from nowhere). 'Snake-oil salesman' became a term of abuse which has lasted to this day. Worse, the system was inefficient. Smart managers started to realize that a better way was possible.

> **In the late nineteenth century in America, the contracting out of sales to external agents, often freelances, was common practice**

One of the first of these was Cyrus Hall McCormick, the inventor-entrepreneur who designed the first combine harvester and, in the years following the American Civil War, turned his design into a global business enterprise. McCormick is best known today as one of the pioneers of mass-production, and the techniques and skills developed by his workmen were later widely copied in the automobile industry. McCormick began with the standard system of using freelance sales agents, but soon ran into a problem; he was selling what was for the time a very high-tech piece of machinery, and his agents knew, if possible, even less about the product than the customers. McCormick began moving back towards direct sales management, employing sales staff in-house, training them in the use and features of the product, and employing creative advertising. McCormick used a battery of marketing techniques including product demonstrations, warranties and credit to buyers, and kept tight control on his sales staff and their methods.

With McCormick, we see in the USA the beginning of a trend towards direct sales management, especially in high-technology and mass volume products. Edward Clark, the lawyer who became Isaac Singer's partner in the sewing machine business, likewise turned from freelance salesmen to directly employed sales staff when he found the former simply could not sell his product. The next major figure in the development of this trend was John Henry Patterson, the founder of National Cash Register. Patterson organized his salesmen as a team, giving them precise areas to cover and definite targets. His salesmen, who were well trained, were instructed not simply to sell cash registers to customers, but to first find out what the customers' needs were in terms of cash control, and then demonstrate how the cash register could meet those needs. Patterson's methods in turn were adopted by the carmaker John North Willys, who used psychology not only to understand his customers but to motivate his sales staff. Willys's view was that salesmen, like all members of the firm, needed to feel part of the firm, part of the 'family', in order to be truly committed to achieving sales targets. Patterson and Willys brought sales management and marketing to a high level of sophistication, and it was observation of their practices and those of their imitators that informed the work of many of the early marketing academics.

## JOHN PATTERSON

**B**ORN IN DAYTON, OHIO IN 1844, JOHN PATTERSON served in the Union Army in the American Civil War and then returned home to set up a small mining business with his brother Frank. Like so many other famous entrepreneurs, Patterson went bankrupt. However, while teaching himself how to manage cash flow, he had come across a device known as a cash register, recently patented by James Ritty. So impressed was Patterson with the machine's potential that he raised some capital and bought Ritty's company, which he re-established as National Cash Register (NCR). By 1900 he had built NCR into an international business with a gigantic turnover. Patterson knew he faced a considerable task in selling this relatively high-tech product to unsophisticated small retailers. His salesmen, who received intensive training before being sent into the field, were instructed first to learn about the customer's business and its needs, and only when they could see a genuine use for a cash register that would benefit the customer were they to make a pitch.

An eccentric who suffered from hypochondria and undertook bizarre diets of hot water and baked potatoes (and often forced his fellow directors to live on the same), Patterson was also a caring employer who was genuinely concerned for the welfare of his workers. When in 1912 he was charged with anti-trust violations after forcing several competitors out of business, his employees sprang to his defence. Soon after, Dayton was afflicted by terrible floods which destroyed part of the town. Patterson shut down his factory and mobilized his employees to aid the townspeople, shipping in relief supplies from New York at his own expense. Shortly thereafter the anti-trust conviction was overturned on appeal. Patterson died while seeking a health cure in Atlantic City in 1922.[4]

## JOHN NORTH WILLYS

**A**LMOST FORGOTTEN TODAY, in the early days of the automobile industry John North Willys was the man who gave Henry Ford a run for his money. Born in 1873, Willys went into business first as a bicycle retailer and then as an agent for Pierce-Arrow and Rambler cars. In 1907 one of his suppliers, the Overland Car Company, went bankrupt; Willys bought the firm, reorganized it and made it into the world's second-largest car-maker. Not a good financial manager, he several times lost control of the company – once to Walter Chrysler – but his sales genius was such that he was repeatedly asked to return. He had an almost instinctive understanding of his market; what is more, he knew how to apply his understanding of psychology to his sales force. He established one of the first large-scale car dealership networks in the USA, backing up his dealers with promotions, advertising and credit plans which helped them attract customers and made it easier for them to sell cars. In an article in *System* in 1917, Willys describes how he developed a 'family spirit' among dealers, engendering loyalty through devices such as newsletters and dealership conventions. In the first of these, in 1916, 9,000 dealers and family members came to the plant in Toledo, travelling on Pullman railway cars paid for by the company, to tour the plant, meet Willys, be entertained and generally made to feel part of the team.

After serving as US ambassador to Poland from 1930–32, Willys returned to take over the company one last time. He suffered a heart attack in early 1935, but continued at his desk until his death later that year.

---

Of all the important figures from the history of marketing, however, there are two men whose philosophies of marketing are timeless. William Hesketh Lever followed his father into the grocery business in Lancashire in the 1870s, and by the mid-1880s he was the leading wholesale grocer in the north west of England. But that, for Lever, was only the beginning. An instinctive marketer (one biographer noted that although Lever was in the grocery business, his true vocation was that of the marketing man), Lever studied the increasing affluence and rising incomes among many of the working classes, and realized that there were opportunities to break through to this group by offering them products which had formerly been unaffordable. The greatest opportunity, he believed, lay in soap. The task was to convince working-class housewives that soap, which they had regarded as a luxury, was in fact a necessity. To do this, he needed not only a high-quality product, but also an image of that product that would prove attractive. He needed, in other words, a brand.

The story of the Sunlight brand is a fascinating one, worthy of much more detailed description than space will allow here. Lever's first step was to find a brand name. Long before advertising agencies moved into the field, trademark agencies not only registered trademarks for businesses but researched and provided lists of potential names for new brands. For a fee, Lever's trademark agencies provided a list of names, none of which initially satisfied him; he then spent two days in his own office, trying to come up with the right name for soap. Only then did he look at the agent's list again, and realize that the name he wanted had been there all along: Sunlight.

Lever then spent several years trying to find a soap manufacturer who could give him consistent quality. In 1885, after several disappointments, he purchased a soap works and began to manufacture his own brand. Lever knew nothing about making soap, but he knew how to manage people who did; he recruited the best technicians and managers he could find, paid them top wages and encouraged them to innovate. The greatest breakthroughs, though, were in advertising and promotions. Advertising campaigns for soap were not new, and some, like those designed by Andrew Barratt at the Pears Company, were highly sophisticated and successful. What distinguished Lever's efforts were the sheer quantity of advertising – in 1905 he is estimated to have spent £2 million on advertising – and the use of every imaginable promotional tool besides, from door-to-door selling to give-aways and prize contests. Again, none of these methods was new in itself; what was remarkable was their combined deployment as part of a larger brand strategy. Lever's methods were first regarded with contempt by his rivals; but as Sunlight's sales grew, contempt became alarm, and alarm gave way to imitation.

Lever was one of the great marketing men of all time. Sunlight was followed by other successes; between 1885 and 1914, Lever launched a major new brand every two years. But what motivated this remarkable figure? Did he sell soap in order to make money? Of course he did: Lever enjoyed prosperity as much as anyone. But he also had a deep belief, based on his personal philosophy and religious convictions, that the products he developed and sold were making life better for the people who bought them. Had he not believed this, it is doubtful if he would have sold them. Cleanliness, hygiene and the prevention of disease were important moral and social issues in Victorian England, and Lever was an archetypal figure of a values set which stressed the importance of a duty to society: the same outlook could be seen in his approach to politics (he served as a Liberal MP), his work in welfare and housing reform at Port Sunlight, the town he built for his workers, and in his efforts to bring prosperity and a higher standard of living to areas of the world as diverse as the Congo, the Solomon Islands and the Outer Hebrides, all places where he had business interests.

While Lever's brands were making history, on the far side of the world another of management's great figures was growing up in poverty in a farming village in Wakayama Prefecture, south of Osaka. Matsushita Konosuke's father had gone bankrupt speculating in the rice market, and the boy was forced to leave school early, taking employment as a shopkeeper's apprentice in Osaka. Matsushita learned the retail business at an early age, and, like Lever, his personal convictions and religious beliefs shaped his approach to business. Founding his own electrical equipment business in 1917, he achieved nationwide success with the National brand of bicycle lamps, and in the 1920s the Matsushita company diversified into many other consumer goods. The company was highly prosperous and grew rapidly. But Matsushita, influenced perhaps by the experiences of his father, detested greed and those who made money simply to become wealthy. He believed that companies like his had a mission to serve and improve the lives of the people, and to overcome poverty. He developed what is still known in Japan as the 'tap water philosophy': high-quality goods should be so cheap and commonly available that people could acquire and use them almost effortlessly, like turning on a tap to get water. Nor was this sense of mission confined to Matsushita himself: he instilled this view in every manager and worker in the firm, and made sure they shared his views.

Matsushita and Lever were different in many respects, but they shared one common value: that the purpose of marketing, mass marketing or otherwise, is to provide products that serve the needs of the people. This sense of belief, of purpose, was conveyed through their brands and supportive advertising and marketing efforts. They were aware of the need for brand image; but they backed up that image with a powerful sense of *brand conviction*. And in that sense, neither man was very far from the views of marketing advocated by both Philip Kotler and Thomas Aquinas.

## Marketing in history

Very little is known about how businesses in antiquity marketed their products and services, as there is a paucity of everyday business records (although archival and archaeological research is slowly changing this). By the time of the European Middle Ages, however, we can begin to see more evidence of marketing practices in the surviving commercial records of businesses, the private diaries and letters of businessmen, and in commentaries by philosophers and theologians. By the late thirteenth century, *practicas* or handbooks on business were beginning to emerge in economically developed areas such as northern Italy; the most famous of these is the *Practica della mercatura* written by the Florentine banker Francesco Balducci Pegolotti, first published around 1340 and widely reproduced (and plagiarized) for more than a century thereafter.

**By the time of the European Middle Ages, however, we can begin to see more evidence of marketing practices in the surviving commercial records of businesses.**

The history of marketing is a vast subject, and could easily form a book in its own right. Here, with limited space, let us look briefly at some of the basics: the 4 Ps – product, price, place and promotion – and the concept of branding.

## Products: specialization and quality

One of the features of businesses in the European Middle Ages was the sharp differentiation between the specialist firms which usually focused on local markets, and the highly diversified businesses which engaged in international trade. Iris Origo, whose account of the business methods of Francesco Datini was referred to in Chapter 2, believes this difference was primarily one of mindset: 'the fundamental distinction between the international merchant and the "little man" did not consist in whether his trade was wholesale or retail, or even in the quantity of his merchandise, but rather in the outlook of the two different kinds of men.'[5] Lack of capital also played a role. Those businessmen who had access to capital and could afford to expand overseas tended to diversify as far as possible, as diversification was an important element in their strategy of reducing risk. The smaller fry, however, were usually restricted to producing a small range of products. Unable to expand the range of their products, they instead emphasized quality.

The modern quality movement has many of its origins in medieval production practices, in particular the role played by the various craft guilds. The small, localized producers of Western Europe did not tend to brand themselves; rather, they relied on 'corporation brands' associated with a particular town or region (see below). One of the core elements of these corporation brands was a reputation for quality, and the craft guilds, to which all producers were required to belong, had an important role in setting and enforcing quality standards, the medieval equivalents of ISO 9000 and its companions. Cloth manufacturers who failed to produce cloth of the requisite weight and colour could be fined or even expelled from the guild and forced to cease trading. In the cloth towns and in many other centres of specialist production, quality was everyone's business; a failure by one business could affect the trade and reputation of many others.

The diversified businesses also practised product specialization. The Medici manufacturing division had a number of manufacturing facilities each producing a separate kind of cloth, and these too conformed to guild regulations. Perhaps the best example of product policy comes from the Cistercian monastic order, where individual monasteries and granges often specialized in particular agricultural products or types of industrial production, usually with an eye to meeting particular local or regional market needs. The Cistercians also operated what was in effect an internal market, where monasteries specializing in, say, mining or wine-making, would also cross-trade with monasteries producing foodstuffs. The overall aim was to produce not only a diverse range of goods, but to produce them in sufficient volume to meet internal needs and to generate a surplus which could be sold in national and international markets.

> Perhaps the best example of product policy comes from the Cistercian monastic order

In an era when prices for many goods, especially agricultural produce, were highly regulated, quality became the primary basis of competition for both individual businesses and guild associations. It became the basis for many famous brands (see below). Indeed, there developed a view, still prevalent in many quarters today, that a brand of sufficient quality will sell itself, without need for excessive advertising. Joseph Rowntree, the Quaker chocolate-maker of the late nineteenth century, was firmly against advertising on the grounds that a high-quality product needed no promotion (he was also convinced that advertising was dishonest). The policy worked, up to a point; after rapid early growth, sales started to level off, and Rowntree reluctantly conceded that quality was not everything and began to advertise.

Quality was also a key feature of the marketing programme of Henry Heinz, the Pittsburgh pickle-maker who launched H.J. Heinz & Co. in the 1880s. His approach was the opposite to that of Rowntree: Heinz argued that his product quality was so good that he should tell the world about it. But the two men shared a conviction, based in part on their religious principles, that products should be of the best possible quality, and that to sell sub-standard goods was to let down the consumer. The same attitude can be found in many Japanese entrepreneurs in that great period following the Meiji Restoration in 1868, when developing a successful business was seen not (or at least, not only) as a path to spiritual enrichment but also to improving national prosperity and making the country strong – making quality products was therefore a social duty. Matsushita Konosuke is a prime example of this; another less well-known one is Torii Shinjiro, who with his son Saji Keizo built up the Suntory distilling and brewing empire. Akadama Port Wine and Torisu Whisky, his most successful brands, might seem odd choices for national necessities; but Torii believed strongly that his goods were improving the quality of life both physically and spiritually (no pun intended) for many Japanese. He was almost certainly right.

One of the first full explanations of the role of quality in marketing was given by Charles Babbage in 1835. In his *Economy of Machinery and Manufactures*, he explains the difference between actual product quality and *perceived* quality. Customers, he says, when assessing the quality of goods before purchase, incur *costs*, in terms of time and sometimes also of money. The level of cost varies according to the good. The quality of loaf sugar, for example, can be verified quickly, usually on sight. The quality of tea takes longer to ascertain, and verification usually requires consumption of some portion of the product. Manufacturers can partially overcome this problem by sending quality signals to the customer, the most common of which is the maker's mark or trade mark (ancestor of the modern brand mark). So long as this mark is backed up by consistent product quality, manufacturers will be able to charge a premium price and make greater profits. For Babbage, as for Heinz and Rowntree, mass-production did not necessarily mean better quality; very often, mass-produced goods were of worse quality than those made under the craft system. This need to improve quality was a minor but significant motivation behind the scientific management movement of the twentieth century.

Price: regulation and value

Customers in the Middle Ages, and probably before that, were much more price-sensitive than has hitherto been realized, especially in commodities markets. Contrary to popular opinion today, prices did fluctuate, sometimes wildly, as local conditions impacted on distribution and affected the supply of goods. Price stabilization was an important policy of most governments in Europe, and was also employed by governments in the Middle East and Far East. Much of contemporary economic theory held that letting prices float could lead to ruinous competition, and also that pricing too low meant that producers did not receive full value for their labour. (Much the same view was advanced by the financier J.P. Morgan in the late nineteenth and early twentieth centuries, leading him to advocate the creation of giant combines that would have monopolies in their markets and set 'fair' prices.) As noted at the head of this chapter, however, a dissenting view following the ideas of Thomas Aquinas held that the fair price was that which was set in the market according to conditions of supply and demand. The tension over what constituted a fair price for goods continued for centuries, and has not entirely disappeared today.

> The tension over what constituted a fair price for goods continued for centuries, and has not entirely disappeared today

Despite widespread price regulation, much attention was paid to pricing, especially in overseas markets. The Medici Bank maintained a market intelligence service, one of whose primary purposes was the collection of price information in overseas markets; the tabulation of this data at head office in Florence played an important role in business policy. Francesco Pegolotti devotes much of his *Practica della mercatura* to giving price information on goods in markets from England across Europe to the Middle East and Central Asia; his price tables were followed and updated by many other writers. Walter of Henley, the fourteenth-century English author on agricultural management, also stresses that familiarity with local prices is among the tasks or functions of the estate manager.

Where price regulation was not in force, most businesses in Europe and in Asia followed an individual price system: that is, they charged each customer a spot price mutually agreed through negotiation (or in other words, they haggled). The price to be paid depended on what each individual customer was willing to pay, modified by what the seller was willing to accept. Although this model continues to be popular (and not just in Middle Eastern bazaars, either), it is very difficult to manage; airlines and hotels, which today use variants on the individual price strategy, have highly complex models which allow them to manage these systems profitably.

Given this complexity, experiments with single-price policies (products have the same price no matter who buys them or when) were relatively rare. The earliest successful use of single pricing seems to have been at the dry-goods store Echigo-ya, established in Edo (now Tokyo) by Mitsui Takatoshi around 1673. The common practice among retailers in Japan at the time was to set prices high and then negotiate discounts with customers on an individual basis. Mitsui set his prices low and refused to give discounts, and became a commercial success because customers knew what they would get for their money.

## MITSUI TAKATOSHI

**B**ORN IN 1622 IN MATSUZAKA, JAPAN, MITSUI went to work at thirteen as a sales assistant in a shop owned by his elder brother in Edo (Tokyo). In his early twenties he returned to Matsuzaka and set up his own shop, which he ran profitably for a number of years. With his accumulated savings as capital, in 1673 Mitsui founded the Echigo-ya dry goods store in Edo, based on the single-pricing principle. This was a revelation in Japanese retailing, and Echigo-ya with its low and predictable prices drew a steady stream of customers, especially from the lower-income groups. Mitsui began to branch out, setting up further shops in Kyoto and Osaka and also moving into money-exchange and banking. The various businesses were combined under a central office which became the founding institution of the later Mitsui *zaibatsu* and thence of the Mitsui group as it exists today. Mitsui died in Edo in 1694, but Echigo-ya lasted into the twentieth century.[6]

Whether Aristide Boucicaut had ever heard of Mitsui is debatable, but his pricing approach was much the same. The son of a Normandy hatmaker, Boucicaut came to Paris in the 1830s and went into the retail business. In 1848, in partnership with his wife Marguerite, Boucicaut opened a drapery shop, Au Bon Marché. Single-pricing was a key part of the Boucicauts' marketing strategy from the beginning, and continued to be so as the shop expanded to become Europe's first department store. Their example was followed by William Whiteley, who brought the department store concept to Britain, and by John Wanamaker, who introduced it to the United States. Single-pricing was taken to the limit by Frank Woolworth, who invented the chain store concept where *every* product was offered at the same price, five cents; after going bankrupt, Woolworth reinvented the idea with two price levels, five cents and ten cents, the famous 'five and dime', and this time succeeded.

## Distribution: challenge and risk

Unsurprisingly, given the low level of transportation technology, distribution was probably the biggest marketing problem of the Middle Ages, and remained so well into the twentieth century (as late as the 1930s, some writers on marketing were still referring to it as 'distribution'). In the West and in Japan we now take distribution almost for granted; yet we ignore it at our peril, as many dotcom retailers have found to their cost. And in countries such as Russia and China, distribution remains a major headache.

The medieval distribution system featured long-distance trade between regional centres handled by wholesalers, who then dealt with jobbers or direct with retailers (store-owners, market-traders, travelling peddlers and so on), who in turn sold goods on to the end customer. In essence, this system was not much different from the present one: the distribution problems faced by the Medici, the salt shippers of the Hanseatic League, the pepper merchants of Venice and Alexandria, and other large concerns were fundamentally little different from those of today. The differences were of degree rather than kind. Risk was of course a major factor, and even in the 1920s marketing writers like Paul Cherington and Fred Clark included the assumption of risk as one of the functions of the marketer.

Another major difference concerned the degree to which manufacturing firms became involved in the distribution chain. Vertical integration was relatively rare. The Medici Bank did its own wholesaling and some of its own transporting, but this was costly and most medieval firms tended to subcontract. The East India Company, on the other hand, began by contracting out shipping from India to Britain but found this to be inefficient and unreliable; by the mid-seventeenth century the company was investing in its own wholesaling facilities. Regulation played a role as well, many governments forbidding foreign ownership of distribution and transport businesses (notably, in modern China the government has been reluctant to allow foreign ownership in these sectors).

> The Medici Bank did its own wholesaling and some of its own transporting, but this was costly and most medieval firms tended to subcontract

There was for a long time debate on the ethics of allowing firms too much control through vertical integration, and as late as 1921 there was a vigorous argument between two noted economists, Lewis Haney and L.D.H. Weld, about the ethics and efficiency of 'integrated marketing' by the big meat-packing firms in the USA such as Armour and Swift.

## Promotion: advertising and publicity

Above-the-line promotion was relatively undeveloped before the eighteenth century. Gutenberg had invented the printing press in the mid-fifteenth century, but there was no overnight revolution: it was many decades before printing became cheap enough to allow for mass advertising. Prior to this period, print advertising was limited to what could be written on signboards or painted on walls. Noticeboards advertising goods and services have been found in the ruins of Pompeii, and almost certainly existed well before that. There was also advertising by voice, through media such as hiring criers to walk the streets and announce the availability and price of goods; whether and how well this worked is not known, but the practice persisted in many cultures for centuries.

From around 1700 onwards, advertising grew rapidly in importance in the West. Advances in the mechanization of printing meant that printed handbills and posters were now cheap to mass-produce, and corresponding improvements in education meant there was a wider audience for mass communications. The Golden Age of advertising between 1700 and 1800 saw printed advertisements for every conceivable product appear in every conceivable venue, and what the early advertisers lacked in scientific application they more than made up for in enthusiasm.

In the nineteenth century, advertising became a considerable force. Newspaper advertisements became a major channel of communication, if a costly one, and poster and billboard advertising became more sophisticated. Products like soap, with large potential markets, became major battlegrounds between manufacturers, and men like William Lever and Andrew Barratt at Pears began spending hitherto unheard-of sums on advertising. Inevitably, a backlash began: politicians and clergymen believed that advertising persuaded people to buy goods for which they had no need, while economists like Thorstein Veblen argued that advertising had no proven efficiency and was inherently wasteful. Many businessmen agreed with him (the problem of whether advertising works and, if so, how you measure its effectiveness remains a vexing one today). It was this questioning of the efficacy of advertising that led writers like Herbert Casson and Walter Dill Scott to begin considering the latest advances in science and applying them to the core problems of advertising and of marketing more generally.

If advertising was underdeveloped, below-the-line promotion was as developed or even more so than today. Many of the methods of promotion we now use, including giving away samples, door-to-door canvassing and product demonstrations, were in use in the Middle Ages and probably long before that. From the beginning of the print media era, around 1700, it was obvious to many that favourable or even unfavourable publicity was in effect advertising without fee, and many entrepreneurs preferred the former to the latter. Dr Henry Bate-Dudley, playwright, journalist, clergyman and duellist (he was known in his own time as 'the Fighting Parson'), launched his newspaper the *Morning Post*, ancestor of today's *Daily Telegraph*, in the mid-eighteenth century by hiring a marching band and parading at the front of it down Piccadilly for several hours. In the century following, P.T. Barnum and Samuel

Colt were masters of publicity. The British department store-owner William Whiteley also shunned advertising, which he saw as wasteful and unnecessary; planting a few stories in the London press gave him the same effect for no cost. The visit of Queen Victoria to Whiteley's store in 1876 and the ensuing publicity brought him thousands of customers.

> From the beginning of the print media era, around 1700, it was obvious to many that favourable or even unfavourable publicity was in effect advertising without fee

For most, however, advertising and publicity were not in opposition; the best marketers were those who knew how to use both to maximum effect. Few better examples can be found than that of Henry J. Heinz. A leader in advertising – he designed the original '57 Varieties' campaign himself after coming up with the slogan while travelling on a streetcar in New York – he was also a master of promotion. At the Chicago World's Fair he gave away a small pin in the shape of a pickle to everyone who came to the Heinz Pavillion: 15,000 people a day jammed the entrance to the Pavillion, and at one point the floor threatened to give way. Heinz also built the Heinz Ocean Pier in Atlantic City, sometimes called the 'Crystal Palace by the Sea' and sometimes, less reverently, 'The Sea Shore Home of the 57 Varieties'. Here, as well as a sunroom and a library, was a restaurant and kitchen which conducted demonstrations and gave away samples of Heinz products; it attracted upwards of 20,000 people a year.

## HENRY J. HEINZ

**BORN IN PITTSBURGH IN 1844, HENRY HEINZ** went into business at the age of eight, selling surplus vegetables from the family garden. By the time he was sixteen he owned several garden plots and hothouses, employed local women to sell door to door, and supplied vegetables on a wholesale basis to several Pittsburgh grocers. In 1869 he and a partner, L.C. Noble, set up a company to bottle and sell horseradish. This failed in 1875, but the following year Heinz was back in business making and selling a variety of tinned and bottled foodstuffs. This time he never looked back.

The idea for the '57 Varieties' brand was Heinz's own. It came to him while riding on a streetcar in New York in 1896, when he saw an advertising card for a shoe store which used the slogan '21 styles', and began musing on whether this might work for his own business. As he tells the story: 'I said to myself, "we do not have styles of products, but we do have varieties of products". Counting up how many we had, I counted well beyond 57, but "57" kept coming back into my mind. "Seven, seven" – there are so many illustrations of the psychological influence of that figure and of its alluring significance to people of all ages and races that "58 Varieties" or "59 Varieties" did not appeal at all to me as being equally strong. I got off the train immediately, went down to the lithographers, where I designed a street-car card and had it distributed throughout the United States. I myself did not realize how highly successful a slogan it was going to be.'

Heinz was also determined to produce the best quality goods, and entered into contracts with farmers that would allow him to dictate what seed the farmers would plant and when it would be harvested; in exchange, the farmers were paid well above the spot market price for their produce. One of his slogans was 'Good foods, properly processed, will keep without the addition of preservatives'.

## The early history of brands

As noted, lack of capital meant that only a small number of firms had the ability to expand and thus most remained highly specialized and localized. In any case, medieval European society was much more group-oriented and corporatist than it is today. These two factors meant that firms preferred to seek alliances and partnerships in order to achieve growth, most commonly through the corporation structure of local craft guilds and guilds merchant.

This meant that few firms had the opportunity to create distinctive brands for themselves. The Medici Bank certainly approached the status of a brand in financial services, as did a few other financial institutions, such as the Society of the Bardi (Florence), the Bank of St George (Genoa) and the Steelyard (the Hanseatic League's office in London). Collectivities of producers, however, were very successful at establishing brands. The cloth manufacturers of Flanders, for example, chose niche product strategies, specializing in fabrics of a certain weave, weight and/or colour. Thus the fabrics became known as cloth of Arras, cloth of Douai, cloth of Tournai and so on, depending on where they were made, and they developed images and reputations for quality based on that name. The same process was repeated in a variety of industries: Bordeaux and Malmsey in wine, Cordoba in leather products, Toledo, Telemark and Dalarna in steel and weapons, and so on. These regional brands remain popular in Europe today, and many such as brie, champagne and cognac have become synonymous with the goods they represent, in the same way that in more modern times Levis became synonymous with blue jeans in the USA and Hoover with vacuum cleaners in Britain. Goods imported from beyond Europe were subjected to the same process. By the seventeenth century the name 'china' was being applied to a range of goods of oriental origin including silk, tea and porcelain, in effect turning 'china' into a sort of prototype global brand.

Branding was also being developed in China at around the same time. This was branding much more as we would recognize it today, with a brand mark serving as indication of quality and linked to a widely held customer image of a product. Brand-marked metal tools and implements began appearing in China as early as the Song dynasty in the tenth century, and corporate brands rapidly became popular in many sectors. Pharmaceuticals were heavily branded, and names such as Lei Yunshang from Shanghai and Tongrentang from Beijing became household names; the latter established multiple outlets and became known all over China. The Caizhi Zhai confectionery company in Suzhou also became known nationally for its distinctively shaped products. Qilu wine and Yipin Zhai calligraphy brushes are later examples of brands reaching national prominence, indicating how strong branding was in Chinese commercial thinking.

**Branding was also being developed in China at around the same time. This was branding much more as we would recognize it today**

## Marketing in the modern age

Enter the psychologists

As noted above, one of the burning questions in business by 1900 was whether marketing, and in particular advertising, actually worked. To answer this question, businessmen and also academics from the newly emerging business schools consulted another new discipline, that of psychology. The emergence of marketing as a discipline coincided with the great excitement then being generated by the works of Freud and his contemporaries. An interest in the workings of the subconscious and responses to stimuli was seen immediately to be of importance in studying customer behaviour, and there was also a strong interest in relationships between producer and customer. Relationship marketing, which became fashionable in the 1990s, was equally a hot topic around 1910. George Orange, author of an article on mail-order advertising for the Harmsworth Business Library in 1911, warned that mass communication does not mean that customers can be treated as a single mass: there is a need to ensure that mail-order advertisements, or 'shots', as he calls them, are personalized and appeal to the individual. He also points out that mail-order customers, if treated well and if a relationship can be developed, have a high propensity to repeat business, which is where the real profitability lies, and urges advertisers not to be seduced by new technology and to stick to first principles. (In the 1980s, W. Earl Sasser was still attempting to drive home the same point in his articles in *Harvard Business Review*.)

One of the most important synthesizers of psychological theory and advertising practice was Walter Dill Scott at Northwestern University. His *The Psychology of Advertising* went through many editions over the course of thirty years, but always maintained the core theme of showing the importance of science for advertising, maintaining that 'no advertisement that defies the established laws of psychology can hope to be successful'. Scott's main achievement is to show the links between psychology, the internal workings of the mind, and perception, the physical stimuli provided by the senses that cause people to respond to advertising. As he says, 'Advertising is an appeal to the senses, a stimulation of the senses by the use of symbols.' Psychology must also be complemented by a study of optics.

Scott developed an early model of how advertising works, which he calls 'attention-comprehension-understanding'.[7] The message must first get the customer's attention, and it must do so by appealing to his or her perceptive senses. He describes attention as the 'gateway' to the customer's mind. Once the message is through the gateway, however, it must still be comprehended; that is, the customer must know what the message is about and what product it refers to. Provided the customer attends to and comprehends the message, however, there is a final hurdle to be got over; the customer must understand what relevance the message has to himself or herself; that is, will the product being advertised satisfy some personal need or desire? Scott comments that 'in advertising we are not dealing with trifling tricks and artifices, but with the fundamental principles of human nature', another basic concept which no advertiser or marketer can afford to ignore.

## Scientific marketing

For Scott and also for Herbert Casson, whose book *Advertisements and Sales* (1913) was the first systematic attempt to apply the principles of scientific management to marketing, there was no question that anyone was 'inventing' the discipline of marketing. Rather, Scott and Casson see themselves as being on a voyage of discovery. Marketing has existed since the beginning of business; but as time passes, economies grow, businesses become larger and distribution chains become longer, it has grown more complex. By employing psychology and the measurement and analysis techniques of scientific management, Scott and Casson hoped to cut through some of the complexity, seek out first principles and create a structure and organization for the mass of accumulated knowledge.

The management revolution was not about reinventing management, but about organizing it and making it more systematic, in keeping with the scientific spirit of the time.

Yet these were not passionless organizers. Behind the prose, one occasionally gets a glimpse of real excitement. C.B. Thompson, a contemporary of Casson who also wrote on scientific management in marketing, describes the 'pride in the efficient management of a business for the sheer artistic satisfaction that comes from doing a thing exactly right'.[8] Casson, always more lyrical, once wrote: 'The business world is sparkling with romance and adventure. There is nothing wonderful in the fairytales of Arabia that cannot be equalled by any department store.'[9]

## As it was in the beginning...

Marketing emerged as a distinct discipline and school of thought at the beginning of the twentieth century. Before that time, marketing was not regarded as something separate, a business specialization in the same way that accounting and engineering were. Rather, marketing was what managers *did*; it was one of their reasons for being managers. Considering this picture, a passage from Peter Drucker comes to mind: 'There is only one valid definition of business purpose: *to create a customer*.'[10] Elsewhere, the great man writes that managers really only have two duties: innovation and marketing. Sam Colt, William Lever, Cyrus McCormick, William Pirrie, Mitsui Takatoshi, Henry Heinz and many others prove his point.

The codification and analysis of marketing during the last century was prompted by two factors: the late Victorian passion for organizing knowledge that was present in society more generally, and the genuine need to come to terms with a changing economic climate and a more complex series of problems that required solution. The result of this process was the development of mass marketing. Today, increasingly, marketers are turning away from generic mass marketing solutions and towards more personalized marketing, based on relationships with individual customers and an understanding of how the goods and services being sold are performing functions that are at least as much social as they are economic. Marketing is turning full circle.

*Notes to chapter 4*

1 Arch Shaw's *Some Problems in Market Distribution* (1912) is usually regarded as the first marketing textbook. The first formal marketing course was taught by Paul Cherington at Harvard Business School in 1908, although some commercial colleges had offered basic training in marketing methods as far back as the 1860s in the USA. Italian *scuole d'abaco* had been providing primers in market knowledge as far back as the fifteenth century.
2 Donaldson, Bill (1996) 'Marketing, foundation of', in Malcolm Warner (ed.), *International Encyclopaedia of Business and Management*, London: Routledge, vol. 4, p. 3209.
3 Urwick, L.F. (1932) *The Management of Tomorrow*, London: Nisbet, p. 81.
4 For more information on Patterson's approach to sales, see Johnson, R. and Lynch, R. (1932) *The Sales Strategy of John H. Patterson*, Chicago: Dartnell.
5 Origo, Iris (1957) *The Merchant of Prato*, London: Jonathan Cape, p. 89.
6 I am grateful to Professor Sasaki Tsuneo for providing the information on Mitsui on which this account is based.
7 This is a direct ancestor of the AIDA (awareness-interest-desire-action) model commonly used today.
8 Thompson, C.B. (1914) *Scientific Management*, Cambridge, MA: Harvard University Press, p. 545.
9 Casson, Herbert N. (1913) *Advertisements and Sales*, London: Pitman, p. 149.
10 Drucker, Peter (1973) *People and Performance: The Best of Peter Drucker on Management*, London: Heinemann, p. 89.

# 5

# Organizations: the building blocks of civilization

> Organization is older than history
> 
> *Edward D. Jones*

The somewhat ponderous term 'organization behaviour'[1] actually describes one of the most complex and fascinating aspects of business: how businesses are structured, how their parts are interrelated, how the human beings who make up the organization's primary elements function and interact with one another. Almost everything about a business – the effectiveness of its communications, the efficiency of its production, the happiness of its members, the satisfaction of its customers and, most of all, the extent of its profits – depends on how, and how well, that business is organized.

Businesses do not function without some form of organization, no matter how 'lean' or 'delayered' or 'democratic' or even 'chaotic' that form may be. Just as anarchy is a form of political system and atheism is a form of belief, early 1990s concepts like the 'fuzzy organization' or the 'chaos organization' or the 'virtual organization' are still, nonetheless, forms of organization. All businesses are organizations. Organization is part of what being a business is all about.

The first writers to explicitly consider business organization in the years before and after the First World War recognized that organization *per se* was nothing new. Edward D. Jones, who wrote a series of articles on the relevance of military history to management in *Engineering Magazine* in 1912, commented:

> The art of administration is as old as the human race. Even the leading wolf of a pack is an administrator. Organization is older than history, for the earliest documents, such as the code of Hammurabi, show the evidences of many generations of systematized social life. The real pioneers are the unknown promoters of the stone age, and the system-makers of the bronze age. Long ago almost every conceivable experiment in organization was first made. The records of history tell us of large units and small ones, of great and slight differentiation of functions, of extreme division and extreme concentration of authority, of mild and severe sanctions, of appeal to system and appeal to passion, of trust in numbers and trust in leadership. Of the vast variety of units of organization through which human intelligence has worked, and through which human purposes have been achieved, or thwarted, the greater part has passed away; and the names of them, even, have been forgotten.[2]

As long as there have been human beings, there have been organizations. Without organizations, the pyramids, the hanging gardens and the Great Wall could not have been built; without organizations, cities could not have flourished and been fed, kingdoms could not have collected taxes and raised armies, and traders could not have found their way from country to country and continent to continent, creating wealth and bringing prosperity. Jones was scarcely exaggerating when he referred to organizations as the building blocks of civilization.

**As long as there have been human beings, there have been organizations**

What is astonishing about the writers on organization during this early period, from around 1890 through to the early 1930s, is the breadth of their interests and the extent of their search for the principles of organization. An array of other disciplines – history, military science, law, political science, sociology, psychology, biology, engineering, economics – was studied and brought into play in order to try to understand a phenomenon that seemed as old as time. In the work of the writers of this time – Henri Fayol, John Davis, Charles Knoeppel, Dexter Kimball, Herbert Casson, Frank Mason, James Mooney, Luther Gulick, Chester Barnard and Mary Parker Follett, to name just a few of the best – one often finds the sense of excitement that is also found in accounts of voyages of exploration and discovery. These people were not *inventing* organization: they were seeking to understand what they regarded as an omnipresent phenomenon.

All these writers start from one fundamental point: the idea, noted above, that organization is a fundamental of human civilization. Organizations are things people create when they join together for a common purpose, be that purpose the gathering of food, mutual defence and safety, education, worship, recreation, or business and economic activity. When undertaking new ventures, rather than creating entirely new types of organization, people sensibly adopt and adapt existing forms. Many of the first businesses were primarily family affairs, and they quite naturally adopted the family concept as their basic organizational model. In other cases, where business was run and managed by governments or by religious sects, the existing models of civil service and temple bureaucracy were adopted. Both these types of business organization existed for thousands of years, and continue to predominate in many parts of the world.

One of the most radical developments in the history of organizations came in the European Middle Ages, when the monastic orders developed a hybrid form of organization, based partly on bureaucracy and partly on the family, which allowed much more flexibility without loss of control. Another powerful influence came in the seventeenth century when the appearance of permanent standing armies led to further developments in the arts of coordination and control. James Mooney, then vice-president of General Motors, noted in 1931 that these two organization forms, the monasteries and the military, prefigured the modern business organization in almost every respect. But other influences have remained powerful, as we shall see.

## Families and partners

The earliest businesses were probably family affairs. The reasons for this are fairly simple. For any business organization to function successfully, it is necessary that the members be able to communicate and work with each other, that they share at least some common assumptions and common goals, and that they trust each other. In cultures which employ the family business model, the latter is often particularly important: one is generally less likely to be cheated by a brother than by a stranger. It may be no accident that the family model is most common where business risks are highest and where laws and regulations are weak. In business as in daily life, the family provides many of its own defences.

Today, we think of family businesses mostly in connection with East Asia, where the 'Chinese family business' is a widely studied phenomenon. Family business has a long history in China, stretching back at least to the Shang period (1700–1200 BC) and probably much further than that. In ancient China, the *zu* (family group) became the main unit of both administration and economic activity. Various experiments with state control of business were made in succeeding centuries, but by the time of the Song dynasty in the tenth century AD, when China was probably the world's greatest economic power, the family model was predominant. It remained so until after 1949, when Mao Zedong abolished private ownership of business and replaced it with state control.[3] In the overseas Chinese communities of East and Southeast Asia, the family model remains common today, and even very large companies like the CP Group in Thailand, the Salim Group in Indonesia, the Kerry Group in Malaysia and Hutchison Whampoa in Hong Kong are managed (at the top levels at least) by members of extended families.

## ROBERT KWOK

**BORN KWOK HOCK NIEN IN JOHOR BAHRU, MALAYA,** in 1923, Robert Kwok was the son of a Hokkien-speaking family from Fuzhou province who had emigrated from China following the toppling of the empire in 1911. His father established a successful food wholesaling business, and Kwok was educated in Johor Bahru and then Raffles College, Singapore, where his studies were interrupted by the Second World War. After spending part of the 1950s in London, he returned to Malaya and established his first business, a sugar refinery. Since then he has built up a network of hundreds of companies with interests in Malaysia (as Malaya became), Singapore, Indonesia, the Philippines, Hong Kong and China.

Like many overseas Chinese business leaders, Kwok manages his business through networks of family and personal contacts. He and two of his sons now reside in Hong Kong, where they manage the affairs of the Kerry group; his eldest son Philip remains in Singapore, looking after the family interests there, and the group's Philippine interests are managed by a cousin. Kwok is also a very active member of the International Association of Fuzhous, the body which supports overseas Chinese with roots in Fuzhou province, and sits on its executive committee.

Kwok is a typical, highly successful example of an overseas Chinese entrepreneur who has built up a large and diversified business using a 'Confucian' model of management that focuses on personal relationships and family ties.

---

In India, the social position of merchants was defined by the rules of caste, and family businesses were often hereditary concerns, sometimes continuing in the same family for hundreds of years. The Jagat Seth, the great Indian banker of the eighteenth century (see Chapter 2), came from a Jain family which had been engaged in the banking trade for decades; he inherited the business from an uncle, and passed it on to his nephews. In the Middle East, too, businesses were family concerns which could pass down through generations. The family business makes its first recorded appearance in Mesopotamia: the international trading concern run by Pusu-ken of Ashur, noted in Chapter 2, which also included Pusu-ken's wife Lamassi and their four sons, is an excellent example. Families were the main business unit in classical Greece and

Rome, and on into the Middle Ages; in the organizational structure of the Medici bank, the top tier of senior managers and principal partners was referred to as the *famiglia*. The family model continues to be an important influence especially in southern Europe, where even very large and diverse businesses such as Fiat continue to reserve important management positions for members of the Agnelli family.

American writers of the mid-twentieth century, including notably Adolph Berle and Gardiner Means and, later, Alfred Chandler, argued that the family business model is incompatible with modern economic conditions, and that a separation of ownership and control, with owners of the business stepping back and delegating control to professional managers, was essential to good management. (Another writer, the Trotskyite-turned-libertarian James Burnham, argued that the separation of ownership and control was an illusion; give people control and in time they will take ownership as well, ousting the former owners from their positions of power.) But the family model works in many instances because, particularly at the small business level, it allows for high degrees of both control and flexibility. Authority tends to flow down from the head of the family, the patriarch or matriarch, but chains of command tend to be short. Because managers know each other well and trust each other, formal planning and responsibilities are rarely necessary; instead, plans and roles evolve on an ad hoc basis, with responsibility delegated where needed. The high degree of trust means lower levels of risk.

## JAMES BURNHAM

**B**URNHAM WAS BORN IN CHICAGO IN **1905** into a well-to-do family (his father was a railway executive). Attending Princeton University in the 1920s he studied philosophy and, like many young middle-class Americans, thought he saw in communism an answer to the ills of society. In 1935 he joined the Fourth International Party and became a strong supporter of its leader, Leon Trotsky, and a frequent contributor to left-wing magazines. His disillusionment with Josef Stalin led in time to a more general disenchantment with communism; he quarrelled with Trotsky shortly before the latter's murder, and began to set out his own view that communism and fascism were just two halves of the same coin.

In the 1940s, Burnham believed that the capitalist system was doomed. The reason for this, he argued, was the failure of the owners of capital, of businesses, to take responsibility for running them. He thought that the delegation of control to professional managers was an evil that would lead to technocracy and totalitarianism. Against Adolph Berle and Gardiner Means, who believed that a separation of ownership and control was essential to good conduct of business, Burnham argued that the separation was a sham; give the managers control, and in time they will seize ownership for themselves as well. Burnham's views were highly influential in right-wing political circles in the 1950s, and he was later awarded the Presidential Medal of Freedom by Ronald Reagan. His worst fears were never realized, but his most famous work, *The Managerial Revolution*, remains both readable and relevant.

---

However, the family business has several drawbacks. First, most family businesses are also hereditary concerns, with control and ownership being handed down from parent to child. This works only so long as the younger generation are content to inherit in this fashion. But children tend to have minds of their own, and often have no interest in taking over the family firm. Hong Kong and Taiwan, where the family business is very common, have higher rates of business closure than either the USA or Britain. The most common reason for business closure in both countries is lack of a son or daughter who will take on the business when the parent retires.

Second, there is no guarantee that the child will have inherited the managerial abilities of the parent; so far as we know, there is no management gene. The problem of incompetent succession has affected many of the great family firms of the past, including the Medici Bank and, even more catastrophically, the great banking house of Fugger of Augsburg. Built up in the early sixteenth century by Jakob Fugger, the business became the Rothschilds of its day, holding the banking business of the Holy Roman Empire and many other governments of Europe (see Chapter 6). His nephew and successor, Anton Fugger, was his equal in managerial talent. But the next in succession, Anton's nephew Hans Jakob Fugger, was a disaster, making a series of reckless loans that nearly bankrupted the house. Thrown out of the business by his family, he was succeeded by his cousin Marx Fugger,

> **The problem of incompetent succession has affected many of the great family firms of the past, including the Medici Bank**

a man of mediocre talents at best who could only look on helplessly as the most powerful business of the age slid into ruin.

Finally, and perhaps of most immediate consequence, there is the issue of the span of control. Even the most brilliant manager cannot be everywhere at once, and as businesses grow there comes the issue of how and to whom authority and responsibility should be delegated. Large extended families can run large extended businesses, but few families are quite big enough to run a multinational. Eventually there comes a time when managers from outside the family need to be incorporated into the structure. One popular early method of doing so was by marriage: talented employees might have their abilities recognized by an offer to marry into the owner's family, an act which also bound the employee's loyalty more closely to the company. This practice is still sometimes observed in the overseas Chinese community of Southeast Asia, where families make 'strategic marriages' in order to cement business partnerships with other families. Women who owned businesses, especially widows who took control of a business after the death of their husband, might also consider marriage to a senior manager in order to secure the latter's business talents. The most famous example of this, perhaps, is the case of Khadijah, the widowed merchant of Mecca, who went on to marry her caravan master and business manager, Mohammed.

The ability of firms to use marriage in this fashion was often constrained, however, not least by the supply of unmarried female relatives, and the willingness or otherwise of said relatives to serve as part of what was in effect a top management compensation package. A rather more enlightened form of alliance was the business partnership. Partnerships between entrepreneurs and between businesses go back into antiquity, but the partnership was raised to a high art in medieval Italy, where both intra-firm and inter-firm partnerships became an essential building block of organization. Entire business enterprises were built using nothing more than networks of partnerships. Francesco Datini, the textiles manufacturer and international wholesaler based in Italy but with branch offices in France and Spain, often had as many as eight partnerships at a time, in each of which he was *capo* or senior partner. In some cases, both he and his junior partner or partners contributed capital; in others, as in his textiles business in Prato, near Florence, Datini contributed the capital and Niccolò di Giunta, the junior partner, provided management skills and specialist knowledge of cloth-making which Datini lacked.

## FRANCESCO DATINI

**BORN IN THE SMALL TOWN OF PRATO**, north of Florence, around 1335, Datini was orphaned when his parents died in the Black Death of 1349. At age fourteen he went to work as an apprentice for a trader in Florence, and at fifteen, using a small legacy left by his father, travelled to Avignon, France, then the site of the papal court and host to a thriving Italian financial and business community. Accumulating a little capital, Datini set up his own business dealing first in arms and armour and later in all manner of goods including cloth and works of art. By 1378 he had also branched out into banking. In 1382 he returned home to Prato, setting up a variety of businesses there and in Florence and then branching out into ventures in Pisa, Genoa and Barcelona. Opportunistic and flexible in his approach, Datini was also a compulsive gatherer of information and maintained correspondents all over Europe who provided him with market information. Datini always remained diversified, manufacturing and trading in many different goods, a deliberate risk-reduction strategy adopted by many of his peers at a time when the risks associated with physically transporting and distributing goods were very high. His use of partnerships allowed him the flexibility to adapt to market trends and lay off risk in a very cost-effective manner. However, another outbreak of plague in 1399–1400 killed off several of his most trusted partners, and he closed his Genoa branch and went into semi-retirement until his death in 1410.

These medieval partnerships were simple devices, yet capable of endless permutation. Partnerships could include any number of partners, though between two and five was most common. Some partners might contribute capital but remain out of the daily running of the business; others, as in the case of Niccolò di Giunta, contributed no money, bringing to the table instead their own skills and ability; others would contribute both capital and management skills. Sometimes the same group of partners would establish more than one business venture, in which case a separate partnership would be drawn up for each venture. In some cases one partner would serve as *capo*, or controlling partner, managing the business and taking the largest share of the profits; in others, the partners would be approximately equal. Partnerships were also usually of very short duration, between two and three years; at the conclusion of the partnership, the partners could reform it on the same terms as before, on different terms, bring in new partners, or dissolve it entirely.

Businesses like Datini's employed partnerships in a fluid manner, forming new ones to take advantage of business opportunities and dissolving them when those opportunities faded. To the modern eye they are complex and dynamic networks, constantly changing form like an amoeba: hell for the business historian who has to try to decipher who was working with whom and when, but absolutely fascinating in their business implications. Endlessly flexible, the medieval partnership businesses functioned by creating a community of interest among the partners, exactly in the way that the 1990s concept of the limited life consortium (LLC) did.

> **Endlessly flexible, the medieval partnership businesses functioned by creating a community of interest among the partners**

Partnerships were an important way of extending the managerial span of control, but they too had their limits; the networks of partnerships could grow only so large before the law of diminishing returns began to set in. The Medici Bank solved this by increasing the size of each partnership, turning each into what was in effect a semi-independent business unit. Partners, particularly at the Tavola, the main banking office in Florence, and at the big silk and woollen cloth manufacturing concerns, were responsible for planning and oversight. Day-to-day management was increasingly directed to *fattori* (factors, or managers), who were usually men of ability promoted from within the ranks. As time passed, *fattori* might be invited to become partners, as in the case of Giovanni d'Amerigo Benci (see Chapter 2). Growth, then, was achieved by creating a pragmatic hybrid structure using both partnerships and directly employed managers, relying on the former for initial control and co-ordination and using the latter as tools to increase the power and reach of management. The combination was a highly effective one and was employed by the large overseas trading companies of the seventeenth century, the Hudson's Bay Company and the British and Dutch East India companies, and became standard practice in large European businesses of any sort down to the late nineteenth century.

## Bureaucracies

Bureaucracy, in modern management-speak, is a dirty word. Over the course of the twentieth century, bureaucracy has come to represent everything that is wrong about business management, and everything that management should not be. Bureaucracy means inefficiency, waste, overmanning, ineptitude. The modern image of bureaucracy owes much to the idea of the 'machine bureaucracy' described by Max Weber, a mechanistic system in which employees and customers alike are treated as cogs on a wheel. Later in the twentieth century, Lewis Mumford created a nightmare picture of the organization as a 'megatechnic wasteland', its life and soul squeezed out by a combination of remorseless technology and cast-iron hierarchy, its members reduced to the level of near-slavery. George Orwell gave us much the same thing in *1984*.

Bureaucracy is also irrevocably associated in the minds of many with government and with civil service inefficiency and incompetence. Yet, like it or not, methods of government administration have played a significant role in influencing management thought and practice, and at times businesses run by civil services have been highly effective. The Egypt of the Pharaohs was a country governed to a very high degree by its civil service, which not only managed to build monuments such as the Great Pyramids and the tombs of Thebes, but also managed the country's export trade and the many business sectors on which the state held a monopoly. In India, the Mauryan kingdom of Chandragupta (founded around 320 BC) had a large staff of paid civil servants who managed the crown's extensive business interests. It seems clear from the writings of Kautilya, the chief minister of the kingdom and head of the civil service who laid down extensive guidelines for administration, that the civil service was designed to run these business interests efficiently and profitably. In the Middle East, as Karl Moore and David Lewis describe in their book *Foundations of Corporate Empire*, business empires such as that of Tyre were organized and managed by the priests of the great Phoenician temples. There was no real difference between temple, civil government and business administration in Tyre, whose priest-managers were all-rounders capable of working in many different fields.

> There was no real difference between temple, civil government and business administration in Tyre, whose priest-managers were all-rounders capable of working in many different fields

## KAUTILYA

ALMOST NOTHING IS KNOWN OF THE LIFE OF KAUTILYA, also known as Canakya, but he was probably a minister in the government of Chandragupta Maurya, first king of the Mauryan or Gupta kingdom which flourished in north India for several centuries from about 320 BC. Chandragupta was an Indian prince who allied himself with Alexander the Great during the latter's invasion of India, and used the resulting political chaos to carve out an empire for himself which spanned much of north India. Kautilya's collected writings, the *Arthashastra*, became the kingdom's foundational political and philosophical text.

Kautilya is particularly interesting on the purpose of administration, which he sees not as simply serving the king's own interests. The king, indeed, is only one element in the administrative system. It is up to the king to provide leadership, but most of all the king is required to be the embodiment of the *dharma*, the rules and customs which hold society together and make life possible. In ancient Hindu thought, the *dharma* were not rules made by men, but were part of the fabric of the universe itself (rather like the later western concept of natural law). Upholding the *dharma* was both a duty and a necessity, not only for kings but for all administrators.

---

In China, as we saw in Chapter 2, the bureaucracy established by the Legalist emperor Qin Shi Huangdi later ossified and became a positive impediment to business, but in the early period it was clearly an efficient method of governance. And Chinese bureaucracy did throw up one outstanding figure at the very end of the Qing dynasty in the late nineteenth century, the talented general, administrator and businessman Li Hongzhang. Almost alone of his contemporaries, Li understood the need for China to modernize and liberalize its business institutions if it was to recover its strength and fend off the aggressive foreign powers. Noting the success of the Meiji Emperor and his followers in Japan, who in just three decades turned Japan from a decaying feudal society into one of the world's foremost economic and military powers, Li tried to work the same magic in China. His commercial ventures, such as the China Merchants' Navigation Company, won him the respect of his western commercial rivals. But as imperial China disintegrated at the seams, Li's talents were needed in too many places at once, and the managers appointed to take over his companies once he moved on were bureaucrats of the worst kind; without Li, the China Merchants' Navigation Company lasted only a few years.

## LI HONGZHANG

**BORN IN 1823 IN ANHUI PROVINCE,** Li passed his civil service entrance exams in 1844 and studied in Beijing, graduating in 1847. In 1853, still a relative junior, Li returned to his home province to help organize forces to oppose the Taiping Rebellion. Although the Imperial army was defeated in Anhui, Li himself fought with great distinction and was promoted several times. By 1860 he was in command of Imperial forces in Shanghai, and later commanded the Imperial armies that finally defeated the Taipings and suppressed the revolt. Loaded with honours, he became one of the leading figures in Chinese administration until his death in 1901.

During the Taiping wars, Li had served alongside western troops, notably the mercenaries of the Ever-Victorious Army led by the British officer Charles Gordon. The experience gave Li an awareness of the power and capabilities of the western nations, and he saw clearly that their pre-eminence was based in large part on their commercial success. Like his contemporaries Shibusawa and Fukuzawa in Japan, Li tried to stimulate the growth of western-style business enterprises, leading to the foundation of experimental firms such as the China Merchants' Navigation Company.

A prophet without honour, Li was one of the first Chinese to realize that western business and management methods could and must be adapted to the needs of China if the country was to combat western encroachment. His western rivals understood his strategy well, and worked hard to forestall him. Had his efforts commanded the support of his colleagues and of the

Empress, and had China been able to stage a Meiji-type economic reform in the 1880s and 1890s, much of the history of twentieth-century Asia might have been rather different.

In the West, during the Middle Ages bureaucracies were themselves effectively organized on the family model, dependent on the 'head of the household', the monarch. (Indeed, in the parlance of the time, the civil service was for long referred to as the 'king's household'.) The twelfth century in England saw major reforms, with talented administrators like Richard Fitz Neal writing the first handbook of administration, the *Diologus de Scaccario* (Course of the Exchequer) and Hubert Walter establishing permanent systems of information-gathering and record-keeping including permanent financial accounts. Both these practices influenced business practice in what we would now call the private sector; by the fourteenth century, business concerns were beginning to keep first financial and then other records on a systematic basis, and the idea of enshrining management procedures in written manuals became more common. Half a dozen manuals of governance and administration survive from this period, most famously a manual on estate management written by Walter of Henley around 1300, which covers not only technical issues related to agriculture *per se* but also concepts of what would later be called personnel management and marketing. Dorothea Oschinsky, the modern authority on Walter of Henley, believes that his treatise, like many others, was used as a textbook by law students at Oxford University, many of whom became stewards and factors after graduation.[4] (If so, then this is another early example of management education.)

By the end of the Middle Ages, England had not only the most efficient and effective government in Europe, it also had a business community that was beginning to punch above its weight. England was a small country with limited population and limited supplies of capital, but by 1500, and especially by 1600, its businessmen were a force to be reckoned with. Several factors contributed to this rise, but the use of systematic management techniques derived from the civil service bureaucracy must be reckoned as one of the foremost of these.

## HUBERT WALTER

**B**ORN AROUND 1140 IN NORFOLK, Walter was brought up in the household of his uncle Ranulf de Glanvill, justiciar (chief minister) to King Henry II. He was a civil servant and judge serving under de Glanvill until 1189, when on the accession of King Richard I he was appointed Bishop of Salisbury (like most administrators of the time, Walter had also taken holy orders). He accompanied the king on the Third Crusade in Palestine where he undertook a variety of tasks, organizing supplies for the siege of Acre, leading a cavalry charge at the Battle of Beit Nuba, undertaking negotiations with Saladin and conducting parties of pilgrims to Jerusalem. Back in England he became Archbishop of Canterbury, serving as justiciar and then chancellor of the exchequer. In both departments, Walter organized the administration and put it on a permanent footing, laying down systems for accounting, reporting and record-keeping that have lasted to this day. Although the English civil service had existed before Walter, it was he who laid the foundations for what was (once upon a time) the most effective government administration in the world. He died, still in office, in 1205.[5]

## Organization and faith: the rise of the monasteries

Meanwhile, a new form of bureaucracy had appeared on the scene. Religious organizations had been involved in management for many centuries. There were the 'temple capitalists' of Phoenicia, already referred to. There were the huge temples of Greek and Roman times (which had their counterparts in India and China), some of which were vast organizations supporting hundreds of priests and acolytes and owning thousands of acres of land. The priests had to be fed and the fabric of the temples had to be maintained, and this required money. To make money, temples went into business, not just agriculture but also shipping and manufacturing. These businesses in turn required management. In Rome, the high priests of the great temples of Jove and Minerva and Venus were also chief executive officers of businesses turning over several million *sesterces* a year.

Christianity started off as a grassroots religion, and for a long time resisted formal structures and authority. But so powerful is the need for human beings to organize that before long dioceses were being created and bishops were being elected. Monks, who withdrew from society to live in isolated communities, were given rules of conduct and governance. Even hermits, who were almost totally solitary, were regulated and classified into different orders (and if an 'organized hermit' isn't an oxymoron, then what is?).

Things changed forever in AD 312 when, during one of the late Roman Empire's frequent crises of imperial succession, the general Constantine, commander of the Army of the Rhine, marched his men southward over the Alps and down to the gates of Rome, where he defeated and killed his rival Maximus at the battle of Milvian Bridge and took the imperial throne for himself. It is debatable whether Constantine was a Christian (one account says he finally agreed to baptism on his deathbed), but he believed that Christianity, handled properly and co-opted by the Roman government, could prove a unifying force that would strengthen the empire. In AD 313 he legalized Christianity and made it the state religion, and endowed its bishops, especially the Bishop of Rome (not yet then known as Pope) with vast amounts of land and other resources. From thence there was no going back; the Catholic church had become involved in business management whether it liked it or not.

Monasticism, the withdrawal from the distractions of every day to seek a life of contemplation so as to draw nearer to God, was a cherished principle of early Christianity. Yet, as the Italian monk Benedict of Nursia discovered in the early sixth century AD (see Chapter 2), even dedicated men of God needed control, coordination, rules of conduct and all the other trappings of organization. The Benedictine rule provided these things through his simple set of rules for the management of monasteries. The rule was widely adopted, and by the later Middle Ages was in use in hundreds of monasteries across Europe.

The Benedictine system provided an excellent basis for organization within the individual monasteries. However, the enforcement of the rule depended on the strength and willpower of the monastery's leader, the abbot. And abbots, like other leaders, could be fallible. Standards were not evenly enforced; some abbots proved unable to master the financial aspects of monastery management and went into debt, while (of more concern to contemporary society) others were lax disciplinarians and failed to restrain their monks from the temptations of gambling, strong drink and women of dubious moral character.

> **The Benedictine system provided an excellent basis for organization within the individual monasteries**

The tenth century saw a massive, Europe-wide reform of the Benedictine Order organized from the monastery of Cluny in southern Burgundy. With the support of the leaders of the church, the abbots of Cluny tightened discipline and sent out tours of inspection to ensure that monasteries were being run according to the rule. The so-called Cluniac Reforms were very effective, but they had the effect of making the Order more bureaucratic. The reforms produced many talented administrators, and not a few Benedictines became bishops, archbishops and popes (and many more took on administrative posts in civil government).

But the Cluny project had its limitations. International in scope, with hundreds of monasteries and many thousands of monks spread all across the West, it attempted to establish control from a single central point. In practice, however, the Abbot of Cluny had limited resources at his disposal. The only way to find out what was happening in a monastery was to send someone there to see the situation in person; and although 'visitors', as these inspectors were known, were regularly despatched, inspections were expensive and time-consuming. Another problem was the continuing influence of local patrons, who expected favours in return for their gifts to local monasteries; the latter were often obligated to their patrons by law or local custom, and this often placed them in conflict with Cluny.

Broad and sweeping though they were, the Cluny reforms never quite reached their goals. Successful organizational change nearly always depends on the enthusiasm of and support for those responsible for carrying out the reforms. Even if change is initially successful, with time inertia begins to set in; the reformers find it harder to gain support, and harder too to keep up their own levels of enthusiasm, or to find successors who can do the same. Thus it was at Cluny.

The Cistercian Order

In the late eleventh century, a small groups of monks, dissatisfied with the autocratic rule of Cluny, broke away and founded their own monastery in the mountains of eastern France at Citeaux. Their movement would have passed unnoticed by history except for the arrival at the monastery gates some years later of a young nobleman named Bernard, who applied to join the monks. This young nobleman, later canonized as St Bernard of Clairvaux, was one of the most dynamic figures of the Middle Ages. Known mainly as a theologian and philosopher, he was also the architect of the Cistercian Order.

Bernard rapidly became famous as a thinker and preacher, and many recruits came to join the new order. Within a few years it became apparent that more monasteries would be needed to house them, and monks went out from Citeaux to found four new establishments at La Ferté, Pontigny, Morimond and Clairvaux (the last with Bernard as its abbot). These four were known as 'daughter houses'; Citeaux was known as the 'founder house'. Continuing increases in numbers of recruits gave rise to still further expansion, and the model of the original foundations continued to be followed. Each of the four 'daughter houses' founded new establishments and became in turn a 'founder house' with 'daughters' of its own. These 'daughters' in turn became 'founders', and so on.

## BERNARD OF CLAIRVAUX

**BERNARD WAS BORN NEAR DIJON, BURGUNDY, IN 1090,** the son of a noble family, and joined the Cistercian Order while in his early twenties. Bernard's organizational and intellectual powers were such that he quickly rose to high positions, and in 1125 he was chosen to lead a new monastic foundation at Clairvaux. Clairvaux became the centre of an astonishing expansion; over the next half-century, hundreds of Cistercian monasteries were established across Western Europe. Bernard himself became the most famous orator and theologian of his day, disputing with Peter Abelard and preaching the Second Crusade in 1147. Pious and ascetic, he was one of a minority of late medieval theologians who believed that trade and commerce were sinful; his inclusion in this book would have horrified him. But the organization which he led not only had a lasting influence on the shape of business organization, but was also a highly successful multinational commercial enterprise in its own right.

---

This was a model of harmonious decentralization such as had never before been seen. Using it, the Cistercian Order was almost immediately successful. By the time of Bernard's death in 1153, there were 330 Cistercian monasteries across Europe; by 1200, there were more than 500 establishments, and by 1400 there were over 750. Every country in Western Europe and most of Eastern Europe had large numbers of Cistercian houses; England alone had more than 80.

> **This was a model of harmonious decentralization such as had never before been seen**

Together, these monasteries represented an immense enterprise. No one has yet taken a Europe-wide census of the Cistercian Order and its holdings, but the larger monasteries such as Fountains and Rievaulx in Yorkshire or Tintern on the Welsh borders could have as many as 500 monks and lay brothers (the latter were subordinate members of the organization who did not take full monastic vows). Landholdings varied depending on the establishment and its location, but the largest houses in England owned as much as 40,000 acres each; and these were dwarfed by some of the huge Continental houses such as Leibus in eastern Germany, whose total landholdings were more than 600,000 acres. The Order as a whole must have owned tens of millions of acres and included hundreds of thousands of monks and lay brothers.

The key to the success of the Cistercians lies in their organization, at both macro and micro levels. As noted above, the system of 'founder houses' and 'daughter houses' was instrumental in the expansion of the Order, and it was retained as the basic framework of the Order's organization. This framework was formalized shortly after the order began to expand, in a document known as the *Carta Caritatis*, the 'Charter of Charity', which spelled out the relationship between establishments.

If Cluny was organized like a monarchy, the Cistercians were organized more like an extended family. Each founder house remained responsible for its daughter houses after their foundation, effectively acting as a kind of parent. Whereas at Cluny virtually all command and control was exercised directly from the centre, with the Cistercians control was exercised at a local level. Because each founder house was also in its turn a daughter house, each supervising monastery was itself supervised, with reporting going on up through the organization to the original four daughter houses and finally to Citeaux.

Further, the relationship between daughter and founder houses was rather different than that between Cluny and its subordinates. First, the daughter houses paid no contributions to their founders; each was a freestanding profit centre and could use its income as it liked within the rules of the Order. Founder houses were required to supervise daughter houses and ensure they kept to the principles of the organization, but they had to use incentives other than financial to achieve this. This alone meant that daughter houses had much more freedom and were much less likely to be involved in tensions with founder houses; relationships were therefore much smoother.

This apparently formless system was given shape by another very simple device, the General Chapter of the Order, a kind of annual general meeting held at Citeaux every year. Every abbot in the Order was expected to attend the General Chapter, or to send a senior representative from their monastery's 'management team'. In this way, the Abbot of Citeaux was able to keep his finger on the pulse of the organization and be personally assured that all the daughter houses were abiding by the Order's rules.

In tandem with the *Carta Caritatis* was a second document, the *Institutiones*, or Rule of the Order. While the first set out the Order's structure, the second spelled out the duties and responsibilities of its members. The Rule combined the features of mission statement and procedures manual, explaining in exact detail not only what was to be done but why it was to be done. The daily lives of monks and lay brothers, business and commercial activities, styles of architecture to be used in monastery buildings, all were regulated and tied to the Order's primary purpose.

Organization at the local level was treated just as carefully as the macro structure of the Order. Unlike the Cluny monasteries, Cistercian houses were always new foundations, usually on land which had not previously been cultivated or settled. Once land had been cleared or drained and put into production, each monastery established production units called 'granges'. Each grange was a self-contained unit, farming about 500–700 acres; if the monasteries were independent profit centres, then the granges can be regarded as production centres, each with its individual accounts and quotas. Nor did the Cistercians often use the Cluny system of tenant farming, where land was parcelled into manors farmed by either free tenants or serfs; they preferred to work their landholdings directly, with monks and lay brothers supervising a paid labour force.

> **Organization at the local level was treated just as carefully as the macro structure of the Order**

As noted in Chapter 2, the Cistercian structure proved to be an extremely powerful vehicle for economic growth and entrepreneurship. Within the structure of the Order, individual abbots were free to choose their own policies and exploit the resources available to them as they chose. In just a few decades, the Cistercians rose to rival the Benedictines in terms of numbers of monks and monasteries, and also economic clout. Before much longer they were moving in on the positions of power in the church hierarchy; archbishops and popes were now as likely to be Cistercians as Benedictines. In time, the organizational systems of both organizations ossified; the sixteenth-century Protestant Reformation dealt them severe blows, and today both orders are only a tiny fraction of their former size. But for a few centuries they were mighty forces in the Christian world.

## Military organization comes of age

Military organizations also began on the family model, with family members and their retainers and servants comprising military units. When large armies were assembled, the commanders were drawn from the most important families and/or those with the largest family forces at their disposal. This was the simplest and most basic military system, and in many parts of the world it continued to be in use down into modern times. In Japan, the military forces of the Shogunate were the extended families and personal households of the *daimyo*, and this system continued right down to the Meiji Restoration of 1868. In India and the Middle East the system lasted until the advent of European colonial rule. The feudal system of the early Middle Ages in Europe was also based initially on family structures. The feudal oath of allegiance which knights took to their lords bound them in a kind of mock-familial relationship; Charlemagne, at least in the troubadour epic *The Song of Roland*, is looked on by his knights such as Roland and Olivier as a kind of pseudo-father.

Other military systems were based on bureaucracy. Ancient Egypt, a rich country which could usually afford to maintain a standing army, initially organized its military forces as a branch of the civil service; so did some of the Middle Eastern states, notably Assyria, and so did the Chinese empire. In these systems there was often no distinction between civil administrator and military general or admiral, and men might well find themselves governing a city one year and leading an army against the barbarians the next year (as in the case of Li Hongzhang).

Standing out from this picture is the military system of Imperial Rome, whose vast standing army was organized on a system quite separate from the civil service bureaucracy. The building block of this system was the Roman legion. Initially the legion was an administrative unit only, and even as late as the wars with Hannibal (third century BC) legions were broken up into individual companies, or cohorts, on the battlefield. By Julius Caesar's day (first century BC), the legion had become a permanent military unit. Each legion had its own supply and logistics trains, and even its own artillery. Its soldiers were rigorously trained, and where possible the cohorts fought together as integrated units on the battlefield. Each legion had its own staff officers, who when larger armies were formed, worked together to provide staff facilities for the generals.

Like all standing armies, the legion system was horrendously expensive, and when the Roman Empire began to fall apart, the legion system disappeared (a version of it, based on regiments of mounted and armoured cavalry known as cataphracts, survived in the Byzantine Empire up to the fourteenth century). The barbarian kingdoms of the early Middle Ages admired the legionary system but could not imitate it, and fell back on the old system of familial and tribal organization.

## The Middle Ages and beyond

By William the Conqueror's day, though, the familial system had been replaced by a largely legal one. Relationships between political leaders (lords) and soldiers (knights and foot soldiers) had been replaced by legal contracts which spelled out duties and responsibilities on an individual basis. Such contracts usually required the soldier or knight to serve for a certain number of days per year at the order of the lord. However, they could not be compelled to serve beyond those limits, and more than one lord found himself deserted on the eve of battle by an army which, waving its contracts in the air, pointed out that its term of duty had expired and it was going home.

**By William the Conqueror's day, the familial system had been replaced by a largely legal one**

Forget what you may have heard about medieval knights spending all their time dashing about in armour fighting tournaments and rescuing maidens. Few had the time; most seemed to spend half their lives in court, arguing over who owed what feudal duties to whom. Fed up with this, kings increasingly began requesting that, instead of coming in person to fight, they pay a compensatory sum of money (known in England as scutage, or shield money). The kings then used this money to hire paid soldiers, with whom they could negotiate better terms. Two-thirds of the army with which King Edward III of England won the Battle of Crécy in 1346 was composed of paid soldiers recruited voluntarily in this fashion.

Suddenly war became good business. Countries with a high population and high unemployment, like Flanders, Genoa and the Swiss cantons, began exporting their surplus young men as paid soldiers. Armies began to be composed almost entirely of mercenaries, of whom there was always a ready supply provided one had the cash. However, mercenary units functioned as private enterprises; their captain was also their chief executive officer, and any contract with the local authorities was made with him personally. The mercenaries themselves owed their sole loyalty to the captain, not his employer. The great Florentine statesman Niccolò Machiavelli warned of the dangers of this in his book *The Prince* in the early sixteenth century, but the full extent of the problem did not become clear until the Thirty Years War in the seventeenth century. During this frightful conflict, political control disintegrated: kings ran out of money and could not pay the huge armies of mercenaries they had hired, and the latter resorted to living off the land. Half the population of Germany, and substantial numbers in neighbouring countries, died in the midst of this anarchy.

During the Thirty Years War (1618–48), some officers did make an attempt to bring greater order to military organization. The Austrian Count Wallenstein, one of the best generals of the war, attempted to set up a standing army organized on Roman principles, with formal systems of supply and logistics. Wallenstein was deeply influenced by the Roman writer Vegetius, whose *De Re Militari* spelled out in detail how the legions were organized. However, this attempt collapsed when Wallenstein was assassinated early in the war. Raimondo Montecuccoli, the Italian general who fought for both Austria and Spain, also attempted to create a permanent force, and later both the Dutch leader Maurice of Nassau and Oliver Cromwell in England created permanent armies whose loyalty was (ostensibly at least) to the state and not to their own leader.

## Frederick the Great and his influence

In the eighteenth century the modern military system emerged in the eastern German state of Brandenburg-Prussia, one of the countries that had suffered most in the Thirty Years War. Successive electors and kings of Prussia had built up a strong standing army as a means of national defence. Frederick II of Prussia, more commonly known as Frederick the Great, brought that system to its apex. In the mid-eighteenth century, Prussia had a population of five million people; from this population, Frederick could regularly raise armies of more than 100,000 troops, and could keep replenishing his numbers even after suffering heavy losses on the battlefield.

Prussian regiments employed a unique system of part-time soldiers, not unlike today's territorial units in Britain. Each regiment had a small central core of permanent troops, which maintained barracks and performed routine duties in the winter. The rest were called up only when needed. In war, the regiments were called up to full strength; but not every soldier attached to a regiment was called up at once. With plenty of reserves waiting at home and a large pool of trained soldiers to draw on, the Prussian army could easily replace battlefield losses. Only fairly late in the Seven Years War (1756–62) did the supply of manpower begin to run dry, while the Austrians and Russians with their vastly larger populations were constantly short of troops.

But as his biographer Christopher Duffy notes, 'Frederick's most remarkable achievement as a wager of war was not so much in surviving the struggle against most of Europe, with its immensely superior resources, as in emerging from the ordeal with a financial profit.' No other country has ever emerged from a war of survival with its accounts in the black; let alone with more money than it began. Prussia had an extremely efficient tax regime, and it was also able to benefit from other resources, notably British subsidies (on the principle that my 'enemy's enemy is my friend', Britain paid Prussia to fight the French), and on asset-stripping captured territories in Silesia and Saxony. Mostly, however, the Prussian financial success stemmed from the fact that the state was supremely well organized. Duffy again comments that Prussia was not so much a state, as an army with a country attached. Like the army, the state was organized to ensure the success of policy.

Prussia had a sound industrial base and was largely self-sufficient in terms of resources: wool for uniforms, lead for musket balls, iron for gun foundries could all be obtained in Prussia. Mills and factories, vast in size for their time, were established for making cannon, muskets, powder, uniforms and other supplies. An efficient quartermaster service kept the regiments in the field well supplied. The only thing Frederick could not control was bread. Grain had to be bought in Poland, so there was some vulnerability. Grain and flour shipped to armies had to be baked into bread; the field bakeries, which produced batches once every three days, were a key blockage in the system. Not only were they prone to breaking down but the bakers, civilians who were fully aware of their importance, were not above going on strike or extorting higher wages from the army quartermasters. Thus the greatest military genius of the age was often at the mercy of a handful of bakers.

Frederick was an autocrat, and tended to direct everything personally; the importance of his leadership can be seen in the fact that if Frederick left the field, the Prussian army seemed immediately to lose effectiveness. (Knowing this, Frederick tended to stay on the field even when wounded.) He maintained control of his state and army through two channels: the formal channel of state government and army staff and quartermasters, and informally through a group of close personal assistants, his corps of adjutants. The former was necessary to ensure organization and planning; the latter was necessary in times of crisis, to cut across the formal machinery and ensure urgent decisions were made and carried out. In these cases, the adjutants communicated Frederick's wishes directly to corps and division commanders. Hans von Winterfeldt, perhaps the most powerful figure in the army after Frederick until his death in battle in 1758, was the most important of these. Talented men like Winterfeldt were difficult to replace, and problems of control became increasingly severe towards the end of the war.

For all its faults, Frederick gave Europe an example of a military organization that, in the right hands, was supremely effective. For Frederick, organization was a tool, shaped to meet his goals. Important here was not only the concept of the *good* organization, but also of the *right* organization; the best and most efficient organization in the world was of no use if it could not meet the goals required of it. This point was not lost on those who commented on his career in later years. The Prussian officer Heinrich von Bülow commented that war should be treated like business (standing the usual metaphor on its head): the military forces at a general's disposal were his 'capital', and should be employed in such a way as to give him the maximum 'return on investment'. His compatriot Karl von Clausewitz famously argued that 'war was an extension of diplomacy by other means' and that armies existed in order to meet the goals of the state. The greatest organizer of the Napoleonic period, Lazare Carnot, invented the concept of the 'nation in arms' and proved how superior organization could be a country's most effective military weapon.

## LAZARE CARNOT

Born at Autun in Burgundy in 1723, Carnot was educated at the Engineering School in Paris, and joined the artillery service as an officer in 1773. He became known as a writer on scientific and military affairs, especially fortifications. He also became involved in left-wing politics, and was friendly with Maximilian Robespierre. Following the French Revolution of 1789, Carnot was elected a member of the Legislative Assembly and became an influential member of the Jacobins, the left-wing party that seized control in 1793; he became a member of the ten-man Committee of Public Safety, headed by Robespierre, that ruled France and used the guillotine ruthlessly to purge political opposition.

In 1793, a coalition of foreign powers had defeated French armies in the field and was poised to invade. Carnot, who possessed both great energy and great organizational abilities, reformed the French army and in the space of just eighteen months raised new armies of hundreds of thousands of men, trained them, equipped them, put them into the field, and found generals to lead them. By 1794 the allies had been repulsed on every front and France was preparing to invade the rest of Europe in its turn.

Carnot was one of the great organizers of all time. He worked almost continuously, and oversaw every aspect of the military machine, including recruitment, training, equipment and promotions, even on occasion taking to the field to oversee his generals directly. He was a great cutter of red tape, and often issued orders in his own handwriting on memorandum paper, with little or no formality and bypassing established chains of command. His memory was prodigious, and he was a master of detail. Most of all, he managed to centralize the control of military affairs, and ensure that the French army was directed by a single controlling will. To his contemporaries he was known as the 'Organizer of Victory'.

---

All these strands of thought coalesced in the figure of Helmuth von Moltke, the chief of the Prussian General Staff and architect of the defeats of Austria and France – the pre-eminent military powers of the middle nineteenth century – which led to the unification of Germany. Moltke and his achievements were discussed in detail in Chapter 3. The line and staff system which he developed had its origins in the staff system of Frederick the Great, and indeed that of the Roman legions. Its followers argued that the system solved one of the greatest problems of organization: the simultaneous need for tight control, to ensure that the organization remained focused on its goals, and flexibility, in order to deal with unforeseen circumstances.

And did it? Harrington Emerson, writing in 1913, believed that the line and staff system meant that military efficiency had reached such a peak that in future all wars would be short and relatively bloodless. A year later there began one of the bloodiest and most wasteful wars in history, fought by armies which, without exception, employed the line and staff principle. Moltke, like Frederick and like Carnot, had made his military system work by not only building a superb organization, but also by placing a brilliant leader – himself – at the head of it. The lesson of the line and staff experiment seems to be that the finest organization in the world is of little avail without the guiding hand to direct it; a great army led by poor generals becomes, in the late Alan Clark's phrase, nothing more than 'lions led by donkeys'.

## Business: the corporate hybrid form

The business corporation that emerged by 1900 had, in the eyes of observers like John Davis and James Mooney, some elements of all these organizational forms. The influence of the family remained important; many businesses were (and still are) run by families, and familial ties of kinship and trust remained important. And even where there was no blood kinship, companies encouraged personal ties of trust similar to those found in families. This often expressed itself in the paternalism found in companies like National Cash Register and Heinz, where the employer saw himself as a father figure to his employees, and at the chocolate-makers Cadbury's and Rowntree in the UK, where the Quaker principles of the owner-managers encouraged close personal relationships between employers and employed. Chapter 5 described how one owner-manager, the car-maker John North Willys, deliberately encouraged his sales teams to think of themselves as 'part of a family'.

Bureaucracy was also important, and bureaucracy found for itself a natural ally in scientific management. In order to maintain the measurement and control systems on which it was founded, scientific management needed a great deal of bureaucracy, and this was (and is) one of the complaints made about it. The early writers on organization were well aware of the dangers. Dexter Kimball, the engineer turned academic whose *Principles of Industrial Organization* (1913) was widely used as a teaching textbook in organization behaviour, supported scientific management and the division of labour, but noted that excessive division and control can impair the functioning of the organization, as it is difficult to find supervisors:

**Even where there was no blood kinship, companies encouraged personal ties of trust similar to those found in families**

> ...with vision, intelligence and leadership, and while no doubt some form of organization must always be employed, especially for the rank and file of the workers, care should be exercised that the administrative methods do not throttle the initiative and enthusiasm of even the lowest subordinate. Genius does not work

well in harness, and men are always more important than machines or methods.[6]

A few years before Kimball, Frank Mason had also warned of the dangers of excessive bureaucracy that accompanied scientific management. In his *Business Principles and Organization*, Mason urged managers to take a systematic approach to organization, but noted again the danger that too much control can lead to loss of coordination:

> One of the advantages of a small concern lies in the fact that the employer can come into personal contact with all of his men. He knows their family history; he knows the difficulties they have to meet; he can sympathize with them in their troubles, and if a dispute arises he can see their point of view. In a large establishment, all this is changed. The men, instead of having dealings with the 'boss' or the 'governor,' which are often terms of affection, now regard themselves as being employed by some vast machine, which they know as 'the company.' The company is looked upon as a machine, as an artificial sort of being that recognizes such things as system, discipline, hard work, but that has no place for any thing like mutual interest, working in harmony, *esprit de corps*. Many managers of even large establishments have attacked this problem of bringing harmony into the interests of employers and of men, with varying degrees of success. Gradually some principles have been evolved which are forming valuable contributions to the science of business organization. At any rate, we can now say that any type of management in which each side spends a large part of its time thinking over and talking over the injustice and the hard treatment which it receives at the hands of the other, must be avoided. The best type of organization is one which calls forth that hearty cooperation on the part of all its members which can only be secured through a genuine, lively and loyal interest in the success and progress of the whole undertaking.[7]

Mason and Kimball spell out the problem that has gripped managers down through the ages. How does the business remain focused on its goals, ensuring that all employees and all divisions and departments are pulling together for the common purpose, while at the same time encouraging such organizational virtues as flexibility, creativity and innovation, avoiding the stifling impact of bureaucracy? James Mooney urged managers to look at two examples where, he believed, these problems had already been confronted: the monasteries and the military. The monasteries, especially the Cistercians, had devolved authority using the daughter house system, backed up by reporting and inspection to ensure that standards were being met and goals achieved. The military had developed the line and staff system whereby individual unit commanders worked in partnership with a small, efficient centralized staff and each unit's goals formed part of the overall objective. Mooney was, with Alfred P. Sloan and Pierre du Pont, one of the architects of the multi-divisional form (M-form) of organization developed at General Motors in the 1920s and 1930s, whereby individual business units within GM became semi-autonomous, working to the direction of the small head office team. Unsurprisingly, elements of both military and monastic organization can be seen in the M-form.

**The military had developed the line and staff system whereby individual unit commanders worked in partnership with a small, efficient centralized staff and each unit's goals formed part of the overall objective**

## JAMES D. MOONEY

**N** **OW ALMOST FORGOTTEN,** Mooney was one of American management's most brilliant minds. Born in Cleveland in 1884, he attended New York University and the Case Institute of Technology and then worked as an engineer. During the First World War he was a captain of artillery in the US Army and served with distinction in France. After the war he joined a small electrical engineering firm which was acquired by General Motors, and came thus to the attention of Pierre du Pont, who was then in the process of re-organizing the business. Du Pont recognized Mooney's potential, and in 1922 made him vice-president of General Motors and president of General Motors overseas with responsibility for all sales and production outside the USA. He grew General Motors' overseas business dramatically during the 1920s and 1930s, and was widely regarded as the firm's foreign ambassador and its keenest intellect. Pierre du

Pont respected him and listened to his advice, and Alfred Sloan relied upon him. His ideas on management and especially on organization theory were among the most advanced of their time, and as well as commanding the respect of heads of state and government Mooney was also on friendly terms with many of the leading management intelligentsia, such as Lyndall Urwick, Luther Gulick and Mary Parker Follett.

In 1940, using his contacts with German industrialists and with President Roosevelt's support, Mooney held meetings with Hitler, Goering and Mussolini in which he broached the possibility of US mediation to bring the war in Europe to an end. Nothing came of these meetings, and Mooney was later libelled in the US press for supposed Nazi sympathies (he sued and won). During the war he served in the US Navy on the staff of the Chief of Naval Operations; in 1946 he became president of the carmaker Willys Overland, and then went into semi-retirement running his own consulting business until his death in 1957. His book *Onward Industry*, later republished as *Principles of Organization*, remains much admired by those who encounter it.

## New thoughts on an old subject

### The administrative approach

The first admission that organization is an essential and explicit part of the task of management comes from the French mining engineer and writer Henri Fayol, whose *General and Industrial Administration*, first published in 1917, became one of the most influential management books of all time. Achieving the balance between coordination and control, between flexibility and structure, is, says Fayol, one of *the* central tasks of top management. In this work, Fayol sets out what he calls his 'Fourteen Points' of efficient administration. At first sight this is an authoritarian and bureaucratic list which includes such concepts as authority, discipline, order and a scalar chain of command. But central to Fayol's conception is unity of purpose. All members of the organization need to know what the organization's purpose is, and to make that purpose their own. Leadership is vitally important; there must be someone to give the organization direction and to ensure it remains focused on its objectives. Morale, *esprit de corps* is another essential feature. The hierarchy of the business exists only and solely to ensure that it meets its objectives, and within that structure employees at all levels should be encouraged to use their initiative and be flexible.

Not for nothing has Fayol's system been compared by one recent writer to that of St Benedict in terms of its principles of command, control and coordination. What is perhaps most important about Fayol's theory is his emphasis on the role of leadership. To repeat the comment made above, the best system in the world does not work without the requisite level of leadership. This idea was later developed in more detail by Chester Barnard, the AT&T executive who became known as one of twentieth-century management's most thoughtful and philosophical writers. Barnard saw organizations as dynamic social systems, naturally resistant to excessive order and structure and requiring constant efforts by their leaders to keep them focused and take them forward towards their objectives. Like the military leaders of the seventeenth and eighteenth centuries, Barnard realized that both strong organizations and strong leaders to guide them were required if things were not to fall apart.

**Leadership is vitally important; there must be someone to give the organization direction and to ensure it remains focused on its objectives**

## The psychological approach

The first application of the new discipline of psychology to business organizations as groups is probably Lillian Gilbreth's *Psychology of Management*. Gilbreth, one of the first women in the USA to be awarded a degree in psychology, returned to university to study the subject after working with her husband Frank Bunker Gilbreth on motion studies. The observation of what people did in the workplace prompted her to question why they behaved as they did. She states the problem thus:

> It has been demonstrated that the emphasis in successful management lies on the *man*, not on the *work*; that efficiency is best secured by placing the emphasis on the man, and modifying the equipment, materials and methods to make the most of the man. It has, further, been recognized that the man's mind is a controlling factor in his efficiency, and has, by teaching, enabled the man to make the most of his powers.[8]

The effect of Gilbreth's work was to begin to turn the focus of organization thinking away from structure and control and towards the individual as the primary element that composed the organization. Many of the subsequent studies belong more properly to the related field of human resource management, but one work in particular, Mary Parker Follett's *Creative Experience*, had an important impact on thinking about organization as well. In Follett's view, people at all levels of the organization should be motivated to work and participate. She saw organizations as being based fundamentally on cooperation and coordination, and believed this to be the single unifying principle which held them together. In a later lecture at the London School of Economics, reprinted in 1937 in *Papers on the Science of Administration*, she speaks of 'the correlation of many controls rather than a superimposed control' and goes on:

> The ramifications of modern industry are too wide-spread, its organization too complex, its problems too intricate for it to be possible for industry to be managed by commands from the top alone. This being so, we find that when central control is spoken of, that does not mean a point of radiation, but the gathering of many controls existing throughout the enterprise.[9]

## The biological approach

The idea that a metaphorical comparison could be drawn between organizations and biological organisms, especially human beings, dates back to the Middle Ages. John of Salisbury, an English Platonist scholar and philosopher of the twelfth century, wrote in his political-ethical work *Policraticus* of how the governance of the state resembles the human body: the prince is the head of the state, the senate is its heart, the agricultural workers and soldiers are equivalent to its limbs and so on. Whether Charles Knoeppel, the foremost proponent of this idea in the early twentieth century, knew of John's work is not certain; but the metaphor is such an obvious one that it was bound to be repeated. The eccentric economist Thorstein Veblen had already begun discussing economic activity in terms of biological evolution as early as 1904, and Harrington Emerson in his later work began to consider the business organization as an evolving biological entity. Knoeppel, who had worked for a time as a consultant with Emerson's firm, was influenced by him, and came to conceive of Emerson's line and staff model in biological terms:

> A close study of the foregoing conclusively indicates the wisdom of following the human body as closely as we can in determining the correct type of man building organization. First in order of importance is the executive, or director of activities, or guide, or co-ordinator, or whatever you choose to call him. Then comes the staff, the counselors who advise, criticise, prescribe and assist the executive in directing and coordinating. Now comes the question of adjusting the remaining two classes of organs, the organs of growth and upkeep and of creation and achievement as Mr. Emerson defined them, or the involuntary and voluntary organs as I had come to consider them, to the staff and the executive.[10]

The biological metaphor, says Knoeppel, is fully compatible with the line and staff model. The brain functions as the staff, providing guidance and control; the limbs and organs execute commands and carry out functions. Borrowing a concept from Herbert Casson, he adds that the heart plays the role of the organizational will and purpose, setting the goals towards which the brain and other components work. As a guiding concept, today this metaphor looks at best naive. Yet it is a vitally important step in the history of thinking

**The idea that we ourselves are organizations and that the larger organizations we create are in some way images of ourselves remains a powerful one**

about organization, because here we see for the first time a concept that can unite the rational and technical aspects of organization with the emotional, social and psychological aspects. The idea that we ourselves are organizations and that the larger organizations we create are in some way images of ourselves remains a powerful one.

## Where are we now?

Nearly a century on, we are still not much closer to a unified picture of what organizations are and how they behave. The Welsh-Canadian academic and writer on organization, Gareth Morgan, has even suggested that we probably never will reach such a picture. Morgan, who has developed a collection of eight separate metaphors of organization, ranging from the machine to the biological organism to the realm of imagination and so on, believes that all these metaphors are equally valid; all have something to tell us about organization.

If that is so, then what is it? The study of organizations down through history shows that the central problem of organization was, is, and probably always will be the combined need to focus energies and attention on the final objectives, while at the same time remaining sufficiently flexible and adaptable to counter challenges met along the way. Strong leadership is necessary to define objectives and provide guidance; at the same time, individuals within the organization must remain motivated.

Different times and places have come up with different solutions. All the organization systems we discussed above were successful, for a time. Then they failed, largely because the guiding hand at the top became a dead hand; lacking guidance and leadership, the perfect organization becomes no more than a rusty implement. Without purpose and leadership, organizations die and become fossilized relics. Morgan may well have been right; there is no one model of organization, only an *idea* of organization that we take and shape to meet our own purpose. In that, he shares common ground with Chester Barnard, Henri Fayol, Charles Knoeppel, Helmuth von Moltke, Lazare Carnot, Frederick the Great,

Bernard of Clairvaux, Francesco Datini and Hubert Walter. Not such bad company to be in, after all.

*Notes to chapter 5*

1. After some consideration, I have used the modern academic term 'organization behaviour' to introduce the topic of this chapter, as it will be familiar to most readers. More properly, we are looking here at the 'study of organizations' or 'organization theory'. Arndt Sorge, writing in the *International Encyclopedia of Business and Management* in 1996, defined organization behaviour as including both the structure and composition of organizations, and the behaviour of individuals and groups within those organizations. This suggested dichotomy is doubtless necessary in terms of academic division of labour, but in practical terms it is somewhat artificial. This chapter follows the viewpoint of the early writers discussed, namely that the structure of an organization and the behaviour of its members are simply different aspects of the same subject: organizations.
2. Jones, Edward D. (1912) 'Military history and the science of administration', *Engineering Magazine* vol. 44, p. 1.
3. In the wake of economic reforms begun in China in 1979, there is evidence that the family model is returning.
4. Oschinsky, D. (1971) *Walter of Henley and The Treatises on Estate Management and Accountancy*, Oxford: Clarendon Press.
5. For more on Walter's reforms, see Cheney, C.R. (1967) *Hubert Walter*, London: Thomas Nelson & Sons. I am grateful to Marilyn Livingstone for drawing my attention to this remarkable man.
6. Kimball, Dexter (1913) *Principles of Industrial Organization*, New York: McGraw-Hill, pp. 158–9.
7. Mason, Frank M. (1909) *Business Principles and Organization*, Chicago: Cree Publishing Co., p. 100.
8. Gilbreth, Lillian (1914) *The Psychology of Management*, New York: Sturgis & Walton, p. 3.
9. Parker Follett, Mary (1937) 'The process of control', in Gulick, L. and Urwick, L.F. (eds), *Papers on the Science of Administration*, New York: Institute of Public Administration, p. 161.
10. Knoeppel, Charles (1918) *Organization and Administration*, New York: McGraw-Hill, p. 42.

# 6

# Finance: making the world go round

> These foreign merchants and bankers arrive without bringing anything besides their persons, a little credit, a pen, ink and paper, and skill in handling, turning and diverting exchanges from one country to another, according to the information they have of the places where money is dearest

Thus a sixteenth-century French writer described the agents of Italian banking firms working in northern Europe at the close of the Middle Ages. He was writing at a time when banking and finance in Western Europe were going through a revolution of sorts, with capital markets expanding rapidly and new financial instruments appearing. And on the back of this revolution, business firms were expanding too, increasing the scale and scope of their operations and moving into new fields and new markets. The steady expansion of capital in the centuries that followed fuelled a global economic expansion that has lasted, with few interruptions, to the present day.

Throughout the history of financial markets and financial management, two themes have been dominant: the need of businesses for sufficient supplies of capital to fund expansion, and the need for capital assets to be kept secure against all manner of hazards, including physical risks and the risk of theft or fraud. These two needs have both dictated the nature and shape of financial instruments and financial markets, and driven the development of financial management by businesses. They have affected everything about the world of finance, right down to the shape of the money in our pockets.

## The evolution of money

The earliest forms of exchange took the form of barter. In barter exchanges, each party must have something that the other wants or needs, and they must be able to communicate with each other, agree on the quantities of goods that can be exchanged (two oxen for one horse, a hundredweight of fish for a barrel of beer, etc.) and then physically deliver the goods. Barter is often described by economists as being a characteristic of primitive economies, but there is still a lot of barter going on today, even in developed, post-industrial nations (much to the annoyance of the tax authorities). Bartering labour for commodities is if anything becoming more common, and there are even websites where such transactions can be arranged.

Nor were the ancient societies that used barter necessarily unsophisticated. Old Kingdom Egypt was, as noted in Chapter 2, a highly organized and highly structured society with a sophisticated civil service, standing army, international trade and the ability to undertake massive projects like flood control along the Nile and, of course, the building of pyramids (not just the Great Pyramids of Giza but a whole range of them throughout Lower Egypt). Money was only slowly introduced into the Egyptian economy, and did not come into common use until after 500 BC, when the state increasingly began to ask for taxes and duties to be paid in silver rather than goods.

Barter worked in Egypt because the Egyptian economy was essentially a redistributive one with state control of most sectors and little private enterprise. In effect, the state ran a central bank, except that rather than controlling the supply of money in the economy it controlled the supply of commodities. Being a large and wealthy state, it had the resources necessary to move and store large quantities of goods. For individual traders in free market economies, though, barter has its limitations. First, goods for barter can often be cumbersome and expensive to store and move. Second, they are often susceptible to damage in transit; oxen can go lame, fish can go off, and so on. Third, and most importantly, in order to make a barter

**For individual traders in free market economies, though, barter has its limitations**

exchange, you need to have something that the other party wants. Suppose you go to market to buy food, and find a dealer offering to sell you two bushels of wheat. You offer him an ox in exchange. Sorry, he replies, not interested; I already have five oxen, and they are eating me out of house and home. What else have you got? You then have a choice between trying to decide what other goods you can part with, or persuading the dealer to take the ox at a lower value (i.e. give you less wheat in exchange).

Though it works fine for individual transactions, over time the barter system is fraught with uncertainties. Very early on, at least four thousand years ago, traders began to adopt items of common value to use as tokens in exchange. These items of common value became what we now know as money. Precious metals, chiefly but not restricted to gold, silver and copper, were most commonly adopted, but wooden and pottery tokens were also known. The dried heads of small fur-bearing animals such as martens were being used as small change by traders in the north Russian city of Novgorod as late as the fourteenth century, and South Pacific islanders were still using cowrie shells as currency in the early twentieth century. Ultimately, the object does not much matter, so long as all members of a society agree to attach an approximately equal value to it. Precious metals were, for one reason or another, adopted as the standard of wealth by many societies and could be exchanged internationally. Silver was recognized as a global currency three thousand years ago, acceptable by businesses in Greece, Assyria, India and China.

Another advantage of gold and silver is that they are durable and imperishable. They can be easily stored, and businesses which make a profit in gold and silver can begin to accumulate capital for further investment. They have, however, two disadvantages. One is weight: transporting even modest amounts of money to and fro requires a considerable amount of motive power. For a businessman in Rome to close a deal worth three or four thousand pounds in Athens, he would have to charter a ship, maybe two, just to move the money. The second is that gold and silver can be easily doctored. It is very easy to melt down gold or silver and add in a small portion of base metal such as lead or tin, which does not change the appearance of the metal when cooled but which devalues the currency and makes a fraudulent profit for the devaluer.

In order to counteract the latter practice, states began issuing gold, silver and copper coins. Originally these were simply slices from a metal bar, stamped on both sides with a metal seal giving the distinguishing mark of the issuing government. The stamps served in effect as a guarantee that the metal was pure (or at least, of a specified level of purity) and that the coin was not a forgery. There were still means of doctoring coins; very small quantities could be shaved off the edges, for example, a practice known as clipping (the penalty for this was death by torture in many jurisdictions). States themselves could and frequently did call in their coinage and remint it with higher portions of base metals, in effect devaluing the currency. The mechanics and economics of this were well known in medieval Europe. In the early fourteenth century, for example, France and the states of the Low Countries reminted and devalued their currencies several times, and there was considerable pressure on England to follow their example and devalue the Long Cross Penny, the standard unit of English currency. The crown refused, pointing out that to do so would decrease the purchasing power of English money on the Continent, and thus increase the price of exports and damage England's highly favourable balance of trade. (This incident will doubtless sound familiar to those following the debate over whether Britain should join the euro.)

One way of determining a coin's true worth, of course, was by weight; doctoring coins with base metals would always show up if the coins were carefully weighed. One of the banker's principal tools was a set of very fine scales, with dried carob seeds used for counterweights (from 'carob' comes the modern word 'carat', still used to determine the purity of precious metals and gems). This method was also sometimes used to determine exchange rates between the coins of different states. Exchange rates were only of small concern during the Roman Empire, when the silver solidus, issued by Imperial mints, was the standard unit of currency throughout the Empire. In the Middle Ages, however, there were hundreds of minting authorities, and a huge variety of coins of different denominations. To save every merchant having to try to work out the value of every different coin, there developed the practice of foreign exchange. It became generally accepted that the standard money of exchange would be the currency of the home country; foreign traders, tourists, pilgrims or whatever would take their money to a *cambio*, or exchange, where it would be weighed and tested and then exchanged for an equivalent value in local currency.

> To save every merchant having to try to work out the value of every different coin, there developed the practice of foreign exchange

For large-scale transactions, all this was extremely time-consuming. During the Middle Ages authorities experimented with 'bulk money', bags of newly-minted coins which were carefully weighed and then sealed and stamped to indicate that they were of a certain guaranteed value. This helped alleviate the quality problem, but not the weight problem.

There had to be a better way, and there was. By around the year 1000, the Chinese authorities began experimenting with issuing small denomination currency made of paper. These were not, as is sometimes assumed, bank notes in the modern sense; rather, they were attempts to establish paper as a unit of currency in its own right. The use of paper was not without its problems; for one thing, paper currency could be easily forged. Sporadic attempts at introducing paper currency continued for some centuries, though, and in the 1290s the Venetian traveller Marco Polo informed his contemporaries that the Chinese were using money made of paper. This was greeted, we are told, with disbelief and derision. But either the tale of the response is untrue, or the Venetians Polo talked to were an extraordinarily ignorant lot. Venice, along with most of Western Europe, had already become a paper economy in which bills of exchange, rather than cash, were used in all but the simplest of transactions.

## The unstoppable rise of credit

The twelfth and thirteenth centuries in Western Europe are sometimes referred to as the Commercial Revolution. Unlike later business revolutions (industrial and information), technology was not at the heart of this new development; the shift in this case was largely mental. During this time, people began to think about money in new ways. Money was no longer just a medium of exchange; it also became, at the same time, a commodity in its own right. Moreover, money no longer had to be represented by metallic currency. Moneys of account began to dominate and then to supersede moneys of exchange, and by 1400 even relatively small companies were conducting their financial business on paper rather than using cash.[1]

The explosion in international trade that followed the conclusion of the First Crusade (1099) made the already prosperous trading cities of Italy into rich entrepots. Surplus wealth was invested in expanding trade still further; it was the availability of venture capital, as much as the desire to explore, that drove Marco Polo to China and Columbus to America. Other capital was invested in expanding manufacturing industries in both south and north Europe. The profits to be made from banking were a lure that few capitalists of the day could resist. Despite prohibitions on usury, the earning of interest on loans, credit began to be increasingly popular and common. Businessmen had always known that by borrowing on credit they could invest in growth and expansion; what had been lacking were lenders willing to take the risk. Now that problem had been greatly reduced.

While there was in general a surplus of liquidity, individuals, companies and even nations suffered from periodic shortages of capital. This was well known, as too was the notion that shortages and abundances of money represented commercial opportunities. Giovanni da Uzzano, writing in 1442, offered this advice:

> Never be eager to remit money when there is dearth, nor to withdraw it when there is abundance. For wherever money is expensive, cash flows in from every place, money is withdrawn

from banks, and therefore abundance is bound to come. And where there is great abundance, cash is drawn away and money is bound to become tight.

As well as providing an early recognition of the nature of economic cycles, Uzzano also shows how early bankers were alert to the opportunities for the employment of money.

Two problems faced the owners of capital. First, thanks to the explosion of credit, the total wealth of Western Europe quickly outstripped the supply of metal coin, and new instruments were necessary. Second, there was the need to find ways of avoiding the restrictions on usury so as to allow lenders to make a profit.

## Commercial paper

The answer was the development of various forms of negotiable, non-currency instruments. One of the earliest was the sea loan. Sea loans began as a form of venture capital. Long-distance maritime trade was an expensive and risky business; to raise capital and spread risk, trading firms invited short-term investment in overseas ventures. Capital advanced at the start of a sea voyage was repaid in full at the end of the voyage, together with a share of the profits. If the ship sank, the investors partook of the loss.

Sea loans were extremely common and popular, as knowledge of the potential for profit became widespread. In the seaports of Italy, not only large capitalists but also small investors – shopkeepers and workers, including many women – handed over their money to bankers to invest on their behalf, further increasing the supply of capital. Profits could be taken in cash, or could be retained as credit balances. Shares in sea loans could be traded and exchanged. It was quickly realized that interbank 'paper' account transfers were more efficient than physically exchanging currency with each transaction. There was no clearinghouse system, but large banks like the Medici Bank in Florence and the Casa di San Giorgio in Genoa performed clearing functions.

The advantages of paper were twofold. First, paper transactions were less cumbersome and risky. Coin was difficult to transport, and could not be recovered if lost, but paper instruments were easy to carry and could be replaced if lost or damaged. Second, they allowed more flexibility. The nature and type of investment was limited only by the imagination of the capitalists (and their accountants). So while on the one hand the new age of credit made business ventures more secure by offering more opportunities to spread risk, on the other hand, for those willing to accept risk, there were more opportunities for profit. Increasing profits fuelled economic expansion still further.

> It was quickly realized that interbank 'paper' account transfers were more efficient than physically exchanging currency with each transaction

Sometimes the profits of a voyage would be remitted in a currency other than the one used for the initial investment. This necessitated another instrument, the bill of exchange. By specifying the rate of exchange to be paid, bills of exchange performed another function; they could effectively function as loans, with the borrower paying back a larger sum than had been lent, but in a different currency. Because exchange rates could, and did, fluctuate, canon law was happy to accept this as a fair reward for risk.

By 1400, bills of exchange were the dominant instrument in international trade, having almost completely supplanted cash. They could be made payable to a named person, or to the bearer. They could be transferred and endorsed, and were commonly used to settle debts and obligations. There is no real evidence for discounting, but it probably did take place.

> Promissory notes were evolved out of letters of credit made payable to a named party. It took only a short time for the next logical step, which was the issuance of promissory notes payable to the bearer.

The second major financial instrument to make its appearance at this time was the promissory note, which played the same role in domestic trade as the bill of exchange did in foreign trade. Coin became restricted to everyday transactions, such as payment of wages or marketplace purchases. It was unusual for coin to be used in commerce; when it was, this was usually because there were no reciprocal credit arrangements, and by 1500 this was becoming rare indeed in Western Europe, and was becoming increasingly less common in India and China. As one economic historian has remarked, 'Credit was the very soul of medieval commerce'.

Promissory notes were evolved out of letters of credit made payable to a named party. It took only a short time for the next logical step, which was the issuance of promissory notes payable to the bearer. Thus were modern bank notes born.

## JAKOB FUGGER

FUGGER WAS BORN IN AUGSBURG, GERMANY, IN 1459, the son or a prosperous businessman who also managed a mint in the silver-mining district of Tirol. At fourteen, Fugger was sent to the family company's branch office in Venice to learn about business, including the study of book-keeping; in 1485 he took charge of the Innsbruck branch, expanding the company's investments in copper and silver mining, and loaning money to Maximilian I, the future Holy Roman Emperor. In 1495 he began developing more mines in Hungary and Silesia, and by 1500 he controlled most of the European copper industry. The trade in copper and silver led Fugger naturally into minting and banking; quite literally, he made money.

Like many other late medieval merchant princes, notably Cosimo dei Medici, Fugger's banking capital was derived from profits made in other industries, usually manufacturing, mining or trade. From 1507 onwards Fugger lent increasingly large sums to the Emperor Maximilian; many of these loans were mortgages on crown lands, and as many of these were never redeemed, Fugger also acquired extensive landholdings. The Imperial connection gave Fugger privileged access to other, more profitable customers. Even more importantly, in an age of political uncertainty and constant change, having a grateful emperor on his books as a client meant that Fugger could enjoy a measure of security and protection afforded to few of his rivals; put simply, if he was threatened either financially or physically, Fugger could call in powerful favours.

Known in his home city as 'Fugger the Rich', Jakob Fugger dominated the European financial world for two decades. A man of fixed purpose and great determination, he tended to set his sights on a goal, develop a strategy and then pursue that strategy unswervingly to its end. The business, like most banks of its day, operated on a network basis with agents in all the major financial centres of Europe; sometimes these agents were directly employed, sometimes they were employed by partnerships established with other banks. As well as transacting business, these agents gathered information. At the headquarters in Augsburg, Jakob Fugger himself kept the firm's master accounts and collated information received from agents abroad; both these things were done on a daily basis. Fugger once wrote that he could not go soundly to sleep at night without knowing that somewhere that day he had made a profit, however small it might be.

This combination of intense monitoring of information and a flexible, far-flung network gave Fugger the ability to respond quickly to crises. On his death he bequeathed to his nephew, Anton Fugger, a fortune worth more than 2 million guilders (over $400 million in today's money).

## Futures

The age of credit revolutionized money. Credit instruments, inter-account and inter-bank transfers opened up vast new opportunities for its exploitation. There is not space here to go into the range of financial instruments which made their appearance between 1200 and 1500, but one type of instrument cannot pass without mention. This was the futures contract.

Futures contracts began in agriculture. All over Europe, as each harvest approached, agents of business concerns would tour the countryside offering to pay farmers in advance for the crops standing in their fields. Large businesses would sometimes buy up the entire crop of a region for several years in advance. Having purchased the rights to these crops once they were harvested, they were then free to sell these rights on to other investors.

It is impossible to estimate how much of the annual harvests of Western Europe was purchased in this fashion, but the total is likely to have been considerable. Futures were quickly introduced into other business sectors as well. Government also got in on the act, selling agricultural futures in order to raise revenue. In 1341, for example, the English crown levied a tax on future agricultural produce. Then, having assessed the value of the tax, it sold the right to collect this produce to private investors for the value of the assessment; the investors had the right to collect the produce and make such profit as they could. International banks and small domestic capitalists alike purchased these rights.

This sort of device worked well for governments of agricultural countries. The city of Genoa, which had no agricultural land to speak of, resorted to more direct measures, selling shares in the government debt to citizens with a promise of repayment with interest. Thus the government bond also entered circulation.

## SIR THOMAS GRESHAM

**GRESHAM WAS BORN IN LONDON AROUND 1519,** the son of a prosperous mercer and sometime Lord Mayor of London. He apprenticed with his uncle, Sir John Gresham, and was admitted to the livery of the mercers company in 1544. In 1552 he was sent to Antwerp to act as royal agent, his primary task being to manage the huge royal debt run up by King Henry VIII. Antwerp was then the pre-eminent money market in Europe, and Gresham's job was to negotiate the renewal of each loan when it came due, paying off high-interest loans where possible by negotiating further borrowing at lower rates. Quite how he managed this daunting task remains obscure, but by 1560 the debt had been largely cleared. Gresham himself had become immensely rich through private business dealings on the Antwerp money markets, and he used some of his earnings to found the Royal Exchange, an establishment which he hoped would help to make London an international financial centre; he also founded an educational institute, Gresham College. In the Victorian period his reputation was revived and he was adopted as a founding father and 'tribal hero' of the City of London.

## Banking: the power behind business

It is seldom appreciated to what extent the history of the world has been influenced by the availability of money. Many of history's great trends and events were dependent on it. Governments must be financed, armies and cathedrals must be bought and paid for. Joan of Arc would never have driven the English out of much of France – nor met her fiery end at Rouen – without the money raised by the banker Jacques Coeur to finance the French armies. The Holy Roman Empire might well have been overwhelmed by Ottoman Turkey without money raised by the imperial bankers Jakob and Anton Fugger. Sir Thomas Gresham helped the government of England break free of its crippling debts and finance its own age of exploration and colonization. The banking house of Jagah Seth helped prop up the failing Moghul Empire in India; when its leaders later switched their allegiance to the British East India Company, the Empire was doomed.

**It is seldom appreciated to what extent the history of the world has been influenced by the availability of money**

In Europe, although joint stock companies appeared in the seventeenth century, and by the early nineteenth century were commonplace in many sectors, banks provided the bulk of the capital that financed the great era of overseas trade and industrialization in the eighteenth and nineteenth centuries. The Grasshopper, the house founded by Sir Thomas Gresham in the sixteenth century, passed into the hands of Thomas Martin early in the eighteenth century; renamed Martin's Bank, it survived the South Sea Bubble and was still trading in the early twentieth century. The nineteenth century saw the rise of the great British banks – Coutts, Barings, Gibbs, Rothschilds – who underwrote the era of Victorian industrial and scientific expansion.

## THOMAS MARTIN

**BORN IN ESSEX IN 1679**, Thomas Martin joined the Grasshopper as a clerk in 1699. Thanks to family connections, he became a partner in 1703 and senior partner in 1711, just before the beginning of the South Sea Bubble (1714–21). During this period of speculation and financial chaos, Martin tried to chart a prudent course. In the early stages, up to late 1715, he seems to have believed that stocks in the South Sea Company would retain their value, and advised clients to buy, though at cautious levels. Later he changed his position, and actively discouraged investment in speculative stocks. How much the Grasshopper suffered from the Bubble is not known; one clerk of the company was later arrested for his involvement in fraudulent promotions, but no scandal seems to have touched Martin. With the collapse of the Bubble in 1721, the Grasshopper seems to have been able to resume normal trading in fairly short order. Martin retired from the Grasshopper in 1725, but remained involved in the bank's management for at least another two decades.

Sometime after his retirement, Martin composed a set of maxims entitled 'Proper Considerations for Persons Concerned in the Banking Business'. The earliest surviving manuscript of these, dated 1746, reads as follows:

1. Some judgement ought to be made of what sum is proper to be out at constant interest.
2. A proportion of bonds, Land Tax tallies, and silver, to be ready on sudden demand.
3. A proportion of government securities, as Navy bills, etc.
4. Not to lend money without application from the borrower and upon alienable security that may be easily disposed of and a probability of punctual payment without being reckoned hard by the borrower.
5. All loans to be paid when due, and ye rotation not exceeding six months.
6. Not to boast of a great surplus or plenty of money.
7. When loans do not offer, to lend on stocks or other securities, buy for ready money and sell for time.
8. When credit increased by accident upon an uncertain circulation, the money may be lent to goldsmiths, or discount bills of exchange.
9. 'Tis prudence and advantage of a goldsmith that depend upon credit, to endeavour as near as possible upon the yearly settlement of accounts to have the investure of that money in effects that are easy to be converted into money.
10. To appear cautious and timorous contribute very much to give persons in credit an esteem among mankind.
11. Avoid unprofitable business, especially when attended with trouble and expense.
12. 'Tis certainly better to employ a little money at a good advantage, if lent safely, in order to have a greater cash by you, tho' possibly you may extend your credit safely.
13. When it shall be thought proper to get in old loans, the demanding of them ought to be in the names of all the partners.[2]

## THOMAS COUTTS

**BORN IN EDINBURGH IN 1735,** Coutts created one of the world's most enduring banking brands. His business partner, his brother James Coutts, was deeply involved in politics and left the management of the bank to Thomas. It was probably through James Coutts's political connections that, in 1760, King George III named Coutts as his personal bankers. The royal business gave Coutts access to the highest levels of the court and government, and over the next four decades he built up an impressive list of clients that included not only the king and the Prince of Wales but also prominent politicians such as William Pitt and Charles James Fox and others including the Duke of Wellington. The bank maintained a reputation for reliability, quality of service, probity and impartiality. By 1800 London was the acknowledged capital of European banking, with established firms like Coutts competing with newer bankers like Baring, Goldsmid and the Rothschilds. Coutts began opening up international links in the 1780s, and by 1800 had developed ties with several Swiss banks; through these, he was able to offer banking services to clients in the Mediterranean and the Levant. With correspondent banks from Lisbon to Bombay, Coutts became the bank of choice for international travellers; British officers serving in Spain were even able to negotiate Coutts drafts with banks in cities within the war zone.

---

Likewise, the very rapid growth of American industry in the period following the First World War is only partly explained by such factors as improved transportation and rapid emigration. All this growth, the railroads and steel mills and factories, had to be paid for; capital had to come from somewhere. Wall Street did not reach its position of eminence until after 1900; before that, the American stock exchange was a small community in which a few score companies at most issued shares. Speculators like Daniel Drew made and lost fortunes there, but Wall Street had little impact on the overall growth of commerce. But banking in America had a long history, stretching back to entrepreneurial bankers like Stephen Girard in the early nineteenth century, and now it was the bankers who came forward to back American industry. Some were content to invest and earn profits without seeking influence. Others, like John Pierpont Morgan, became powerful forces shaping the nature of American business.

**Speculators like Daniel Drew made and lost fortunes there, but Wall Street had little impact on the overall growth of commerce**

J.P. Morgan was much more than just a banker; he was also an idealist. He believed in neither state intervention nor unbridled competition. The state, he believed, was not competent to be involved in the economy and business (and given that on three separate occasions he personally bailed out the nearly bankrupt US Treasury, it is easy to see why he felt this way). In terms of markets, he saw competition as wasteful and potentially ruinous. Why should companies dissipate their energies in competition with each other? By combining their efforts, they could achieve economies of scale, improve the quality of their goods and their distribution, provide more products for consumers and do so at lower prices. Everyone would benefit: the businessman would make a profit, and the people as a whole would see their standard of living and their prosperity improve. This philosophy was by no means unique to Morgan. In the late nineteenth century competition was seen by many as an inherent evil in the free market system: to some it was a necessary evil, part of the price to be paid for economic freedom, but to others, on both right and left of the political spectrum, it was a force which should be curbed and controlled. But unlike many observers, J.P. Morgan had the power to act.

He turned his attention first to the railways. The growth of the American railway industry in the two decades after the American Civil War is one of the bleaker chapters in the history of business. This was the age of the robber barons, of takeovers achieved through fraud and deceit, of watered stock, insider trading and bogus share issues, and of companies wrecked and lives ruined in a scramble for territory, position and power. Morgan brought the railway companies to heel. He first established an alliance with other bankers which refused to underwrite further expansion unless the railway owners were prepared to make terms. He then established a railway cartel, buying up some of the smaller and unprofitable lines and combining them under single management, and persuading the bigger fish in the pond, men like James J. Hill and Edward Harriman, to join forces with him. By the mid-1890s, the Morgan-backed Northern Securities Company controlled many of the major railways in the USA, setting prices and schedules and bringing order out of chaos.

Morgan then turned his attention to other industries. The major American steel corporations, including that of Andrew Carnegie, were combined in the gargantuan trust, United States Steel, then the world's largest company. The mining and smelting industry merged to form another trust, ASARCO, led by Daniel Guggenheim. A shipping trust was established, International Mercantile Marine, bringing companies on both sides of the Atlantic together in a loose alliance. Together with John D. Rockefeller, Morgan merged the oil industry into yet another trust, Standard Oil. His aim was clear; in the interests of rational financing and management, as much of American industry as possible should be rationalized into monopolistic organizations for the good of businesses, society and the people.

Morgan's efforts were thwarted, in the end, because Americans as a whole had a suspicion of monopoly, and did not accept his view that the trusts benefited the common good. His belief in tight monetary controls aroused passionate opposition from small businesses, which wanted easier access to capital. Crusading journalists, known as the 'muckrakers', roused public opinion against trusts, and they had the backing of President Theodore Roosevelt, who introduced tough new anti-trust legislation. Many trusts such as Standard Oil and Northern Securities were forced to disband by the courts and government. International Mercantile Marine failed when two major British shipping lines, Cunard and Furness Withy, suspicious of Morgan's motives, refused to participate. But even though the edifices he built did not always survive, Morgan had succeeded in lodging the idea of big business firmly in the heart of American business culture. Though Standard Oil had split, its descendants remained powerful forces in the American economy. Other great companies of today, like AT&T and General Electric, also started with backing from Morgan.

## J.P. MORGAN

**UNUSUALLY AMONG NINETEENTH-CENTURY CAPTAINS OF INDUSTRY,** John Pierpont Morgan was not entirely a self-made man; his father, Junius Morgan, was a wealthy banker, and the son was educated at good schools in the USA and Europe. He showed early promise as a banker; as a child, he kept a ledger of his purchases of sweets, and also built a diorama of Columbus's discovery of America and charged other children to see it. In the 1850s the Morgans made an important alliance with the great British banking houses of Rothschilds and Barings, with which J.P. Morgan worked closely in later years when bailing out the US Treasury (his thanks was to be accused in the press of being a British agent).

As noted above, Morgan viewed unrestrained competition as being intrinsically harmful. In an often quoted passage concerning the railway industry, he remarked: 'The American public seems unwilling to admit ... that it has a choice between regulated legal agreements and unregulated extralegal agreements. We should have cast away more than 50 years ago the impossible doctrine of protection of the public by railway competition.' He was by no means alone in his view. He succeeded in creating his giant monopolistic trusts in part because other captains of industry agreed with his assessment, and not only in the USA. In Britain, the amalgamation movement exemplified by Alfred Mond of ICI (later caricatured as Mustapha Mond in Huxley's *Brave New World*) and William Lever at Leverhulme believed competition to be almost sinfully wasteful; in Japan, the development of the *zaibatsu* integrated industrial groups, though they were not inherently monopolistic, was part of the same view that big conglomerates could serve society more effectively than small competing businesses.

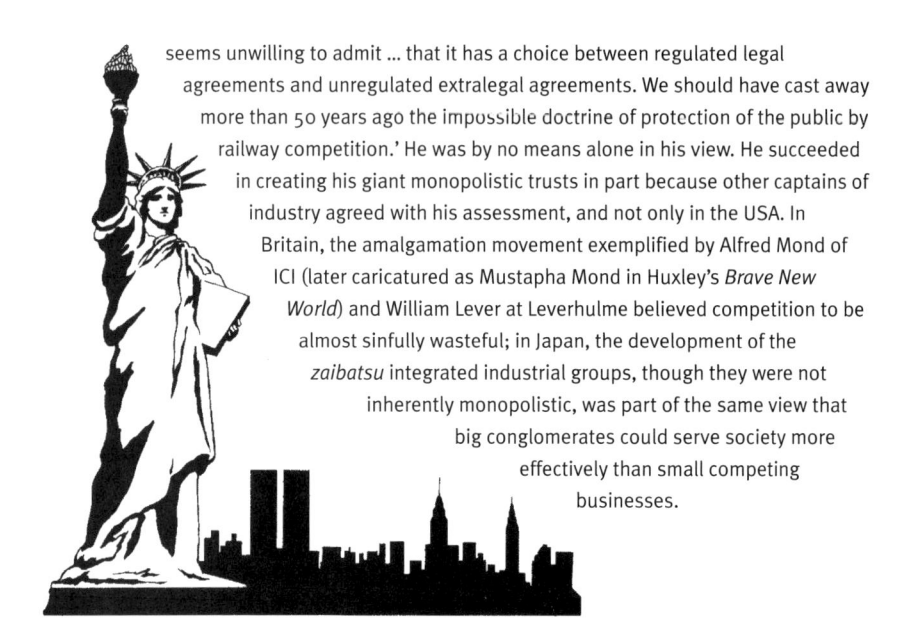

J.P. Morgan's career and the passionate opposition he roused brings into sharp relief many of the issues which have characterized financial management from the beginning and which continue to do so today. What is the relationship between capital and society? What responsibility do the providers of capital have to make sure that money is used properly and ethically? Where is the balance to be found between control and financial efficiency on the one hand, and freedom and entrepreneurship on the other? Should bankers encourage entrepreneurship and com-petition despite the obvious risks, or should they seek order and rationalization so as to achieve the greatest good for the greatest number? Not only business managers but private bankers, central bankers and government regulators continue to seek the ultimate answers to all these questions. At the time of writing, given the performance of exchange rates and stock markets over the past few years, they are no closer to succeeding.

**Should bankers encourage entrepreneurship and competition despite the obvious risks, or should they seek order and rationalization so as to achieve the greatest good for the greatest number?**

## Accounting and control

We have seen how the growth in the supply of capital, primarily through instruments of credit, fed the growth of business, especially in the West, after about the year 1000. With this growth and increasing complexity of financial affairs, however, the need for more sophisticated forms of financial management and control became more and more important. Here, the need for security and safety was the primary driving force.

> *Who shall doubt the secret hid*
> *Under Cheops's pyramid*
> *Was that the contractor did*
> *Cheops out of several millions?*
> *Or that Joseph's sudden rise*
> *To comptroller of supplies*
> *Was but a fraud of monstrous size*
> *On King Pharaoh's swart civilians?*
> 
> Rudyard Kipling

The first form of financial management was accounting. Simple income and expenditure accounting has been around for centuries; clay tablets and other written documents from Egypt and Mesopotamia containing records of accounts show that accounting has a history of at least four millennia. As Rudyard Kipling humorously(?) suggests in the quote above, fraud too is an ancient practice, and accounting was devised not only as a means of recording assets but also as a check against deceit. The famous Domesday Book compiled by William the Conqueror's officials is effectively a valuation of property, and as noted in the previous chapter, the administrative reforms in England in the twelfth century were founded in part on the institution of systematic accounting and record-keeping; in later centuries, English revenue officials used recorded tax values as a basis for calculating new values and checks to prevent deception and underpayment. A considerable advance came with the development of double-entry book-keeping in the fourteenth century, an invention usually credited to northern Italy (though forms of double-entry book-keeping have also been noted in Japan by the Tokugawa period). The Florentine friar Luca Pacioli is sometimes credited with inventing double-entry book-keeping, but it seems likely that the system goes back to around 1300; Pacioli's book *Summa de arithmetica*, published in Venice in 1494, is the earliest known written account of how the system works. By 1600 the double-entry method was in widespread use in Europe.

For our purposes, of equal interest to how control was maintained is the question of who maintained it. Up until the fifteenth century, almost without exception, accounting was one of the functions of top leadership; the head of the family business, one of the senior partners, etc. Francesco Datini, devolving day-to-day management of his businesses to his partners, reserved for himself two functions: keeping the books, and gathering and assessing market information. Datini kept centralized accounts for all the partnerships, with detailed cost and price information. In woollen cloth manufacturing, for example, his accounts showed both the cost of each stage of production and the consolidated final production cost, giving him exact information about the financial status of the business.

In larger and more complex businesses such as the Medici bank, it was no longer possible for head office to control every aspect of the accounts, though consolidated accounts were still prepared and checked by one of the senior partners, the *famigilia*, usually the general manager Giovanni d'Amerigo Benci. Divisions prepared their own accounts and forwarded these to head office in Florence. However, as a safeguard against fraud and incompetence, head office always nominated which partner in each division or overseas office was to be responsible for preparing the books. As often as not, that partner was a junior member of the Medici family or someone with close ties to the family who could be counted on to be loyal. Although junior clerks were often used to prepare the actual books, they had little power and their work was closely scrutinized (and not just for frauds; mathematical errors could be just as costly).

With weak regulatory structures, trust was everything in the Middle Ages and for long after. Managers of agricultural estates, as described in

Walter of Henley's tract on the subject around 1300, had enormous financial responsibilities. Landowners were frequently away on military service, attending parliament, carrying out functions as sheriffs, acting as justices of the peace and so on, and responsibility for accounting and financial management fell on their stewards. Fraud was an ever-present risk. To lay this off, landowners either appointed junior family members, or recruited outsiders and paid them high wages to ensure their loyalty.

## The rise of the accounting professional

The system of centralized accounts, with the accounts themselves prepared at the highest level of the firm, satisfied the needs of the firm's owners. It did not necessarily satisfy the needs of the suppliers of the firm's capital, and as banks began to play a major role in financing expansion and as joint-stock companies grew in numbers and size, both bankers and shareholders wanted to know that their money was being spent properly and was not being used incompetently or fraudulently.

The need for greater transparency was recognized early on, and became more urgent following the two great financial scandals of the early eighteenth century, the Mississippi Bubble in France and the South Sea Bubble in England, when dozens of banks and thousands of investors lost their money to fraudulent promoters. There were calls for regulation, particularly from the church, but most of these calls were based on moral and ethical grounds rather than purely economic considerations. Banks were reluctant to see government intervention in business as this could hurt their own prospects; bankers like Thomas Martin and Thomas Coutts urged that investors should simply take greater care and do business only with people they could trust.

**The need for greater transparency was recognized early on, and became more urgent following the two great financial scandals of the early eighteenth century**

Throughout this period, the profession of independent accountant grew slowly in terms of numbers and prestige. By 1800, independent accountants were carrying out a variety of functions, usually at the behest of the courts, including winding up insolvent businesses and examining disputed accounts in cases at law; many British accountants, carrying on a tradition that had lasted since the Middle Ages, also practised as estate managers (in the rural shires of Britain today, it is still not uncommon to find small joint accounting and estate management practices; some also sell property, act as insurance brokers and even conduct auctions). In 1854 the Institute of Accountants in Glasgow petitioned for a royal charter, the granting of which made the institute the world's first formally recognized accounting body; the term 'chartered accountant' dates from this time. Other accounting bodies followed suit in Scotland and England, and later on the Continent and in North America. These societies became responsible for setting accounting standards and establishing professional qualifications, largely as they still do today.

Around the same time, the role of the accountant took on a new dimension when, in 1849, the London accountant William Deloitte was approached by the shareholders of Great Western Railway for assistance in preparing the company's accounts. Great Western was experiencing financial problems at the time, and the shareholder-auditors lacked sufficient experience to deal with the complex accounting problems this caused. Deloitte, who already had a reputation for probity and accuracy, performed the task so well that the directors appointed him permanent auditor to the company, probably the first time that a permanent external auditor had been appointed in this fashion. What is more, they recommended that every firm should appoint an external auditor, and that this practice should be enshrined in law; as it duly was a few years later.

## WILLIAM DELOITTE

**DELOITTE WAS BORN IN LONDON IN 1818.** Little is known of him until he established his own accountancy practice on Basinghall Street, London, by 1845, specializing in insolvencies (his offices were located conveniently close to the bankruptcy courts). In 1849 he assisted the shareholder-auditors of Great Western Railway in preparing the company's accounts, and was appointed the company's permanent external auditor; this practice was later established in law. Over the second half of the nineteenth century, Deloitte served as external auditor for many large companies, especially in transportation and engineering. His own business grew and he took on a large number of staff, although unusually for an accountant of his time he rarely took in partners. He continued to be an innovator in accounting practice, developing the double-account system for auditing railway companies (this again was adopted in law as standard practice) and also devising a standard system of hotel accounts. He was also called in to investigate several major frauds, again mostly in railway and steamship companies. By the time of his retirement in 1897 he was the most high-profile accountant in Europe. He left behind a number of accounting and auditing methods which have had lasting impact on management reporting and control. The firm he founded is today part of the global accounting and consulting business, Deloitte Touche Ross.

---

The appointment of external auditors seems unremarkable now, but in fact it was a great leap forward in terms of transparency and openness about financial management. It also opened up new opportunities for accountants to render professional services. A few years after Deloitte, another great British accountant, Edwin Waterhouse, who co-founded the Institute of Chartered Accountants of England and Wales and helped establish a formal training programme and examinations for candidates to the profession, began offering advisory services for partnerships wishing to convert to limited liability companies. Other accountants began following suit, and to the accounting profession much credit must be given for overhauling the antiquated legal structures of many British businesses and greatly promoting the growth of shareholder investment. In the early years of the twentieth century men like Arthur Cutforth, Lawrence Dicksee and Gilbert Garnsey improved professionalism and training in accounting, and also began disseminating new accounting practices among managers more generally; Dicksee in particular promoted general accounting knowledge through his writing and teaching.

The USA lagged behind until the beginning of the twentieth century; in 1850, there were only eighteen registered accountants in the entire country. Small wonder that in 1860, the journalist Henry Varnum Poor wrote of the lamentable state of financial management and disclosure among the American railway companies; even where regulations required them to disclose their accounts, few did so, and few states had the mechanisms or the expertise to force greater transparency. By 1885 there were still only just over 200 accountants in the USA. The formation of the American Association of Public Accountants gave the profession a boost, but it took government intervention in the form of the anti-trust acts of the 1890s and 1900s to force companies into greater transparency, and only then did accountants begin to move into the formal auditing roles they had held in Britain for many years previously. By this time, too, British-style accounting standards and accountancy professional bodies had been adopted in many other countries, most notably Germany and Japan.

> The USA lagged behind until the beginning of the twentieth century; in 1850, there were only eighteen registered accountants in the entire country

## EDWIN WATERHOUSE

**BORN IN LIVERPOOL IN 1841**, Waterhouse was educated at University College London and then apprenticed as an accountant for three years before setting up his own practice. In 1867 he joined with two partners, establishing the accounting firm Price, Holyland and Waterhouse; in 1874 this became Price, Waterhouse & Co. In the mid-1870s Waterhouse became the managing partner, taking control of the business following the death of Samuel Price in 1887. Price, Waterhouse & Co. became a leading firm of auditors, specializing particularly in banks and railways. Like other large accounting firms of the day, they were often called upon to research firms which were prospective targets for takeover, and to investigate potential cases of fraud. Waterhouse, who emphasized accuracy and detail in his work, was in the forefront of the movement which called for greater transparency of company accounts and the publication of detailed financial statements. By the 1880s, British capital was also seeking outlets in the USA, and in 1890 Price, Waterhouse went international, opening its first office in New York. Today the firm of PricewaterhouseCoopers is one of the largest accounting and consulting businesses in the world.

### The rise of the finance professional

More complex capital markets, more complex ownership structures and more regulations all led in time to the development of corporate finance as a distinct branch of management. But the development was a long time in coming. Even into the 1930s, like the Italian banker-entrepreneurs centuries before, presidents and chairmen of large companies preferred to manage corporate finances directly. Finance, like marketing, was seen as being at the core of the management function, and responsibility for it went right to the top. Although large – sometimes very large – accounts departments were maintained, the responsibility of these was to gather and tabulate information, not to make decisions and set policy. Separate finance departments did not begin appearing in most firms until after the Second World War. Today, of course, finance is very much a separate province in most firms, and financial managers are almost a breed apart.

Is this a good thing? The need for specialist expertise cannot be denied; but then neither can the central role of money, the need for both access *to* capital and the secure and effective management *of* capital, in making organizations function. Is it right that something so vital should be so heavily devolved to a specialist department? And, are finance departments – and the business schools that largely train their members – really understanding what is happening today within their profession?

Today, managers are rethinking the role of money. Another revolution, that based on information technology, is (potentially at least) enabling money and credit to take new forms and be traded in new ways. Vital questions need to be asked, including (but not limited to) the following:

- If money is a commodity, then what new forms – in the modern case, enabled by technology – might this commodity take? We read frequently of electronic cash, or e-cash; but should this more correctly be referred to as e-credit? When will e-credit become endorsable, discountable and tradable on open markets, and who will be the first to make a profit doing so?
- If money is a means of exchange, then is a cashless society possible? What does 'cashless society' mean, given that even bank notes are essentially credit instruments? Did we not reach a 'cashless society' some centuries ago? If so, what is stopping us from inventing and exploiting further forms of money?
- How will wealth expand in the future? Who will have it and how will they acquire it? Does it really 'take money to make

money', or can new credit instruments be used to 'create' wealth in new ways? And what comes next, after credit?

- Who will take the lead in this field; business or government? The experience of centuries past suggests governments are not really interested in new and uncontrollable forms of wealth, which are difficult to tax and which upset economic policy. Business, then, will have to lead.

- How will the new wealth be employed? In the great Age of Credit in the Middle Ages and the Renaissance, much surplus wealth was spent on art; it is fascinating to think that, without the bill of exchange and the promissory note, the great works of Leonardo and Michelangelo might never have been painted. Are we today on the verge of a new Renaissance?

Some – possibly all – of these issues are beyond the power of the individual manager to control; but they are nonetheless part of the reality that confronts us in a changing world. In this instance, the imagination and creativity shown by our ancestors in creating and exploiting wealth can be inspirational when examining our own futures. All of the questions above, albeit in different forms, faced managers in the twelfth century, and the eighteenth, and the nineteenth. The answers our predecessors devised cannot be used as exact guides to our own problems, but they show us some interesting parallels. Even more, in the midst of so much change, they can show us which things are constants and can be relied upon. In finance even more than in most branches of management, there are first principles that can be depended on.

## FINANCIAL MARKETS: DEJA VU ALL OVER AGAIN

THE COMPARISON BETWEEN THE ASIA CRISIS AND THE DOTCOM BUBBLE in our own all too recent memory on the one hand, and the Dutch tulip crisis and the South Sea Bubble, has been made often – by me in Chapter 1 of this book, for starters – and I will not repeat it again. And yet on another level, the comparison cannot be made *too* often. As my friend Stephen Adamson at

Ernst & Young, who has been one of the key figures in rescuing the Thai banking industry from its own excesses and the folly of foreign investors, tells everyone who will listen, bubbles will be repeated, over and over again, until finance professionals learn to study and recognize the telltale signs of bubble-dom.

Medieval theologians recognized that greed and money are inseparable. Some, like Thomas Aquinas, argued that money has no real value outside the things it will purchase for us; money alone has no inherent good, and the greedy are in the grip of a delusion. Others, like Bernard of Clairvaux, believed that the acquisition of money was such an intrinsically greedy act that it must be considered a sin in its own right. Today, we can be sceptical about whether those who acquire money are sinful; but plenty of 'em sure are deluded.

We pride ourselves on the sophistication of our financial markets, and how far we have come in terms of harnessing the power of capital. But consider the phenomenon known as 'burn rate' which made a (fortunately brief) appearance during the dotcom bubble. This phenomenon, which I am convinced started as a joke, came to be taken seriously by not a few merchant banks and venture capitalists: briefly stated, the concept held that the potential value of a dotcom business could be gauged by how quickly it was spending, or 'burning', its invested capital.

If you were to approach a group of seventeenth-century merchant bankers and explain the concept of burn rate to them, they would howl with laughter. Banking was about *making* money, not about spending it! As Thomas Martin of the Grasshopper said, 'Avoid unprofitable business, especially when attended with trouble and expense.' The mark of a successful banker was in how much profit you made, not in the volume of capital passing through the doors. For these guys, on the other hand, burn rate was how many witches you could get through in an afternoon. What is there to choose between us in terms of ignorance and superstition? Probably not much.

## *Notes to chapter 6*

1 Moneys of exchange are those used in everyday transactions, represented physically by a coin or banknote. Moneys of account are usually large monetary units, unrepresented by physical money, used in commercial transactions. The pound sterling was a common money of account in England in the Middle Ages, despite the fact that until 1350 the largest denomination coin was the penny. The tael of silver and the lakh of rupias were moneys of account found in China and India, respectively.

2 Quoted in G. Chandler (1964) *Four Centuries of Banking*, London: B.T. Batsford. 109–10.

# 7

# Roads to victory

> No plan survives contact with the enemy
> *Field Marshal Helmuth von Moltke*

Strategy is one of the most discussed and least understood concepts in business today. Everyone talks about it; the word trips off the lips of governmental policy-makers and management gurus with almost astonishing ease. All business leaders have, or say they have, an idea of what *their* strategy is; but try to pin them down on what *strategy* itself is, and the answers start to become notably more vague.

For starters, few in the business world seem to be capable of making a distinction between 'strategy' and 'tactics'. Both are concepts drawn from military science. Strategy comes from the Greek *strategia*, meaning generalship or the movement of armies on a broad scale; even as late as the Byzantine empire, the word for general was *strategos*. Tactics is also derived from the Greek *taktika* and refers to the deployment and handling of forces when in contact with the enemy (it has the same root as 'tactile' and other words signifying touch). Confusion between the two terms abounds in management literature. Textbooks on marketing and advertising

> **It takes a strong sense of purpose and of mission to achieve long-term growth and success in this or any business environment**

strategy, for example, frequently treat both the planning of advertising campaigns and issues of timing and placement of advertisements as part of 'strategy'. I once sat in on a meeting where a company was planning a takeover of another, and senior management discussed their 'strategy' for handling the takeover. It was like listening to someone discuss their strategy for driving a car.

Words can and do change their meanings, and just because military science offers one set of meanings for terms does not mean business and management must slavishly follow those definitions. Fair enough; but what must be of concern here is the confusion of ends with means. Tactical plans for outmanoeuvring a competitor, securing a source of supply, achieving a certain share of a certain market, etc. are often confused with the company's wider goals. It takes a strong sense of purpose and of mission to achieve long-term growth and success in this or any business environment. A sense of strategic vision and knowledge of how to achieve that vision are essential. And in order to have these things, it certainly helps to know what strategy is, where it comes from, and what its first principles are.

## The late arrival of strategic thinking

Most of the disciplines of management which we have considered here developed in their modern, codified form during the period from about 1900–1930. Strategy was a late arrival on the scene. The first person to articulate the idea of business strategy is usually said to be Alfred Chandler, the great Harvard business historian whose book *Strategy and Structure* (1962) gives us a starting definition: strategy is 'the determination of the basic long-term goals and objectives of an enterprise, and the adoption of courses of action and the allocation of resources necessary for carrying out these goals'.[1] Chandler also offered a truism that has remained at the root of much strategic thinking since, namely that 'structure follows strategy'; successful firms first determine their goals and their strategies for reaching them, then select a model or form of organization that is best suited to those needs.

Chandler's is a highly-rational concept of strategy, and it appears to assume that there is a neat linear process: set goal, allocate resources, work out method of reaching goal. Michael Porter, in the late 1980s and early 1990s, went so far as to offer ideas of 'generic strategies', such as cost leadership, differentiation, cost focus and focused differentiation. Make two simple decisions concerning competitive scope and competitive advantage, click on the right option and bang, there's your strategy.

But earlier writers who had touched on strategic issues had their doubts. Herbert Simon, the great postwar American philosopher of organization, had earlier described the problem of what he called 'bounded rationality', meaning basically that organizational decisions are nearly always made on the basis of less than complete information. Earlier still, in the 1930s, the British industrial economist Philip Sargant Florence, considering the efficacy or otherwise of large-scale organizations, posed three problems which needed to be faced when designing and setting strategy: (1) the need to match the goals of the business with those of consumers, which were in turn difficult to analyze and homogenize; (2) the need to know the organization's span of control (i.e. once a strategy had been designed, did the organization have the managerial skill and ability to implement it?); and finally, (3) the need to make sure that the organization's goals were also harmonized with those of its members, so that the latter would be willing to pull together to help achieve the required results.

These three factors, said Florence, meant that there was no such thing as an 'optimum strategy'. Nor, it appears, does structure necessarily follow strategy; the relationship between the two is complicated, and sometimes indeed the process works the other way round, with strategy of necessity being dictated by the organizational resources and tools available. Resetting and reconfiguring the organization every time there is a change in strategy is a luxury few companies can afford. Echoes of Florence can be found in the recent writings on strategy of Henry Mintzberg, who argues that most managers most of the time make up their strategy on an *ad hoc* and intuitive basis. He believes this is a good thing: excessive formal planning of strategy leads organizations to become rigid in their approach and unable to respond to new challenges and opportunities.[2]

As a result of critiques like that of Mintzberg, writers on strategy have become cautious about adopting firm definitions of their subject. Roger Mansfield, writing in the *International Encyclopedia of Business and Management*, says that business strategy 'would seem' to include the following:

1. an evaluation of the company's present position and an audit of its strengths and weaknesses
2. scanning the environment to note potential opportunities and threats
3. the establishment of strategic objectives
4. the establishment of a plan for meeting those objectives
5. communication of the plan to the relevant departments and people
6. implementation of the plan
7. monitoring the progress of the implementation as it goes on
8. reassessment of the plan at various stages and adjusting it to fit new circumstances.

1 and 2 together form the famous concept of SWOT analysis. SWOT stands for Strengths, Weaknesses, Opportunities and Threats; or, depending on your level of cynicism, Silly Waste Of Time.

And finally, my own two cents (my privilege as author): I don't believe the four 'generic strategies' Michael Porter offers are strategies at all. I think they are strategic *principles*, which firms can use in given situations to meet given needs and on which strategies can be founded, but they are not strategies themselves. In order to be considered a strategy, any concept must meet the goals test: that is, it must be possible to ask the question 'strategy for what?' and receive a comprehensible answer. On this basis, differentiation and cost focus are no more strategies *per se* than are principles such as concentration of force and maintaining secure lines of communication, commonly found in military strategic thinking.

> **In order to be considered a strategy, any concept must meet the goals test: that is, it must be possible to ask the question 'strategy for what?' and receive a comprehensible answer**

But this idea of strategic principles is important; again, it is the nomenclature that is at fault, not the ideas themselves. If most strategy is conducted with bounded rationality, and if there is no optimum strategy, and if most strategic thinking is done *ad hoc* and on the fly, then there is surely a great necessity for some principles on which we can fall back when doing our strategic thinking. And with great respect to Michael Porter, we need more than just four principles, more than just a Boston Box from which we pull out the right option. Strategy is both more simple and more complicated than that. To *understand* the concept of strategy, then, it is time to take a look at its sources.

## Strategy in the classical world

The pre-eminent Roman writer on military affairs, Vegetius, actually had relatively little to say about strategy *per se*, but he did strongly argue that strategy must be conducted according to first principles: his favourite maxim is that 'war must be conducted according to principles, not chance'. Vegetius's main emphasis is on the organization and management of armies, and he takes the pragmatic view that no strategy has a chance of succeeding unless the army is fit for the tasks required of it.

There was, however, great interest in the Roman world in the subject of strategy, and writers looked to their own history and that of the Greeks for examples of sound strategic thinking. One popular source was the Greek general Xenophon, a relatively junior officer in a corps of Greek mercenaries hired to fight on one side of a civil war in the Persian empire around 400 BC. The party for which the Greeks were fighting was defeated, and the Greek force negotiated a safe passage home; however, the Persians reneged on the deal and the leaders of the Greeks were assassinated during negotiations. Xenophon, as senior surviving officer, took over the contingent of about 10,000 troops and fought his way across Asia Minor to the sea, an epic which he later recounted in his book the *Anabasis*. Xenophon was widely admired for his singleness of purpose and strong will, which played an important part in forcing his way past obstacles.

Other works of history were widely studied, including the account by Josephus of the revolt in Judea in AD 70, the military histories of Tacitus, the account of Alexander the Great's campaign by the historian Arrian, and Julius Caesar's autobiographical account of his campaigns in Gaul. A common lesson from all these campaigns, especially those of Caesar, was the need for thorough preparation before embarking on a campaign. Caesar was also praised for his ability to manage all his resources; infantry, cavalry, auxiliary troops, artillery, engineers and so on, and keep them supplied and in good heart in the field.

One of the most influential works was the account by the historian Livy of Rome's long war with Carthage. The achievements of the great Carthaginian general Hannibal were studied carefully, but attention too was paid to his Roman opponents, particularly the consul Fabius Maximus, later nicknamed Cunctator (the delayer). Following Hannibal's annihilation of the Roman field armies at Cannae in 216 BC, Fabius took command of the few remaining troops and fought a masterful campaign of delays and rearguard actions which prevented Hannibal from achieving his main objective, marching on Rome. A key lesson from the Fabian experience was the need to deny the enemy access to his objectives.

**A key lesson from the Fabian experience was the need to deny the enemy access to his objectives**

Vegetius summarized many of these approaches. Although there was plenty of other late Roman writing on the subject, including the *Strategemata* of Frontinus and the writings on strategy of the Byzantine emperor Nicephoras Phocas, Vegetius's *De Re Mitliari* remained popular thanks to its accessibility and simple style. In the Middle Ages, every warlord (or noble with pretensions to being one) seems to have read it, and copies were to be found in libraries across Europe; it was also well known to Machiavelli, of whom more follows.[3]

## Eastern approaches

It was in East Asia, however, that strategy first became a high art. The book known as *Sunzi Bingfa* (The Military Methods of Master Sun, more usually known in the West as the *Art of War*) attributed to Sunzi (Sun Tzu) became a classic, and was studied intensively by generals and officers from the Han dynasty on down. Whereas Roman writers had studied strategy through example and precept, Sunzi goes immediately to first principles:

> The art of war, then, is governed by five constant factors, to be taken into account in one's deliberations, when seeking to determine the conditions obtaining in the field. These are: (1) The Moral Law; (2) Heaven; (3) Earth; (4) The Commander; (5) Method and discipline. The Moral Law causes the people to be in complete accord with their ruler, so that they will follow him regardless of their lives, undismayed by any danger. Heaven signifies night and day, cold and heat, times and seasons. Earth comprises distances, great and small; danger and security; open ground and narrow passes; the chances of life and death. The Commander stands for the virtues of wisdom, sincerity, benevolence, courage and strictness. By method and discipline are to be understood the marshalling of the army in its proper subdivisions, the graduations of rank among the officers, the maintenance of roads by which supplies may reach the army, and the control of military expenditure. These five heads should be familiar to every general: he who knows them will be victorious; he who knows them not will fail.

To put it in more modern terms, for a strategy to succeed, there must be a firm goal in which all believe, good knowledge of geography and the environment in which the campaign will take place, strong leadership and strong organization. Sunzi agrees with Julius Caesar on the need for full preparation:

> Now the general who wins a battle makes many calculations in his temple ere the battle is fought. The general who loses a battle makes but few calculations beforehand. Thus do many calculations lead to victory, and few calculations to defeat: how much more no calculation at all! It is by attention to this point that I can foresee who is likely to win or lose.

At the conclusion of preparations, the general must act swiftly and with purpose, striking hard at the enemy and avoiding delay. The commander should keep his mind focused at all times, on the ultimate goal, victory over the enemy, and not be sidetracked into other activities. It is also critical, says Sunzi, to remain flexible and adaptable, and to be able to change plans in the face of changing circumstances.

Sunzi also advocates the use of stratagem and deception, arguing that these are often cost-effective means of achieving aims. He emphasizes that the aim of warfare is not to fight battles: it is to force the enemy to your own will: 'Thus the highest form of generalship is to balk the enemy's plans; the next best is to prevent the junction of the enemy's forces; the next in order is to attack the enemy's army in the field; and the worst policy of all is to besiege walled cities.' He comments that 'the clever combatant imposes his will on the enemy, but does not allow the enemy's will to be imposed on him'. Finally he describes his five essentials for victory:

> Thus we may know that there are five essentials for victory: (1) He will win who knows when to fight and when not to fight. (2) He will win who knows how to handle both superior and inferior forces. (3) He will win whose army is animated by the same spirit throughout all its ranks. (4) He will win who, prepared himself, waits to take the enemy unprepared. (5) He will win who has military capacity and is not interfered with by the sovereign. Hence the saying: If you know the enemy and know yourself, you need not fear the result of a hundred battles. If you know yourself but not the enemy, for every victory gained you will also suffer a defeat.

If you know neither the enemy nor yourself, you will succumb in every battle.

## SUNZI

**SUNZI HAD TRADITIONALLY BEEN IDENTIFIED AS SUN WU,** chief minister of the state of Wu in the sixth century BC, near the end of the Spring and Autumn period. However, textual scholarship suggests that the book which bears his name was probably composed around two centuries later, during the height of the period of conflict known as the Warring States period. The book was heavily edited by Cao Cao, one of the great generals of the Three Kingdoms in the second and third centuries AD, who used it as a manual of strategy and encouraged his commanders to read it. Along with other works such as *The Thirty-Six Stratagems* and the *Romance of Three Kingdoms*, it became one of the foundational texts of later Chinese strategic thinking; in the twentieth century it was studied closely by both Chiang Kai-shek and Mao Zedong. Sunzi was also studied by Japanese military leaders, and during the twentieth century the book was translated into many western languages and is now taught at most military academies. Along with other works such as Miyamoto Musashi's *Book of Five Rings* and the *The Art of War* of Karl von Clausewitz, it has also crossed over into business strategy, and popular versions have been produced for business leaders in both Asia and the West.

Sunzi's work was widely admired and imitated, and in later years dozens of other Chinese writers on strategy appeared. One of the most important and widely read was the *Thirty-Six Stratagems*, a series of maxims which, as the title suggests, focus mostly on the use of deception, guile and bluff. The stratagems themselves have picturesque titles such as 'beat the grass to startle the snake' or 'point at the mulberry and curse the locust'. Their common theme is the old Chinese concept of paired opposites, usually employed to convince the enemy that you are intending one thing when you are in fact intending another. Stratagem 7, 'create something out of nothing', exhorts generals to employ the resources they have to hand in unconventional ways; a commonly cited example is that of the general Zhang Xun who, besieged and running out of arrows, ordered his troops to make life-sized dummies of straw, dress them in soldiers' uniforms and post them on the battlements. The enemy obligingly fired arrows at the dummies, whereupon

Zhang Xun's soldiers pulled them out and replenished their ammunition supplies.

Literature also provided fertile subject matter for strategy. The historical novel *Romance of Three Kingdoms*, set in the 'Three Kingdoms' era when China briefly broke apart following the end of the Han dynasty in the third century AD, featured Zhuge Liang, statesman and general of the state of Shu, who for nearly thirty years held off the powerful rival kingdoms of Wei and Wu. Like Sunzi and the *Thirty-Six Stratagems*, the *Romance of Three Kingdoms* has been widely read in China down through the years and continues to be popular with Chinese business leaders. Later writers drew a number of principles of strategy from his work, of which these are the most important and widely followed:

- In terms of guiding purpose, the ruler should be as unerring as the North Star.
- Ties of respect and loyalty should bind the ruler to his subjects.
- Educate the people to win them over.
- Seek out the worthy and employ the talented.
- Do not be swayed by emotion.
- Rectify oneself before giving orders.
- Act decisively.
- Be far-sighted and plan carefully.

## ZHUGE LIANG

**BORN ABOUT 180 AD IN NORTHERN CHINA,** Zhuge Liang rose quickly to positions of power and by the age of twenty-seven was chief minister and general to Liu Bei, the king of Shu. He spent the next thirty years supporting Liu Bei's bid to re-unify China under his rule and fighting against powerful rival generals such as Cao Cao of Wei and Sun Quan of Wu. Despite being a harsh disciplinarian with distinct Legalist tinges to his leadership style, Zhuge Liang was strongly influenced by Confucian ethics and believed in the need to win the hearts and minds of the people. His name has become a byword in China for successful generalship and leadership.

## Daoist and Buddhist strategy

As will immediately be seen, these principles focus not so much on the actions of the organization but on the nature and behaviour of the leader. The foundational Daoist text the *Daodejing* (*Tao Te Ching*), a title which translates roughly as 'The Classic of the Way and Virtue', has also had an important impact on Eastern strategic thinking. One of the most important Daoist concepts in this regard is the emphasis on the intangible, as the paired opposite of the tangible. The *Daodejing* gives examples:

> Thirty spokes converge upon a single hub;
> It is on the hole in the centre that the use of the cart hinges.
> We make a vessel from a lump of clay;
> It is the empty space within the vessel that makes it useful.
> We make doors and windows for a room;
> But it is the empty spaces that make the room livable.
> Thus, while the tangible has its advantages,
> It is the intangible that makes it useful.

From this premise, the *Daodejing* goes on to discuss the opposite of action, *wu-wei* or 'non-action'. According to this the ruler does not do things; rather, he causes them to happen. In a society or organization which is focused on the *dao* (the Way), right things happen naturally and of their own accord without need for the ruler's intervention. The task of the latter, then, is solely to guide the organization along the Way and in accordance with the principles of virtue. The key strategic concept here is that there is a time for both action and non-action, and it is important to be able to recognize which is which.[4]

The importance of virtue is also implicit in Buddhist thinking in China. Buddhism became influential in China around the sixth century AD, though Buddhist ideas and scholars had been known before that. A number of Buddhist schools developed, some strongly faithful to the original ideas of Indian Buddhism, others, such as Chan (better known today by its Japanese name, Zen) adapting considerably to Chinese culture. Buddhism has as one of its central tenets the personal search for enlightenment, and many of the Chinese schools focused on 'strategies' for achieving enlightenment. The school of Linji, which still survives today, used allegories and stories, such as the tales of the Seven Sages of the Bamboo Grove, to instruct and enlighten. Linji also used unorthodox pedagogical methods such as suddenly striking students with a stick during lessons, or shouting things such as, 'If you meet the Buddha on the road, kill him!' How students dealt with these interruptions was viewed as a measure of their progress towards enlightenment. Buddhist and Daoist ideas were and remain important sources of inspiration and strategic thinking for managers in the East, where strategic principles are often enshrined in popular maxims and precepts.

### The way of the warrior

The idea that success depends to a degree on personal virtue and enlightenment is found even more powerfully in Japan. *Heiho*, the way of the warrior (today better known as *bushido*), was influenced by both Buddhism and the indigenous faith, Shinto. The primary emphasis in *heiho* is on preparedness, including both physical and mental preparation. The two most widely-studied works were the *Gorin-no Sho* (Book of Five Rings) of Miyamoto Musashi, and the *Hagakure* (In the Shadow of Leaves) by Yamamoto Tsunetomo.

Miyamoto, a semi-legendary figure whose fame rests on his reputation as a swordfighter and duellist, might more properly be regarded as a tactician; the thrust of the *Gorin-no Sho* is on how to win swordfights. But the path of the warrior, he insists, is not about learning how to win one fight; it is about reaching a state of preparedness and ability which enables victory at any time, under any situation. Patience and preparation are essential virtues: 'You must walk down the path of a thousand miles step by step, keeping at heart the spirit which one gains from repeated practice with whomever one can get to practise with, and knowledge attained from whatever experience you can come by, without impatience.' Constant practice and constant learning are also essential: there is no one right way to fight a sword duel, says Miyamoto, but rather many different schools, all of which have knowledge to impart. In the final chapter, the 'Book of Emptiness', he urges the importance of dispelling illusion, learning, clear thinking and a pure heart, all of which allow the fighter to focus on the goal.

The *Hagakure* was written around 1716 by Yamamoto Tsunetomo, a *samurai* who later became a Buddhist monk and, while in seclusion, wrote down his thoughts on the role and duties of the warrior. Like many contemporary philosophical writings, the *Hagakure* is a set of allegorical tales and sayings intended to guide the reader towards understanding rather than to instruct in a didactic manner. The work achieved notoriety for its blunt opening statement: 'The way of the *samurai* is found in death.' However, he goes on, this does not mean that the aim of the warrior is to die; rather, it is that the warrior should be ready and willing to meet death in the service of his master, and that there comes a time in every warrior's life when death is a duty. The famous case of the Forty-Seven Ronin, which occurred a few years before the writing of the *Hagakure*, illustrates this precept well.

> **Like many contemporary philosophical writings, the Hagakure is a set of allegorical tales and sayings intended to guide the reader towards understanding rather than to instruct in a didactic manner**

## MIYAMOTO MUSASHI

**B**ORN IN 1584 IN THE VILLAGE OF MIYAMOTO IN HARIMA PROVINCE, Miyamoto trained as a swordfighter and fought his first duel at the age of thirteen. He went on to fight sixty-six duels, emerging victorious from all; on one occasion he fought and defeated in turn every member of a fencing school in Kyoto. Retiring at the age of thirty, Miyamoto spent the next several decades as a fencing master, and in 1640 retired to a Buddhist monastery where he spent his remaining years in contemplation and in writing down his thoughts on the art of the sword. In the twentieth century Miyamoto became the subject of much popular literature and film, which sometimes portrayed him as a kind of Robin Hood.

The *Hagakure* continues to be read and admired by Japanese businessmen primarily for its views on the cultivation of self and its emphasis on preparedness. Over and over again, Yamamoto chastises *samurai* who have failed to prepare themselves either mentally or physically and then, in a crisis, flinch from their purpose and fail to do their duty and achieve their goals. Like Miyamoto, who wrote that a journey of a thousand miles begins with a single step, Yamamoto believed that even the hardest task could be accomplished by working a day at a time; tomorrow, he wrote, is also just a single day. The Buddhist influence in his thinking comes out strongly when he emphasizes that fitness for purpose must be inner as well as outer:

> If your strength is only that which comes from vitality, your words and personal conduct will appear to be in accord with the Way, and you will be praised by others. But when you question yourself about this, there will be nothing to be said. The last line of the poem that goes 'When your own heart asks' is the secret principle of all the arts.

## THE FORTY-SEVEN RONIN

IN 1701, A DAIMYO IN ATTENDANCE AT THE COURT OF THE SHOGUN IN EDO quarrelled with one of the Shogun's officials and drew his sword. For this offence, he was condemned to death. His *samurai* retainers, who numbered forty-seven, now became *ronin* or masterless men, effectively social outcasts. Living in great poverty for the next two years, they hatched their plans and eventually confronted the official whom they believed to be responsible for their master's death and killed him. All forty-seven then committed ritual suicide, or *seppuku*. This incident quickly became widely known, and the *ronin* were widely praised for their singleness of purpose and their attention to their duty. In the twentieth century the story was turned into a film by the director Kurosawa Akiro.

## From Machiavelli to Moltke

The first modern western writer to consider strategy explicitly was the Florentine politician and diplomat Niccolò Machiavelli. Writing while in exile after his patrons, the Medici family, had been expelled from Florence, Machiavelli produced three major works: *The Art of War*, a discussion of military organization, and two treatises on statecraft, *The Prince* and *The Discourses on Livy*. *The Prince* was regarded as a sensation when it was first published some time after Machiavelli's death, particularly for its argument that the prince (or general, or any other leader) is justified in using deception, lies, dishonesty, and even cruelty and torture if these means are necessary to achieve his ends. For this Machiavelli was stigmatized for generations as an immoral and even evil man. In fact, his views were based on pragmatism: immoral means are sometimes necessary to achieve moral ends. The prince who does *not* use dishonesty or cruelty when these means could have saved his people, and who instead loses the war and causes his city to be delivered over to fire and sword, is in Machiavelli's eyes a worse offender than the cruellest tyrant.

Key components in Machiavelli's view of strategy are strength of purpose and flexibility. In both *The Prince* and *The Discourses*, he emphasizes two concepts: *virtú* (ability or capacity), and *fortuna* (serendipity or luck). The possession of *virtú* is essential if a leader is to be successful; it is *virtú* that allows leaders to recognize and seize opportunities and to out-think and outfight their opponents. *Fortuna* plays an important role in every strategic calculation, in that unexpected events can upset even the most carefully-laid plans. However, says Machiavelli, *virtú* allows leaders to recognize when chance has given them an opportunity, to take advantage of *fortuna* by reacting more quickly than competitors or opponents.

> Key components in Machiavelli's view of strategy are strength of purpose and flexibility

## NICCOLÒ MACHIAVELLI

**MACHIAVELLI WAS BORN IN FLORENCE IN 1469**, and began his career in the Florentine civil service when the city was ruled by Lorenzo dei Medici, son of Cosimo dei Medici. He retained his post following the overthrow of the Medici and the establishment of a republic in 1494 and went on to achieve high rank, serving as secretary to the body known as the Ten of War and representing Florence on diplomatic missions abroad. After the return of the Medici in 1512 Machiavelli was removed from office, and in 1513 he was arrested, imprisoned and tortured.

Released, he retired to his country estate at San Casciano, near Florence, and it was here that he produced his most famous writings: *The Prince*, *Discourses on the First Decade of Livy* and *The Art of War* (only the latter was published in his own lifetime). He recovered some public favour after 1521, but died shortly after the second overthrow of the Medici in 1527.

........................................................................................................

Despite his unsavoury reputation, Machiavelli and his ideas were well known in the seventeenth century, when writers like the Italian soldier of fortune Raimondo Montecuccoli and the Dutch leader Maurice of Nassau began writing some of the first manuals of military strategy and organization. However, the first great strategic thinker of the modern period appeared in the following century in Prussia in the person of its king, Frederick the Great. Frederick created the first coherent body of strategic thought and practice, much of which was written down in his *Instructions to Generals*, a document which Frederick composed shortly after the Seven Years War and continued to revise until his death in 1786.

Frederick's principles of strategy depended to a large degree on planning and organizing. The Prussian system of military organization, described in more detail in Chapter 5, was intended to be sufficiently flexible to meet any eventuality. Frederick's view of organization depended on discipline and control, but even more on developing in each military unit a sense of *Korpsgeist*, the ability of members of an organization (such as an army regiment) to identify with the organization and put its interests over their own. Like Machiavelli's *virtú*, Frederick also believed that an essential for success was for leaders to cultivate the capacity to seize opportunities and take advantage of changing circumstances; like Napoleon, he believed that to a large extent leaders make their own luck.

Frederick believed in concentration of authority and singleness of purpose. His position as both king and commander-in-chief of the Prussian army gave him absolute control over policy and strategy. Where possible, he exercised control in person and alone; he regarded councils and committees as chiefly being excuses for doing nothing. However, he was not afraid to devolve command to trusted subordinates. One of his major problems was that, as the war went on, many of his best generals such as Hans von Winterfeldt and William Keith were killed and could not be replaced.

Frederick also placed much emphasis on studying his rivals and learning their capacities. He knew how they would act and react, and knew the patterns of their behaviour, sometimes better than they did themselves. At the Battle of Leuthen in December 1757, Frederick, outnumbered two-to-one by the Austrians under Archduke Charles, knew his rival well enough to know that the latter would stand his position while the Prussians made a highly risky march across the enemy's front before turning to attack their flank. When the Prussians did attack, it was a well-organized blow with infantry, cavalry and artillery working in close co-ordination; the result was Austria's worst military defeat of the war.

After the war, Frederick returned to Leuthen and stood on the spot where Archduke Charles had directed the Austrians, then ordered his own army to march towards him following the original Prussian line of march. By literally standing in his opponent's footsteps, Frederick was able to understand how and why his opponent had failed.

Though he believed in conducting war according to principles, Frederick also knew when to break his own rules. Opponents did sometimes regard him as mad, but there was always a calculating logic to his decisions. At the Battle of Rossbach in November 1757, Frederick's army encountered a French army. Without waiting to form up for battle, as was the convention of the day, Frederick attacked immediately; his cavalry at once destroyed the French vanguard, and by nightfall the French were in total retreat. They suffered 10,000 casualties; Frederick suffered fewer than 600. At Leuthen, again, he adopted the then new technique of ordering his artillery to advance along with the infantry to engage the enemy at close quarters.

Frederick's methods and strategy were widely studied and analyzed. Heinrich von Bülow, writing in the first years of the nineteenth century, when Prussian armies had been heavily defeated by Napoleon, analyzed Frederick's successes in terms of his having a military 'system'. Bülow is sometimes credited with being the first to employ the term 'strategy' in its modern sense by defining Frederick's aims and methods as part of the larger military system. He argued that war needed to be treated like business; the military force available to a nation was its 'capital', which needed to be kept in circulation. Concentration of capital and assets at the appropriate points would yield a return on investment, and capital had to be flexible so that it could be concentrated quickly where needed. This new approach emphasized strategic goals over processes and methods. Bülow believed that Frederick had been successful because he had followed this principle; his successors, who lacked both Frederick's strategic insight and his ability to keep his organization fit and flexible, had been defeated as a result.

> Bülow is sometimes credited with being the first to employ the term 'strategy' in its modern sense by defining Frederick's aims and methods as part of the larger military system

## HEINRICH VON BÜLOW

**HEINRICH VON BÜLOW WAS BORN IN PRUSSIA IN 1757**, into a distinguished Prussian military family; his elder brother Friedrich became a noted general and commanded an army corps at Waterloo. Bülow served in the Prussian army from 1773–89, and on retirement devoted himself to writing on military issues. He published his major work, *The Spirit of the Modern System of War*, in 1799, and went on to write a further fifteen works, culminating in 1806 with a study of the defeat of the Prussian army by Napoleon the previous year. This last work was a scathing criticism of the Prussian army and state; the criticisms were largely valid, but Bülow had overplayed his hand. He was arrested on charges of insanity in early 1807 and was imprisoned first at Kolberg and then at Riga, where he died, apparently as a result of his maltreatment in prison.

Another student of Frederick the Great's ideas was the Swiss officer Antoine-Henri Jomini, who served in Napoleon's army from 1805 until the summer of 1813, when he defected to the Russians. Jomini was convinced that warfare, which appeared chaotic, was in fact governed by enduring principles. In particular, he believed that strategy should be formulated and carried out according to universal scientific precepts.

Jomini's idea of strategy consisted of 'bringing superior force to bear on a point where the enemy is both weaker and liable to crippling damage'. The issue that preoccupied much of his later work was how this could be done. He was the first to develop the concept of logistics, 'the practical art of moving armies', which included a whole variety of sub-disciplines such as planning, supply management, movement, intelligence, communications and record-keeping. Jomini saw logistics as a staff function, or, in modern terms, a managerial task; the commander-in-chief had an oversight or general management role, while individual staff officers looked after specialist functions. Careful management of the organization and logistics of an organization was seen as a pre-requisite to the achievement of strategic goals. In a similar vein, Jomini also wrote extensively on the nature of organization.

## ANTOINE-HENRI JOMINI

**BORN IN SWITZERLAND IN 1779**, Jomini joined a banking firm as an apprentice while in his teens. He also became involved in revolutionary politics and supported the pro-French republican movement in Switzerland. In 1803, greatly influenced by the career of Napoleon, he published his first work on military strategy. In 1805 he joined the staff of General (later Marshal) Ney, one of Napoleon's most prominent commanders. He served with great distinction in the French army, but during the summer of 1813 he quarrelled with Napoleon's chief of staff, Marshal Berthier, and defected to the Russians. During more than forty years in Russian service, he served as aide-de-camp to Tsars Alexander I and Nicholas I, organized the Russian military academy and served in the Crimean War of 1854-5. After returning to France, he was military adviser to Emperor Napoleon III. He died in France at the age of 90.

The most important writer on strategy of modern times was another Prussian officer, Karl von Clausewitz. His book *Vom Kriege* (translated into English as The Art of War On War), today studied by cadets at nearly every military academy, has been referred to by almost every subsequent writer on strategy. Deeply influenced by Kant and other German philosophers of the Enlightenment, Clausewitz applied techniques such as critical reasoning to war, looking for a bridge between theory and practice and trying to come to terms with the moral and psychological aspects of war.

Central to Clausewitz's view of strategy and warfare in general was the relationship between theories of war and war itself. War is not an independent phenomenon: it is waged for a purpose, one that is determined by the will of the commander. If organization is subordinate to strategy, then strategy too is subordinate, to purpose. There is a difference between the purpose of war and war itself; the latter is simply 'an act of violence meant to force the enemy to do our will' (he also refers to war as 'a continuation of diplomacy by other means'). It is easy to set a purpose for war, and easy too to make plans for the defeat of the enemy and set these plans in motion. However, it is another matter to carry out these plans as intended, and leaders are constantly beset with the problem of staying true to their own purposes. In taking this view, Clausewitz acknowledges a debt to Machiavelli, whose works on war and politics were familar to him.

> **If organization is subordinate to strategy, then strategy too is subordinate, to purpose**

The key factor is 'friction': 'countless minor incidents – the kind you can never really foresee – combine to lower the general level of performance, so that one always falls far short of the intended goal'. Friction, says Clausewitz, is what distinguishes real war from war on paper. Strategic planning is based on statistical facts; but real war can never amount to more than probabilities. Many factors lead to friction, but none is more important than the moral factors, the courage and ability of the leader, the experience and spirit of the troops. Should these fail at any point, previously determined plans will be jeopardized. As a result, he says, 'Everything in strategy is very simple, but that does not mean that everything in strategy is very easy'.

## KARL VON CLAUSEWITZ

**CLAUSEWITZ WAS BORN IN BURG, GERMANY IN 1780,** the son of an army officer. He was commissioned in the Prussian army in 1793 and attended the military school in Berlin from 1801–4. He joined the general staff in 1804, serving under General Scharnhorst, and worked with Scharnhorst to reorganize the Prussian army following the defeat by Napoleon in 1806. In

1812 he served with the Russian army that defeated Napoleon, and in 1815 he was a senior staff officer in the Waterloo campaign. In 1818 he was appointed director of the War College in Berlin, where he began writing his major work, *Vom Kriege*. He died of cholera while serving with the Prussian army during the Polish revolution of 1830–1.

And so we come to Clausewitz's greatest student, Helmuth von Moltke. One of the great strategists of all time, Moltke combined effortlessly two cardinal virtues: he was a meticulous planner and preparer, and he was endlessly flexible and adaptable in his strategic thinking and implementation. His planning skills were legendary; as he himself later wrote:

> The means of mobilizing the North German army had been reviewed year by year, in view of any changes in the military or political situation, by the Staff, in conjunction with the ministry of war. Every branch of the administration throughout the country had been kept informed of all it ought to know of these matters. The orders for marching, and travelling by rail or boat, were worked out for each division of the army, together with the most minute directions as to their different starting points, the day and hour of departure, the duration of the journey, the refreshment stations and place of destination. At the meeting-point cantonments were assigned to each corps and division, stores and magazines were established, and thus, when war was declared, it needed only the royal signature to set the entire apparatus in motion with undisturbed precision. There was nothing to be changed in the directions originally given; it sufficed to carry out the plans pre-arranged and prepared.

Yet this is the same Moltke who wrote that 'no plan survives contact with the enemy'. He was deeply impressed by the Clausewitzian idea of 'friction', the accumulation of minor but unforeseen incidents that throws any given strategy off track. As a consequence, he preferred to focus on specific goals rather than on generic strategies. His plans were based on known factors insofar as possible, but they tended to be loosely structured, allowing for flexibility and quick decisions; thus he preferred to issue general directives rather than operational plans, specifying outcomes but leaving the manner of execution up to the officers in charge. Almost none of the major battles of the Franco-Prussian war went according to his meticulously laid plans, but by reacting rapidly and communicating orders quickly, Moltke was able to turn uncertainty to his own advantage.

## The influence of Moltke

As noted in Chapter 3, the influence of Moltke's ideas and achievements was widespread in management thinking in the early twentieth century. Edward Jones, the professor who wrote on organization behaviour in *Engineering Magazine* and was quoted at the head of Chapter 5, analyzed the Moltke recipe for success in some detail. After paying credit to the efficiency and meticulousness of the advance planning, he then notes how in the implementation phase, every emphasis is on flexibility and efficiency:

> In contrast to the rigid plan of mobilization imposed by central authority, when the campaign is once under way, and changing and uncertain conditions have to be dealt with, the headquarters becomes responsible only for the general features of the plan of operations.
>
> Authority immediately passes down the line to army commanders, and regimental and company officers, lodging as close as possible to the time, place, and agencies of specific action. The army then becomes, not a mechanism under the thumb of a single leader, but an organism with great liberty of action, and corresponding responsibility, resting upon the parts.
>
> It is reputed that von Moltke once said that nothing should be ordered which it was conceivable could be carried out by the

proper officers without orders. Certain it is that the orders from headquarters in the Austrian and Franco-Prussian wars were very few in number, and composed of but a few sentences each. Passing from higher to lower units, orders from the leaders of separate armies, corps orders, and division orders, were, of course, progressively firmer and more detailed.

In the modern tactics of engagements, a similar rule as to the location of authority is followed. While each army headquarters retains sufficient control to insure harmony of plan, details of execution are intrusted largely to the officers on the field, and in direct command of the minor divisions of troops. The old ramrod drill movements of troops on the field of battle are no longer possible. Discipline is now interpreted broadly that each individual shall apply sound principles in every emergency, remaining as continuously in touch with authority as this will permit. The fear of minor mistakes is as nothing, with modern military administrators, in comparison with the fear of crushing out the spirit and energy of troops and lower officers by unduly suppressing initiative.[5]

Analyzing the relevance of Moltke's system to business management, Jones picked out six basic strategic principles to which Moltke always adhered:

1. leaders must always act swiftly and decisively
2. every officer must be prepared to take the initiative when required
3. preliminary planning and preparation are essential
4. detail should be subordinated to overall goals when planning and acting
5. discipline must be maintained in order to focus the organization on its goals
6. force should be concentrated at the appropriate time and place; the organization that follows this principle successfully may defeat a rival many times its own size by obtaining local superiority.

## Strategic principles reviewed

Common to the works reviewed above are a set of related ideas which we can consider as principles of strategy. Not every writer considers all of these principles, but they are sufficiently common in strategic thinking down through the ages that we can consider them as generic. What follows is a brief review of these principles and their suitability or applicability to business strategy today.

### 1 Focus and purpose

This is mentioned continually. Xenophon was praised for his stern resolve in getting his army through against impossible odds, in the same way that the resolution displayed by Zhuge Liang helped him defeat his enemies. Sunzi, Machiavelli and Frederick the Great all believed that leaders must display resolve and remain fixed on their purpose; von Bülow spoke of the army investing its 'capital' in order to see a 'return on investment'. Yamamoto believed that everything must be subordinated to the way of the Samurai, and Karl von Clausewitz argued that strategy must always be subordinate to purpose.

> **A strategy without a high-order purpose is an empty shell. Strategy is about long-term vision, not short-term gain**

A strategy without a high-order purpose is an empty shell. Strategy is about long-term vision, not short-term gain. Firms may and frequently do set their sights too high and fail, but an equal danger lies in setting sights too low and failing to fulfil potential. The first step in any strategy process must be the establishment of a purpose and goals; once this is done, it is important to remain concentrated on those and not be sidetracked by minor issues along the way.

### 2 Leadership

Fixing and maintaining purpose is a prime requisite of leadership (see Chapter 10). This is argued strongly by Sunzi and Frederick the Great, and Machiavelli and von Clausewitz say that it is the prince's qualities of leadership that make the difference between success and failure by overcoming *fortuna* or 'friction'. Many of Zhuge Liang's principles of strategy are concerned with leadership.

Strategy-setting and guidance towards implementation is one of the core tasks of leadership; many great business leaders of the past have concerned themselves with little else, devolving lower-level management tasks to subordinates. Strategy is the province of the general or the chief executive; only he or she can take the final decisions about the organization's purpose, and only he or she can muster and coordinate all the resources necessary to achieve that purpose.

## 3 Requisite organization

The idea that the organization should be fit to meet its purpose is found in authorities as various as Vegetius, Sunzi, Frederick the Great and von Clausewitz. On one level, the members of the organization must be appropriately trained and skilled; on another, the units of the organization must be capable of working together effectively in order to meet the goal set for it. The Prussian army created by Frederick and led by his successors was efficient, well-trained and well-organized by many of the standards of its day; but it was not fit to compete on equal terms with the armies of Napoleon, which were organized along different principles, and so disappeared in blood and flame on the battlefields of Jena-Auerstadt in 1805. It is not enough that the organization be efficient according to some generalized set of criteria; it must be right for its purpose.

Alfred Chandler said in 1962 that structure should follow strategy. For the military strategists, the picture is not so simplistic; structure and strategy are inextricably mixed. To set an existing organization a strategy which that organization is manifestly unfit to meet is to doom it to failure. One would not, for example, expect that the Women's Institute would be able to organize a manned mission to Mars, and so one would not set it that task. And though some work could be done in terms of structure, training and skills provision for the Women's Institute, those would probably never be sufficient to allow its members to walk among the foothills of Olympus Mons. Any strategy set for the Women's Institute should then be consistent with its organizational capabilities, actual or potential. (Whether the WI would make a better job of organizing a manned mission to Mars than would Nasa is a separate question entirely.)

## 4 Deployment of resources

Julius Caesar was widely cited for his ability to marshal all the elements of his army – legions, auxiliaries, cavalry, artillery, ships, supply train, etc. – and make them work together as a coherent force. Jomini, the inventor of logistics, sought to harmonize the efforts of the army so that all units worked together, and the great exponent of this in practice was Moltke. The *Daodejing* reminds us that intangible as well as tangible resources need to be considered.

Twentieth-century strategists and military scientists sometimes refer to a further concept, 'economy of force', which, simply stated, says that for maximum efficiency the level of force used should be exactly that required to achieve the objective with certainty, no more and no less. Gauging this level is always difficult, but it is clear that by coordinating the efforts of different people and different departments and concentrating them on an objective, the efforts of those individuals can be greatly magnified. Jomini and Moltke both wrote of the need for concentration of force, focusing on the objective required. In business management terms, the principle of deployment of resources suggests that the organization needs first to know exactly what resources and capabilities it has at its disposal, and second, to know how to use each resource to it maximum effectiveness in concert with other resources.

## 5 Self-knowledge

This concept is widely found in Eastern writings, notably in Sunzi, the *Romance of Three Kingdoms* and Miyamoto's *Book of Five Rings*. It is largely absent from Western thought. Put simply, it is essential that the leader and, indeed, the individuals under them know their own inner strengths and weaknesses, and their own failings.

**This sort of personal SWOT analysis does not feature much in western management thinking, but it is worth considering**

This sort of personal SWOT analysis does not feature much in western management thinking, but it is worth considering. Simple factors like fatigue, depression and ill health can have a powerful bearing on both the design and implementation of strategy. Knowing one's limitations and working within them should be considered a sign of strength, not weakness.

## 6 Knowledge of the environment

Both Sunzi and Frederick the Great urged that a full analysis of geographical and environmental factors such as terrain, hours of daylight and weather be considered when planning strategy. Environmental factors are a primary source of uncertainty, but close study of the environment can reduce much of that uncertainty by allowing contingency plans to be laid should the weather change, a wide river be encountered, etc.

Environmental scanning is a core feature of techniques such as SWOT, and its necessity is widely known to managers. Such scanning should be thorough, and should be focused particularly on areas where the greatest risks may lie. Contingencies should be considered and options rehearsed as part of the planning process.

## 7 Knowledge of the enemy

A little surprisingly, only Sunzi and Frederick consider this idea explicitly, though the need for what we would now call military intelligence is implicit in most writings on strategy. In business terms, it is important not only to know the capabilities of the competition, but also their own likely responses to any competitive opportunities or threats. This means not only gathering hard data on the competition (turnover, number of employees, market share, etc.) but also the management style and culture, the composition of the board of directors and the attitudes of shareholders. Some large firms conduct dummy planning exercises where they try to guess what competitors will do next, and then analyze the gap between their own predictions and actual events to refine their own intelligence and planning systems.

## 8 Preparation

Thorough preparation was a feature of the campaigns of Caesar and Frederick the Great, and Sunzi advised meticulous preparation before taking action. Preparation was one of the principles advocated by Zhuge Liang, and Miyamoto Musashi advocated constant training and readiness. Moltke's attention to detail in planning has already been noted.

Following Moltke, thorough planning has become a feature of military operations worldwide, and operations such as D-Day or Desert Storm are preceded by months of intensive planning by large teams. Staffwork of this kind is usually less meticulous in businesses, the more so as modern theories of organization tend to emphasize 'lean' headquarters operations and devolution of responsibility to lower levels. That works fine, so long as responsibility for strategy is devolved as well. This can work counter to the principle that strategy is a prime function of leadership. Violation of the principle of thorough preparation can only increase the risk that the strategy will not be successful.

> **Violation of the principle of thorough preparation can only increase the risk that the strategy will not be successful**

## 9 Virtue

This again is primarily an Eastern concept, though Machiavelli introduces the idea of *virtù* with a slightly different meaning. Daoists and Buddhists both believed that inner virtue was crucial to success, and both Miyamoto and Yamamoto promote the need for inner strength and duty as an ideal.

Do you have to be virtuous in order to succeed? As Chapter 9 suggests, business success and ethical behaviour do not always go hand in hand. But virtue in this sense should not be read necessarily in terms of 'right' and 'wrong', but rather as an inner calm or inner strength that can be relied on in times of crisis. This is a personal attribute, but 'virtue' can also be an organizational concept. Morale and *esprit de corps* are manifestations of virtue, and play a major role in keeping the organization focused. Andrew Grove, the CEO of Intel, has written of what he calls 'strategic inflection points', times of crisis and paradigmatic change which require all an organization's resources to come through successfully; he describes the transit of a strategic inflection point as 'like passing through the valley of death'. Organizational toughness and inner strength are required to succeed.

## 10 Flexibility

Clausewitz, and after him Moltke, discussed the concept of friction, the accumulation of unforeseen happenings which inevitably throws any strategy off track. Other western writers including Frederick the Great and Machiavelli speak of the need for flexibility, as do Sunzi and Miyamoto. The *Daodejing* puts a different spin on the topic by suggesting that there are times when it is best to act and other times when it is best to remain inactive.

Put simply, an organization which is flexible can adapt its strategy to meet new circumstances without losing sight of its goals. Lack of flexibility means that the organization either loses sight of its goals as it struggles to meet new events, or pursues its goals single-mindedly and without adaptation until the accumulation of friction forces it to a halt. Flexibility is largely a matter of organization, but not solely. Strategies and plans too must be flexible; there is always a danger that plans will become a straitjacket, forbidding initiative and reaction to opportunities. To Machiavelli, an ability to take advantage of *fortuna* is one of the single greatest strategic assets an organization or leader can possess.

## 11 Imposition of one's will on the enemy

This is a core concept in Sunzi's idea of strategy. Its flip side, denying the enemy access to his objectives, was the great achievement of Fabius Maximus in the war against Hannibal. More basically, this principle suggests that organizations should always attempt to wage competition on ground of their own choosing and by means of their own devising, trying to avoid confronting the enemy's strength. For example, when taking on a rival brand supported by very large-scale advertising, one strategic option may be to support one's own brand with even more advertising; but it may be more effective to use less advertising and undertake other forms of promotion which would raise the brand's profile equally effectively and less expensively. Planners and analysts need constantly to look for spots where the competition is weak and seek ways of exploiting those. It is here that the use of 'generic strategies' like those proposed by Michael Porter run into trouble; it is not enough to decide what strategy one wishes to adopt in isolation – account must be taken of the strategies of competitors as well.

## 12  Use of stratagem and deception

Sunzi, and many other Chinese writers after him, believed the use of stratagem and deception to be legitimate if they entailed the ultimate ends to be achieved. Machiavelli argued much the same thing. The view was considered acceptable in Chinese culture, but not in the West, where the large deception is frowned upon.

There are obvious legal, moral and ethical reasons why many forms of stratagem are wrong and should not be used. Consideration might be given, however, to harmless deceptions which can be practised in order to disguise, even if only temporarily, one's true intentions in competitive situations. This is not 'cheating', any more than not showing one's opponents all one's cards in a game of poker is cheating. Opponents may complain when they lose, but that is their problem.

## 13  Speed and surprise

Sunzi believed that once preparations were complete, the army should move rapidly to achieve its objectives, and Machiavelli argued much the same thing; what they argued, Moltke practised. Sunzi also believed in the need for surprise; one's opponents should not be forewarned. Buddhist teachers like Lingi regularly used surprise as a tactic for eliciting a response. Swift action usually achieves surprise in any case, and is associated with decisiveness; it also has a strong moral effect on opponents.

> **Although slow, deliberate movements are sometimes called for, in the main, slow implementation of a strategy increases the level of friction encountered and gives competitors more time to respond**

Although slow, deliberate movements are sometimes called for, in the main, slow implementation of a strategy increases the level of friction encountered and gives competitors more time to respond. Rapid action is usually cheaper and more effective, and not only impacts on the morale of competitors but also can raise the morale of one's own organization; nothing cheers people up like success.

## Conclusions

The foregoing is by no means a complete picture of strategy. What this chapter suggests is that, by going back to the roots of strategy, it is possible to get a broader and deeper picture of what strategy is. Strategy is both simple and complex; or, to quote Clausewitz again: 'Everything in strategy is very simple, but that does not mean that everything in strategy is very easy'. At its simplest, strategy is about setting a goal and devoting all energies and resources to achieving that goal. At its most complex, strategy involves not only working to keep the organization focused on the goal and ensuring that its parts work together to that aim, but also dealing with the fact that all strategy unfolds in dynamic situations, that unexpected frictions will certainly occur, and that competitors and rivals will also be pursuing their own strategic designs which will conflict with one's own. Strategies are comparatively easy to set; they are hell to implement.

Generic strategies, or concepts of specific 'business' strategy, have inherent dangers. As the example of the ages shows, it is far safer to seek and adhere to fundamental strategic principles which have been tried and tested in the past; and then, having understood these principles, design a strategy which conforms to them but which also fits to one's own needs and goals. That may be an *ad hoc* and intuitive way to approach strategy, but none better has been devised yet.

*Notes to chapter 7*

1 Chandler, Alfred D. (1962) *Strategy and Structure: Chapters in the History of the American Industrial Enterprise*, Cambridge, MA: MIT Press, p. 13.
2 Of particular interest on this is Mintzberg, Henry (1993) *The Rise and Fall of Strategic Planning*, New York: Free Press.
3 Nearly all of the works above are available in modern editions and translations; Xenophon, Josephus, Arrian, Tacitus, Caesar and Livy are all published in paperback by Penguin.
4 Daoism became known in the West during the European enlightenment, and one author believes that the concept of *wu-wei* is the origin of the idea of *laissez-faire*, popularized by the physiocrats of eighteenth-century France; see Clarke, J.J. (2000) *The Tao of the West: Western Transformations of Taoist Thought*, London: Routledge.
5 Jones, Edward D. (1912) 'Military history and the science of business administration', *Engineering Magazine*, vol. 44, p. 186.

# 8

# The quest for the best of all possible worlds[1]

> Joy in work comes in the main from the sense of good leadership, of accomplishment, of personal progress, of security, of team work. Evidently the responsibility for the intelligent leadership which will make these things possible goes much farther than the personnel department
>
> *Henry Post Dutton*

The greatest changes in business over the past few centuries have been not economic, but social. In Western Europe, and then in the USA and Japan, an array of factors – technological developments, growth in the size and diversity of markets, an emphasis on large-scale organization, increasing division of labour and, perhaps most importantly, broader changes in social values and ways of living – have changed the relationship between people and their work. These changes, which began with the Protestant Reformation of the sixteenth century and were greatly accelerated by the Industrial Revolution, were not at first generally recognized. By the time Karl Marx and his colleagues in the Socialist International began to analyze the problem and offer their solutions, the problem of labour was an explosion waiting to happen; the efforts of statesmen and businessmen to solve the problem by force was like striking matches in a fireworks factory. The ensuing crisis spread far beyond the workplace. It may seem an exaggeration to state that the lonely deaths of the Tsar of Russia and his family in Siberia can be blamed on excessive division of labour, but there is a causal chain nonetheless.

The management response to the crisis in the twentieth century was to develop a new managerial discipline or set of practices. Known first as labour management, then personnel management and more recently as human resources management (with the term 'human capital' coming into vogue, human capital management must surely not be far away), this discipline was an attempt by management to focus specifically on the problems of labour and the management of people at work. As such, it was laudable, and doubtless did much to remedy the many problems that had occurred. However, even at the time, writers on management like Henry Post Dutton, quoted above, warned that the responsibility for personnel management must go beyond the personnel management department itself; employee relations were the responsibility of all managers, and the personnel department was simply a tool for ensuring that personnel management was better organized and more efficient.

In our own time, human resources management has become a highly specialized field with its own body of theory and practice. At the same time, team management and group working are becoming ever more common. If these methods of working are to be successful in the long term, however, it seems logical to assume that the diffusion of HRM practices is going to have to become much more widespread. Every group leader, every team manager, is also in part a human resources manager. There is an argument, strongly expressed in some cases, that HRM needs to come down from its ivory tower and start engaging with all of management more directly. I do not propose to get into that argument here. Rather, I suggest that managers who want to know more about the management of people can, if they wish, derive a fair amount of useful knowledge by studying how and why the discipline developed in the first place.

**Every group leader, every team manager, is also in part a human resources manager**

The study of human resources management is a study of cause and effect. So long as workplace relations were harmonious, so long as the workers were satisfied – or appeared to be – there was no need for many specific management practices; such practices as did exist were governed by family ties, custom and personal values. Once problems of labour efficiency and labour unrest began to grow, management faced a challenge to which it had to respond in a more systematic way. This chapter is the story of that challenge, and of how management faced it.

## Managing face to face

In the earliest and most widely used type of business organization, the family business, employee relations were largely a matter of face-to-face contact. Bonds of loyalty and trust held the organization together. Paid employees, not bound to the owner by blood ties, were nonetheless treated as family members. In exchange for their wages they owed the owner their loyalty; the owner assumed the right of direction in the workplace and, it was also generally recognized, had the right to ask employees to take on extraordinary tasks such as working overtime.

In return, the owner owed the employees a duty of care. In many family organizations, the owner was expected to take responsibility for the workers' family and personal lives. This can still be seen in Chinese family businesses especially in Southeast Asia, where it is not uncommon for workers to ask their managers to help them sort out family or personal problems, and it is accepted that workers have a right to call on their bosses at their homes, or even at otherwise sacrosanct locations such as the golf course. The same ethos long prevailed in Japanese businesses, where old-style entrepreneurs like Matsushita Konosuke urged workers to regard themselves as part of a family, and it is only recently that changing social values in Japan have begun to weaken the familial bonds between employer and employee.

### SAKUMA TEIICHI

**B**ORN NEAR TOKYO IN **1848,** Sakuma came from a *samurai* family in the service of the Shogunate, and as a young man fought in Shogunate's armies against the forces of the restored Meiji Emperor. After the war and fall of the Shogunate, Sakuma went into business, setting up a print shop and then moving into publishing. These businesses were very successful and Sakuma later diversified into insurance and banking. Sakuma was one of the first to realize that old-style paternalism was not well suited to changing conditions, and despite being a large-scale employer, was an early supporter of labour unions (to the dismay of his fellow industrialists); he encouraged his print shop workers to organize and later backed the national trades union organization. He is sometimes referred to as the Robert Owen of Japan.[2]

---

Employers were also expected as a matter of course to provide for their workers if the latter became ill, elderly or infirm. Relics of this practice still remain. Workers on many large country estates in Britain still receive housing as part of their benefits, and are usually allowed to remain in their estate homes after their retirement; pensions are provided to employees and their relicts. These practices are by no means universal, but they are accepted as approved practice, and the landowner who fails in his duty to his tenants in this manner can expect to be cold-shouldered by his neighbours. Another, quite different relic can be found in China. After 1949, Mao Zedong made a deliberate effort to break down the Confucian-based sense of loyalty to family which had predominated in Chinese culture, and replace it with loyalty to the Communist Party. To reinforce this point,

> This 'cradle-to-grave' security system is known as the 'iron rice bowl', and its entrenched position in most large state companies is continuing to prove a huge obstacle to economic reform

the Party took over many of the functions of the family business, including the provision of housing, education, retirement benefits, health care and even sometimes meals to workers. This 'cradle-to-grave' security system is known as the 'iron rice bowl', and its entrenched position in most large state companies is continuing to prove a huge obstacle to economic reform.

The other major form of early business organization, the bureaucracy, featured a much more formal and ritual relationship between management and workers. In some cases, workers thought of their work as a religious duty, as in the case of the temple bureaucracies of Egypt and Phoenicia. In others, they might owe a personal loyalty to the king or emperor who employed them. More sophisticated bureaucracies cultivated a sense of loyalty to a higher ideal. In Kautilya's India, bureaucrats of the Mauryan kingdom regarded themselves as upholders of the *dharma*, the sacred rules and customs by which not only society but the universe as a whole was governed. The civil service of Imperial Rome owed loyalty not only to the emperor but to the gods and, increasingly, the idea of Rome as an unchanging, eternal, divinely sanctioned presence. In England, the development of effective government and administration in the twelfth and thirteenth centuries may in part have been due to the view that in England, unlike other European countries, the king was not an absolute master, but ruled to some extent by the consent of his people; kings came and went, but government had to go on. (Later, Charles I would try to overturn this view and insist on his divine right to rule. It cost him his head.)

Within bureaucracies, the ties of loyalty tended to be rather one-way. Whereas family-style businesses have traditionally been (and still are) reluctant to dismiss employees outright, preferring to use negotiation, conciliation, changes in roles and jobs and other devices to resolve problems, bureaucracies are more ruthless; those who fail to do their duty are kicked out. At least, that is the theory: most studies of bureaucracies show that members tend to develop quasi-tribal loyalties over time, and in practice it can be almost impossible to fire a civil servant or make one redundant. But this is a defensive routine which members of bureaucracies develop over time, precisely as a response to the fact that bureaucracies are perceived to owe their members little or no loyalty. Though a feature of bureaucracy, this tribal defensive mechanism is not part of the bureaucratic structure *per se*.

Within the majority of businesses and similar organizations, work was craft-based; division of labour was limited, and employees were multi-skilled and capable of carrying out many different tasks. This applied equally to the manufacturing of consumer goods such as furniture or shoes, and to government and administration; we saw in Chapter 5 how administrators like Hubert Walter in medieval England were expected to be able to run accounting and tax offices, dispense justice, conduct diplomatic negotiations and, when need arose, pick up a sword and go out to smite the infidel. Management was correspondingly more flexible. Most organizations were small, and relationships between managers and employees were conducted face to face, but that is only part of the picture. Even in large organizations like the Medici Bank, spread across Western Europe and the Mediterranean, organizational flexibility meant employee relations could be conducted on an ad hoc and personal basis.

Part of the success of these methods of managing people must also be laid at the door of a general ethical view, common to nearly every culture across the world until the sixteenth century. People were not considered to live or work in isolation; they were part of a community, and whatever their rank or social standing, they owed a duty to that community. There were of course plenty of people who rejected this belief, but they were generally regarded as social deviants. Despite numerous exceptions, on the whole the system worked.

Those exceptions tended to take place in industries where large-scale organization and division of labour were required. Chief of these was the textile industry which, in an era prior to mechanization, required some sixteen separate processes, many of which in turn required skilled specialist craftsmen. It was in these industries that workers were more likely to feel alienated (to use the Marxist term) from their employers and less likely to identify with the latter's interests, while the intervening distance meant that paternal care by employers was either absent or ineffective. Weavers, numerous and well organized, were leaders in most of the major incidents of worker unrest in the industrial centres of Flanders and northern Italy through the Middle Ages.

## The spirit of capitalism

In the sixteenth century, the Protestant Reformation in northern Europe challenged this ethic and ultimately doomed it, especially in the West. Max Weber, sometimes regarded as the father of modern sociology and author of the study *The Protestant Ethic and the Spirit of Capitalism*, first published in 1905, saw the Reformation as a crucial turning point in promoting self-interest and self-reliance. Early Protestantism as expressed by Martin Luther and John Calvin had, says Weber, built-in ethical safeguards to curb excessive displays of self-interest, but by the eighteenth century these were breaking down. Weber, who despite his generally enlightened views was in the last analysis a defender of the old European order, blamed America for this. The atmosphere of freedom and the need for self-reliance on the American frontier encouraged self-interest, and Weber here quotes Benjamin Franklin as the originator of the phrase 'time is money'. Under the capitalist ethic, Weber says, the making of money became not a means to a higher end, but an end in itself. The acquisition of wealth was not just the activity of a few, but one of the ethical and social core values of the new society, in which everyone aspired to riches and dreamed of attaining them.

> **Under the capitalist ethic, Weber says, the making of money became not a means to a higher end, but an end in itself**

Weber is exaggerating – people have *always* wanted to get rich – but he has a point about the making of money becoming not just more acceptable but a virtue in its own right. The get-rich-quick speculations of the Dutch tulip market and, later, the Mississippi and South Sea bubbles show some evidence of this. In the eighteenth century, Adam Smith had defined the notion of self-interest as lying at the heart of much economic activity, and before him, Josiah Tucker had described how 'self-love' carried within it the seeds of conflict in the workplace. The Industrial Revolution, in its infant years when Smith was writing *The Wealth of Nations* in the early 1770s, kicked the process along. The new group of factory owners made money on a scale and speed unparalleled until the software entrepreneurs of the late twentieth century (and unlike the latter, the factory owners' wealth did not exist solely on paper). No accurate record of the personal wealth of Richard Arkwright remains, but it is certain that he went from being a near bankrupt barber and innkeeper to one of the four or five richest people in England in the space of about fifteen years.

## JOSIAH TUCKER

**BORN IN WALES IN 1713**, Tucker went to Oxford and went on to a career in the clergy, spending the last thirty years of his life as Dean of Gloucester. He was an economist of some note, and his *The Elements of Commerce, and Theory of Taxes* (1755) was read by and influenced Adam Smith. Tucker was an admirer and defender of merchants and men of business: it was he who first coined the term 'nation of shopkeepers', and while Napoleon Bonaparte would later employ the term as an insult, Tucker meant it as a compliment.

One of the basic principles described by Tucker is 'self-love', which, loosely defined, is the motivating force that causes people to seek wealth or personal benefit through economic activity. Commercial activity, says Tucker, is motivated by this self-love, which Adam Smith renamed 'self-interest' and which later economists would describe as the profit-seeking motive of the entrepreneur. In general terms, self-love creates a public good, in that it leads people to undertake commercial activity which enriches the people and the nation. However, both workers and employers were motivated by self-love. This raised the prospect of conflicts of interest, with resulting tensions between the parties as each tried to maximize their own self-interest at the expense of the other. This passage later caught the attention of Karl Marx, and influenced his ideas on the relationship between capitalists and proletariat.

........................................................................................................

Arkwright himself was no better and no worse than the average mill-owner, and the Industrial Revolution did produce some outstanding examples of good labour management, notably Samuel Oldknow and Robert Owen (of whom more anon). But there were many others who did not achieve this standard. The industrialists of the time, in Britain, Europe and later in America, no longer felt personal responsibility for their workers. Labour management was concerned with efficiency; labour was seen as an asset solely in terms of the value that could be extracted from it. In practical terms, this took the form of recruiting large numbers of untrained men, women and children and 'pressing' or 'driving' them to achieve the maximum possible output.

Working conditions were so poor in the early and mid-nineteenth century that people in industrialized nations began quite literally to shrink; archaeological evidence from exhumed skeletons shows that the workers and their families of this period were on average several inches shorter than the peasant farmers of the Middle Ages, thanks to poor diet, sanitation and medical care. Legislation, for example, to restrict child labour and determine maximum working hours had some effect as the nineteenth century wore on, but by the 1880s the combination of poor working conditions, lack of job security, and the rise of revolutionist doctrines such as Marxism, anarchism and syndicalism, was leading to widespread worker unrest. Output gains were no longer being realized – in most firms, the workers were being sweated to the limit – and it seemed to some as if the entire industrial project was in danger of stalling.

From the 1880s onward, workplaces increasingly became places of confrontation and violence. Strikes were bloody, especially in the USA, where workers and police seemed well-provided with handguns; when the police brought up machine guns, strikers broke into local military arsenals and wheeled out cannon. Deaths were common, as in the strike at Carnegie's Homestead steel mills in 1892 or during the Pullman strike of 1893. Good leaders tried to maintain good employee relations, but were often let down by their subordinates; the car-maker John North Willys prided himself on good relations between himself and his workers at the company's plant at Toledo, Ohio, but when Willys left to go to New York and establish a subsidiary, relations went downhill quickly and less than a year later Toledo was paralyzed by a violent strike. Daniel Guggenheim, whose mining company ASARCO was during the first years before the First World War rocked by strikes that threatened anarchy in mining communities, with armed miners and security men stalking and murdering each other in the streets, metaphorically threw up his hands and called on the government to intervene in the labour market for the protection of workers; in effect, Guggenheim admitted that the workers often had justice on their side but he himself could not control his own managers.

> **Good leaders tried to maintain good employee relations, but were often let down by their subordinates**

## DANIEL GUGGENHEIM

**B**ORN IN PHILADELPHIA IN **1856**, Guggenheim joined his father's lace-importing business and spent a number of years in Switzerland as a buyer. In the 1870s the company diversified into silver and lead-mining in the American West, and after taking over the firm from his father Guggenheim greatly expanded its efforts, opening a number of mines and smelters and negotiating a highly profitable copper mining concession in Mexico. In 1899 he took control of the J.P. Morgan-backed mining and smelting company ASARCO and became the largest mine owner in the world. In the following decade his company was racked by bloody strikes; Guggenheim initially favoured the use of force to put down the strikers, but later changed his mind. In 1915 he stunned the United States Industrial Relations Commission, before which he was testifying, when he said that employees were justified in organizing, as many capitalists were too arbitrary in their treatment of their workers:

'There is today too great a difference between the rich man and the poor man. To remedy this is too big a job for the state or the employer to tackle single-handed. There should be a combination in this work between the Federal government, the state, the employer and the employee. The men want more comforts — more of the luxuries of life. They are entitled to them. I say this because humanity owes it to them'.

The widespread disappearance of the social contract between employer and worker had much to do with the problem, but so too did the increasing division of labour. It was widely believed that highly divided labour systems required workers of less skill and training: it was easier to run a machine which stamped soles out of leather than it was to make an entire shoe. This led to the process which modern political economists like to refer to as 'deskilling', in which tasks were divided up into smaller and smaller sub-units, each of which was assigned to a worker whose sole function it was to carry out that task. But there were two problems here. First, this minute division of labour tended, as Marx observed so very well, to alienate workers from their work. How can one take pride in the shiny new automobile that has just rolled off the assembly line, if one's sole part in that process was to tighten the nut behind the steering wheel? How particularly, when the profit from the sale of that automobile goes straight into the pocket of an employer who may, today or tomorrow or next week, cut your wages or dismiss you altogether? The lack of connection was shrewdly exploited by Marx, and even more so by his colleague, the fox-hunting communist Friedrich Engels, who argued that the only real security for workers would come when they controlled the means of production directly.

Engels was also one of a long line of writers to suggest that deskilling was the wrong way to go about achieving efficiency (and as a factory owner, he was presumably in a position to know). There is in fact no such thing as unskilled work. This is implicit in Adam Smith, who acknowledges that even in the most menial tasks some skill is required, and explicit in the writings of the economist Nassau Senior in the 1820s, who wrote forcefully of the need for workers to be fully trained and skilled in those elements of work for which they were responsible. A strong argument was made that the division of labour was in fact a *narrowing* of skill, in that the range of activities in which workers were required to be skilled was less than before; but there was also a requirement for a *deepening* of skill, in that workers had to be very proficient indeed in that narrow range of tasks. So intricate were the new industrial enterprises with their minute divided tasks that the failure of a single piece of machinery could bring the entire plant to a halt. Every worker had to play his or her part, keeping the system going and keeping the machinery running smoothly, and to do this effectively required high levels of skill.

## The crisis of output

By the 1880s and 1890s, factory managers in the rapidly growing American economy were running into a persistent problem; they were at or very near their output ceilings. Productivity in many sectors was levelling off. Most plants were highly inefficient, being focused solely on speed and volume of production; waste was high, overmanning was high and product quality was often very poor. Turnover was king, and as long as production targets were met, few managers were interested in the methods. But increasingly, those targets were not being met, and in the engineering profession thoughtful minds began considering solutions. In 1886, Henry R. Towne, president and co-founder of the Yale Lock Company in Connecticut, presented a paper before the American Society of Mechanical Engineers in which he called on members to look to ways of organizing engineering shop management on a systematic and, indeed, scientific basis. Towne's paper met with some resistance – several members apparently argued that engineering and science had nothing to do with one another – but on the whole the Society decided to take Towne's plan ahead.

Towne believed that the key to unlocking greater productivity lay in motivating the workers. Further, the first and most obvious method of motivating people was to pay them according to their productivity: the more the worker achieves, the more he or she earns. Towne believed the solution was the introduction of a bonus system based on productivity. Piece-work systems had already been experimented with in both the USA and Britain, with mixed results, generally because once a piece-work system became successful and workers started to increase their earnings, employers could seldom resist the temptation to cut rates; the end result was that the employer saw increased output and profit while the worker ended up working harder than before for the same money.

Alternative systems which were introduced attempted to circumvent this problem. The first such system was introduced by Towne himself in 1889, and was known as 'gain-sharing'; it was in essence similar to a profit-sharing plan, except that the workers received pay increases when costs went down, rather than when profits went up. The second plan, perhaps better known, was devised by another American engineer, Frederick Halsey, who called it the 'premium plan', based on additional pay for workers who could complete their tasks in a shorter time. A variant of the premium plan known as the Rowan Plan was introduced shortly thereafter in David Rowan & Co., a marine engine manufacturer in Glasgow.

The Towne and Halsey schemes were both tried out in factories and both yielded results, in terms of both higher wages and increased productivity. Indeed, one of the enduring features of the various schemes which emerged over the next thirty years is that, when first introduced, with full novelty value and under the close scrutiny of their inventors, they worked well: or at least, statistics were produced which indicated that they worked well. Yet, many of these schemes never took off. In the case of the Towne and Halsey schemes, the calculations necessary to work out the bonus paid to the workers were highly complex, and few cases could be found where either employers or workers were sufficiently trusting to adopt them. The constant bugbear of employment relations schemes, the fear by either management or the workers that the other side was 'getting too much', was already rearing its head.

## FREDERICK HALSEY

**Now largely forgotten**, Frederick Halsey was one of the architects of scientific management. Born in 1856 in Unadilla, New York, he studied mechanical engineering at Cornell University and then worked with an engineer at the Rand Drill Company in the USA and Canada from 1880–94. He then became a staff writer with *American Machinist*, becoming editor of the journal in 1907. His 'premium plan' was popular and was adopted in factories in the USA, Britain and Germany, before being gradually supplanted by the piece-rate systems developed by Taylor. Some still argue that the Halsey plan was superior. However, the system lost the support and interest of its founder, who devoted much of his later life to a passionate crusade against the metric system.

## Scientific management and labour

The third solution was developed by Frederick Winslow Taylor while working at the Midvale Steel Works in Philadelphia from 1885–95. This system started as a fairly simple piece-rate system, first introduced by Taylor at a meeting of the American Society of Mechanical Engineers in June 1895. In the first instance, Taylor's aim was to come up with a simpler and more easily adaptable piece-rate system which could overcome the problems of rate-cutting. To do this, Taylor proposed to couple the piece-rate system with a systematic time study of each work task using properly scientific methods of inquiry (from which comes the name 'scientific management', by which Taylor's system is better known). By this means, both employer and manager would know exactly how long a task should take. Rates could then be set in the light of something like 'perfect knowledge', which would enable the workers to make a good living wage and would allow the employers to make good but not excessive profits. One of Taylor's main goals was to reduce uncertainty in the workplace, and he calculated that his system would achieve three results:

> **Taylor proposed to couple the piece-rate system with a systematic time study of each work task using properly scientific methods of inquiry**

1. men working in scientifically managed workplaces would earn wages superior to those in other workplaces
2. scientifically managed workplaces would have higher levels of output and be more profitable
3. scientifically managed workplaces would be more attractive to workers, not only for their higher wages but for the security they offered.

Yet even in the discussion of the Taylor system which followed his initial paper of 1895, it became clear that the success of the system was dependent on two factors: a high level of skill on the part of the workers, and a corresponding reduction in levels of labour turnover, to cut down on training and recruitment costs. From its very inception, therefore, scientific management required a high degree of labour management. Within a few years, Taylor and his colleagues, notably Henry Lawrence Gantt and Harrington Emerson, were including chapters on 'labour management' in their works, and the dependency of the scientific management system on good labour management was widely recognized even by the turn of the century.

Was scientific management fair to labour? The debate erupted almost at once, and continues to this day. Certainly there is no doubt that Taylor thought it was. He has been heavily criticized, especially by British writers like Frank Watts and the husband-and-wife consultancy team, the McKillops; the latter cite reported comments such as 'It does not do for a man to get rich too quickly' as evidence that Taylor was not on the side of the worker. But Taylor was from a Pennsylvania Quaker family, an austere man in terms of personal life and habit, and he did not believe that *anyone* should get rich too quickly. In 1895, he defended his paper on the grounds that it would improve the lot of the manual worker. He also argued throughout his career that scientific management was dependent for its success in the first place on the cooperation of the workers; if the shop floor workers rejected the system, then it could not be employed at all.

This point was taken up with some passion by scientific management's most prominent *rapporteur*, C. Bertrand Thompson, who argued that 'scientific management does not work except with the heartiest consent and help of the men under it'. Thompson's belief in scientific management was so strong that he believed that it could make trade unions unnecessary, as the workers' lot would be sufficiently improved to eliminate most grievances, though he conceded that some form of worker representation would still be required.

These were deeply held convictions, but even the most ardent supporters of scientific management could not but acknowledge the elitist element of the discipline. The emphasis on excellence was summed up by Gantt in 1905: 'the only healthy industrial condition is that in which the employer has the best men obtainable for his work, and the workman feels that his labour is being sold at the highest market price'. He argues that the employer has a duty of efficiency to his men: 'The duty of an employer to his employees then demands that he shall maintain his plant and system of management at its highest efficiency, for only thus can he afford his men employment during times of sharp competition.' He continues:

> In order to get the best results, which, in case of a machine is the maximum product from it, and in case of a labor operation is its most efficient performance, four things are necessary:
>
> First – complete and exact knowledge of the best way of doing the work.

> Second – an instructor competent and willing to teach the work man how to make use of this information.
>
> Third – wages for efficient work high enough to make a competent man feel that they are worth striving for.
>
> Fourth – a distinct loss in wages in case a certain degree of efficiency is not maintained.[3]

This last point in particular was seen as a threat by opponents of scientific management. Robert Hoxie, the economist asked by the US government to look into the issue, noted in his book *Scientific Management and Labor* how the American trade unions, notably the emerging American Federation of Labor led by Samuel Gompers, were concerned not so much by the *theory* of scientific management as by how it was put into practice. Many union leaders had in fact no objection to practices which gave their workers more security and higher wages. What they saw happening before their eyes, however, was employers introducing Taylor-type piece-rate systems, then, as before, cutting the rates as soon as higher levels of productivity were reached. Even where scientific management methods were honestly introduced, problems still arose; the work studies were not always correctly handled, and unfair rates could be introduced from the start, and even when the right rate was introduced, workers did not always meet targets, meaning punitive measures were then introduced.

When scientific management crossed the Atlantic and began to be introduced in British plants, the attitude was even more hostile. One of the first to comment on the effect of scientific management on labour was the Fabian socialist Sidney Webb, in *The Works Manager Today*. Webb, somewhat surprisingly, was cautiously in favour of scientific management, but argued that it would function correctly only if the workers fully supported it and management played fair with the workers. The chocolate-maker Benjamin Seebohm Rowntree, a notable exponent of improved labour relations (see below), approved of the technical aspects of scientific management but believed the difficulties of the piece-work scheme were too great to be overcome, and professed himself in favour instead of profit-sharing schemes and co-ownership. American defenders of scientific management in turn rejected Rowntree's ideas as being 'unfair' to individuals in that those who worked hardest had to share their profits with those who did not pull their weight. The debate thereafter degenerated into a clash of cultures, exemplified in the writing of one of the most vociferous British opponents of scientific management, the engineer Frank Watts. Watts, whose book *An Introduction to the Psychological Problems of Industry* (1921) is one of the first evidences of backlash against scientific management, accused Taylor of destroying craft work and deskilling the worker: 'His solution unfortunately involved the atrophy of the spontaneity and initiative of his workmen. The philosophy underlying his methods seems to have been that the world is made up of a few supermen and a multitude of creatures intended by Providence to be drudges.' He continued:

> The psychological dilemma concerning the monotony of repetition-process work is this: either the worker employs all his powers on the task, in which case there is established an undesirable limitation and stereotyping of mental process so that the movements of his mind tend to become unduly circumscribed and uniform, *and this is bad for the worker;* or the mechanical processes tend to be carried on automatically while the conscious attention is given to other things, which means that only a small portion of the worker's energy is given to the work, *and this is frequently bad for his employer.*[4]

## The concern for social justice

Could a system which was unfair to workers be said to be efficient, even if that unfairness was only a perception on the part of the workers themselves? Harrington Emerson, an engineer but one for whom efficiency was always much more than just a technical concept, argued that it could not. He made the point emphatically in his book *The Twelve Principles of*

*Efficiency*: fairness and efficiency had to go hand in hand. The 'fair deal', for Emerson, lay at the heart of efficiency. Managers treated their machines with care, he said; the very least they could do was treat their workers in the same way:

**Could a system which was unfair to workers be said to be efficient, even if that unfairness was only a perception on the part of the workers themselves?**

> As to the man, the worker, without whom industry would collapse, all conditions ought to be standardized. Drinking water ought to be germ-free, life-destroying dust should be sucked away, safeguards should surround moving machinery, work illumination should be adequate, not ruinous to eyesight. Working hours should be reasonable and without overtime except in great emergencies, means should be provided for ascertaining directly his needs, his wishes, of listening to his recommendations...These general welfare considerations have their effect on the contentment of the worker and not one of them is recommended from any patronizing or altruistic motive. A locomotive or other machine is cleaned, housed, kept in repair, given good fuel and good water because its efficiency is thus increased; and in the interests of plant efficiency men should be treated at least as well as we treat machines. It is for mutual, not one-sided, benefit that the workers' counsel is considered.[5]

Emerson rejected piece-work and all other forms of productivity pay, an important distinction between him and the Taylor school. Piece-work, said Emerson, was open to abuse; even where the system was not being abused, the possibility of abuse was *perceived* by workers and they would never fully trust it. Instead of trying to drive workers with the stick or lure them forward with the carrot of bonuses, said Emerson, employers should seek to create workplace conditions in which workers will feel secure and will be willing to work. In other words – just as in the family businesses of the past – employers should develop bonds of trust with their employees, and that trust must in turn be based on a sense of equity and justice.

In stating that employers should give as much care to their human capital as they did to their machines, Emerson was repeating a common enough view at the time; the former were equally as valuable as the latter, and deserved as much attention. But Emerson's real innovation – one which is still not widely recognized to this day – is that the worker and the firm operate in a partnership. Labour markets are not straightforward exchanges; indeed, labour *per se* is not a commodity. In labour markets, employers buy *output*, but what workers sell is *time*:

> The worker is selling time, just as a coalmine operator sells coal; but the purchaser is not buying time nor coal; he buys output and heat units. The equivalency between operation and time (not wages) is of transcendent importance, exactly as equivalency between heat unit and fuel is of importance.[6]

Emerson believed that a fair organization was an efficient one. For the British critics of scientific management, the problem was not so much Taylorism itself, though this remained the focus of their attacks, but the much larger question of the widening of the gap between workers and employers and a need to re-establish that bond for social as well as economic reasons. Frank Watts and Benjamin Rowntree would be called paternalists today, but their view that employers had a duty of care to their employees was honestly held and had a history stretching back to Robert Owen in the early nineteenth century.

## Towards personnel management

For all these reasons – the need to improve workplace relations and end the damaging strikes, the need to find ways of increasing output, the need to ameliorate workplace conditions and bring social justice back into management – observers increasingly saw the need for the development of more specialist managerial skills for handling labour. The first ever 'employment management' department was that developed at National Cash Register by John Patterson in the 1890s. Patterson was a highly paternalist employer, but he recognized the need for a systematic approach to labour relations, and he also recognized that better relations would lead to great efficiency and profitability. One feature of the Patterson system was the emphasis on employee involvement. Patterson treated his employees as if they were dependants or family members; but he listened to their views, consulted them on important decisions, and made them feel valued. In Britain, Cadbury's was close behind NCR in developing two labour departments, one for male workers and one for female workers, and Edward Cadbury developed a formal employee suggestion scheme whereby employees were urged to put forward their ideas for improving operations and working conditions, with small bonuses for those whose schemes were adopted successfully. In both cases, corporate leadership placed great stress on developing bonds of trust between management and workers; the labour management departments were vehicles for helping to build that trust, rather than dead-ends into which labour problems could be shunted.

Employment management grew steadily in importance. The first major employment managers' association was established in Boston in 1910, under the chairmanship of Meyer Bloomfield (there may have been an earlier association in Detroit, but it does not seem to have had much impact), and the movement slowly spread to other cities (and to the UK, where the Institute for Labour Management was established in 1913). Developments in this field were given a considerable boost by the First World War. Even before America's entry into the war, the drying up of the supply of immigrant labour from Europe had caused something of a crunch in the labour market, and firms began quickly to realize that their success depended on recruiting and retaining high-quality labour. It is at this time that the first training programmes for employment managers began to emerge, at the Tuft School of Management at Dartmouth College and at the Wharton School in Pennsylvania, and also at Bryn Mawr College for female employment managers.

**The first major employment managers' association was established in Boston in 1910**

The coming of age of the employment management movement can be said to be marked by the publication of a special edition of the *Annals of the American Academy of Political and Social Science* in May 1916, co-edited by Bloomfield. A leading article by William Redfield, US Secretary of Commerce in the Wilson administration and a strong supporter of the personnel management movement, reiterated Emerson's point that if an organization's people are as important as its machines, then they deserve the same care. Dryly, he comments that from his own business experience:

> I have always felt that the last concern in the world with which I should want to compete would be that which paid high wages, which sold the best quality of goods, and which had such management as to lead its men upward all the time. I have never found any difficulty, as a salesman, in competing with a cheap shop.[7]

The following five years saw a flood of literature on this new discipline, much of it extraordinarily good and forward-thinking. Ordway Tead was the leading guru in the field in the period after the First World War, who urged all companies to set up personnel departments to coordinate the development of better relations, with a view both to increasing productivity and improving the lives of the workers. Tead, like most writers of the period, makes the point that employment management or personnel management cannot succeed unless it has the backing of top management and is considered a principal executive function. Here again, the personnel department is a tool which top management uses to achieve its aim of growing better relations with employees; setting up a personnel department is not an end in itself.

## Growing people with the business

Throughout the early 1920s, the practice of personnel management continued to develop. The pages of journals such as *Industrial Management* and *System* are full of news on this subject, and the former even developed a special section related to personnel management. One of the major ongoing themes at this time is *continuity*. Employers were urged to hire for the long term. The orthodoxy of the 1920s was to get employees and keep them. High labour turnover was associated with high costs; far better to invest in selecting and recruiting the *right* employees, train them to the necessary standard, and make them part of the business. Promotion was nearly always internal; businesses were proud of the fact that they did not have to go outside the firm to recruit talent. Two prominent business leaders of the time, Henry Ford and Thomas Watson, chairman of the newly-founded IBM, argued that business talent should be incubated or 'grown' within the firm rather than recruited from outside.

## MUTO SANJI

**Born in 1867**, Muto studied at Keio University where one of his teachers was Fukuzawa Yukichi. He then worked in the USA for three years before returning to Japan and joining Mitsui Bank in 1893; in 1894 he took over a Mitsui subsidiary, the cotton spinning firm Kanebo. The company was in a severe state of disorganization, and Muto began a systematic process of reconstruction. From 1900, he began introducing scientific methods of workflow analysis and working practices, including time and motion studies and standardization of tasks and processes. Although his approach to management was scientific, Muto recognized that the system could not work unless the workers were motivated, and that to achieve full motivation, it was necessary to see that the workers were satisfied and happy. At Kanebo, Muto not only paid high wages (he did not adopt the piece-rate system of bonuses) but provided many facilities including housing and education, encouraging his workers to feel part of the company 'family'. Muto thus combined the best of scientific management with the best of Japanese management culture.

Much attention was also paid to making the workplace as attractive as possible for employees. In a move away from the scientific management view that proper remuneration alone would attract and keep good employees, American managers in particular began to recognize the importance of the workplace as an environment, and as a community. In the first place, the role of personnel management began to expand to take on a whole host of functions such as health and safety and welfare management, dedicated to ensuring that employees felt safe, comfortable and secure both in the workplace and outside it. In the second, the first steps were taken towards trying to establish the kind of workplace coordination within and between work teams and departments which became a hallmark of human resource management in the latter half of the century.

> American managers in particular began to recognize the importance of the workplace as an environment, and as a community

## The whole employee

In 1927, five employees of the Western Electric Company began to take part in an experiment at the company's Hawthorne Works in Chicago, which aimed to study the effects of fatigue and monotony on workplace performance. By the time the project was finished, ten years later, its scope had been widened to include nearly every factor, psychological and physical, personal and professional, in work and home life, which might affect the employee and his or her performance, and more than 20,000 people had been studied and interviewed. The experiments had attracted the notice of such luminaries as the British management consultant Lyndall Urwick, the Australian psychologist Elton Mayo and Harvard University faculty including Fritz Roethlisberger and Thomas North Whitehead. In the process, a new discipline, industrial psychology, was born, the term 'human resource management' began to be used, and the entire discipline can fairly be said to have come of age.

Perhaps the important outcome of the Hawthorne studies was the view that the management of the workplace depends ultimately on the management of people, and that the human factor may be the most important single ingredient in terms of success or failure. On mechanization, for example, Elton Mayo concludes:

> The general conclusion with respect to the mechanization of industry that seems to be indicated by these inquiries is that the mechanization itself is of no great importance in an industry that sets itself, intelligently and diligently, to discover what human changes of method must accompany the introduction of repetitive methods of work. We cannot make individuals stupid; we may make them dissatisfied, psychoneurotic, or restless. It is urgently necessary that industry should give as much attention to human as it has to material inquiry. With the institution of adequate researches, physiological, psychological, and social, society has nothing to fear from industrial mechanization.[8]

Henry Post Dutton, the author of one of the better management textbooks in the early 1920s (*Factory Management*, published in 1924 and quoted at the head of this chapter), had already anticipated some of the themes that would be confirmed in the course of the Hawthorne studies. Dutton, influenced by the psychological thinking of the time, argued that people do not work (or join any organization) solely for material benefit; there are deep and powerful social needs as well, such as security, a sense of advancement, the need to 'count for something', the desire for praise and appreciation, and the desire for companionship. The factory system, he says, contains many elements which seem to run counter to human instincts: 'The deadly humdrum of daily dependability, so necessary to effective production, is in itself galling to the neck of the man whose ancestors but a short span of years ago, as history goes, were free nomads, and who still feels occasionally the urge for adventures in new fields. And on individuals of only ordinary capacity, the strain of modern life, of the support of a family, the uncertainties of unemployment and of illness and old age, tend to force a preoccupation which gradually crowds out of life all the spontaneous play elements which should enrich it, with a consequent immense loss to society of motive force, of imagination and daring and desire to excel and to achieve.'

The answer, says Dutton, not unlike Emerson a decade before, is to humanize the workplace. The Hawthorne experiments bore this out.

Places of work are human spaces. Anyone attempting to avoid that fact will run into the kinds of problems noted by the industrial psychologist W.J. Watson in 1931, who described how a group of British workers quietly rebelled and set about sabotaging a new productivity system based on scientific management:

**Places of work are human spaces**

> So, what we did was to ignore the regulations, and if we wanted to sharpen a tool, we simply cajoled the tool-room foreman to allow us to touch it up ourselves. If the time-limit on a job was excessive, we went 'ca'canny' to hang the time out, and if the time was insufficient, we also adopted 'ca'canny,' and lodged a complaint with the foreman. Should the 'feed and speed' man attempt to interfere, we either threatened him with, and sometimes applied (if we were big enough), physical violence, or we politely invited him to increase the speed himself, knowing full well (having provided for it) that as soon as he did so the job would be spoilt. When the bonus clerk came along to time the job with a watch, it was not difficult to persuade a clerk who knew nothing about such things that the metal was 'tough,' by manipulating the tool so that it would not cut. The charts disappeared from the machines, despite the vigilance of the management. Harassed by the employers and bullied by the employees, the 'feed and speed' men had such a rotten time of it that no one could be persuaded to accept the position. One I knew personally became mentally deranged and another worried himself into an early grave. By such tactics – passive resistance and sabotage – the system was rendered almost unworkable.

This description will doubtless cause many managers to shudder with horror, imagining it happening in their own workplace. As Taylor himself had said, without the cooperation of the workers, scientific management will never work, and Watson shows clearly what happens when managers try to press ahead without the informed consent of their employees. But Watson also had doubts about the work of him and his colleagues; in particular, he felt that research on workplace behaviour tended to bias its own results (a view confirmed by the Hawthorne researchers, who found that many productivity increases had to be attributed to the fact that the workers, aware that they were being studied, found renewed interest and stimulus in their own work and began to work harder and faster). Interviewing employees and observing them cannot tell the researcher or, more importantly, the personnel manager everything that is going on in the minds of the former.

> Even though the conscientious investigator *does* soak himself in the conditions of the factory wherein he is conducting experiments, and himself carry out the operations, even though, during the months he is pursuing his studies, he actually *lives with* the workers, he is not, after all, 'dependent upon what the merest breath of adversity may in a moment dispel', and he is ever conscious of the fact that he is an industrial psychologist studying the worker, and not himself a wage earner. Consequently, with the best intentions in the world, he cannot hope thoroughly to understand the psychology of the workers; the most he can do is to diagnose the wage-earner and his working conditions, postulate theories as to what is wrong, and suggest methods of improvement – the *wage-earner alone actually knows*.[9]

## Alternative approaches

By the late 1930s, then, personnel management was moving towards its modern form, and after the Second World War would emerge, renewed and reinvigorated, as human resource management as we know and love it today.

Today's HRM model (with a lot of embellishments and additions) is essentially the one advocated by Emerson and Dutton. It relies at its base on a knowledge of the psychology and motivations of employees and seeks to provide a workplace in which employees feel motivated and voluntarily give of their best efforts. It also seeks to increase the potential productivity of employees through methods such as training, and it seeks to create more efficient employee management through methods such as recruiting high-quality workers and decreasing employee turnover. That, at least, is the theory; in practice, only a tiny handful of companies have a human resource policy that meets all or even most of these goals. Before looking at some of the historical implications for better human resources management, though, let us look quickly at some of the alternate approaches which have been tried and either discarded or failed to catch on.

> **In practice, only a tiny handful of companies have a human resource policy that meets all or even most of these goals**

## Profit-sharing and co-partnership

Profit-sharing and co-partnership, mentioned above, were primarily British experiments which developed in the mid to late nineteenth century and reached their heyday in the first two decades of the twentieth century. There were many different forms of profit-sharing and partnership schemes, from simple partnership, whereby employees were paid a bonus as a proportion of either gross or net profit, to partnerships which gave employees shares and paid dividends. William Lever, who disapproved of profit-sharing, introduced a limited form of partnership at Lever Brothers, but the most outstanding example of the practice was developed by the department store owner John Lewis in 1928. Lewis, who greatly admired Robert Owen, saw management as a form of stewardship and believed that businesses were like living things and had independent existences and, in a metaphorical sense, lives of their own. His ideas on partnership were based partly on ethical views and partly on the need for greater harmony and efficiency in the workplace. Lewis believed that all businesses were founded on a triangular relationship between profit, knowledge and power. In his view, effective partnership schemes require all three; simple profit-sharing schemes will be less acceptable because, in a democratic system, happiness requires that people have access to knowledge and have a degree of control over their own lives. Allowing worker participation in management increased that control, even if only to a limited degree.

## JOHN LEWIS

**JOHN LEWIS WAS BORN IN LONDON IN 1885**, the son of a department store owner, and joined the family business at age nineteen. He almost immediately quarrelled with his father, whom he later described as 'a second-rate success in a first-rate opportunity'. He was told to take charge of a newly acquired subsidiary, the Peter Jones department store in Chelsea, and immediately turned this into a successful enterprise. In 1926 he took over the entire business, and in 1929 launched his great experiment, the John Lewis Partnership, which made every employee a shareholder in the business. During the 1930s the company expanded rapidly; several of its larger stores were badly damaged in the Second World War, but the company made a swift recovery after the war. Lewis always believed that a key to the company's success was the strength of commitment by its employees, who saw success as linked to their own. The John Lewis Partnership continues today, though several attempts have been made to dissolve it.

---

Not every manager was willing to go as far as Lewis. Christopher Furness, chairman of the international shipping giant Furness Withy, had introduced a partnership scheme in the early part of the century, but it foundered when it became apparent that Furness, when handing over shares to employees, had no intention of handing over any portion of control as well. Otherwise progressive employers like Edward Cadbury and Benjamin Rowntree, while admitting the theoretical merits, showed little interest in implementing the concept in their own business.

> **Profit-sharing spread the money around without loss of control: it was thus advocated strongly by liberal politicians and business leaders as a means of redistributing wealth and thereby countering socialism**

Profit-sharing spread the money around without loss of control: it was thus advocated strongly by liberal politicians and business leaders as a means of redistributing wealth and thereby countering socialism. Procter & Gamble was the first large US firm to introduce profit-sharing, in 1887, and Henry Dennison launched a high-profile profit-sharing scheme at the Dennison Company in the 1920s, but there were few other imitators. Profit-sharing schemes were widespread among British firms, and the concept was also popular on the continent, where Ernst Abbé, the inspirational leader of Carl Zeiss Jena, introduced a profit-sharing scheme in the 1890s. Profit-sharing was also an implicit part of more radical forms of organization such as the Oneida Company and the Bat'a Corporation.

## ERNST ABBÉ

**BORN THE SON OF A TEXTILE WORKER IN 1840**, Abbé won a scholarship to the University of Jena, where he studied physics and thermodynamics. Becoming a teacher at Jena, he specialized in optics and managed the university's astronomical observatory. A local craftsman and lens-maker, Carl Zeiss, then asked Abbé to help solve a problem of image defraction; the two men got along well, and Zeiss invited the young professor to become a partner in his business. Zeiss retired a few years later, and Abbé became sole proprietor and general manager. Under Abbé, Carl Zeiss Jena became one of the most innovative companies in Europe, launching a new product every year and creating a culture of innovation in which workers were encouraged to experiment and learn.

Abbé was a strong believer in industrial democracy. He believed that workers had the right to be heard and represented on major issues that affected the business. He paid high wages: profit-sharing was considered an additional perquisite, not the main form of remuneration. He also set up an employee sick fund in 1875; a company pension scheme was established in 1888; paid holidays and compensation in event of layoffs were introduced, and in 1900 the working day was cut back to eight hours. The reforms at Zeiss attracted attention throughout Germany, and served as models for social legislation in several German states.

Profit-sharing was and continues to be a subject of vigorous debate. On the surface, it looks a good idea: if the company does well and makes a profit, then the employees, whose labour contributed to that profit, should share in it. However, there are two main objections. The first, heard strongest in the USA, was that profit-sharing was unfair to individuals. If 10 per cent of the workforce work hard and force productivity and profits up, the resulting profit is distributed not only to them but to the 90 per cent who simply went along for the ride. American individualism revolted against this (or at least, was used as a convenient excuse to avoid giving away profits to workers and keep them for shareholders) and profit-sharing never took off.

The other objection became clear in time; profit-sharing is all very well when the company does well, but what if it has a bad year? There can be many reasons why a company's profits will decline, even temporarily, and not all are the responsibility of the employees. Why should hard-working staff in a widget factory have their bonus cut in half because the market for widgets has dried up following the collapse of several widget-using companies in Australia? In cases such as this, the theoretical injustice can also mean real physical hardship if bonuses and wages decline steeply and without warning. William Lever was against profit-sharing for just this reason, preferring to plough profits into permanent facilities for employees, and Ernst Abbé paid his employees high wages as well as a share of the profits, preferring to see the latter as a form of bonus. The perception of equity, then, often turned into a reality of inequity, and few profit-sharing schemes survived for long.

## Welfare schemes

In the late nineteenth and early twentieth century, before state welfare provision became general in the West, worker welfare schemes were the mark of every progressive employer. George Cadbury was a leader in this field in Britain; following the example of Robert Owen and Titus Salt, he built a complete village for his workforce on a greenfield site next to the company's new factory at Bournville, near Birmingham. Cadbury became widely studied as a model of employee welfare, and his methods were adopted in Europe and the USA. His fellow Quaker and chocolate-maker, Joseph Rowntree, also developed welfare schemes, though not on the same scale, and these were carried on by his son Benjamin.

**In the late nineteenth and early twentieth century, before state welfare provision became general in the West, worker welfare schemes were the mark of every progressive employer**

## GEORGE CADBURY

**CADBURY WAS BORN IN BIRMINGHAM IN 1839**, the son of John Cadbury, a Quaker and chocolate-maker. His father died when Cadbury was twenty-one, and he and his brother Richard took over the management of the firm. The business had gone into decline, and the brothers worked twelve hours a day, six days a week, to turn it round. A devout Quaker, Cadbury taught Sunday school every week and abstained from alcohol, tobacco, coffee and tea.

Cadbury is most famous for planning and building the model town of Bournville. When, in 1879, it became clear that the company's factory in central Birmingham was not large enough to support continued expansion, the Cadburys built a much larger factory on a greenfield site on the outskirts of the city. Along with the factory they built large-scale housing and public amenities for their workers. Bournville became one of the most famous of the late Victorian 'social experiments' which combined industrial management with social reform. However, Cadbury's experiment was never just about social reform. What was good for the community was good for the company, and vice versa; the innovations that pleased Cadbury most were those which benefited employees and the firm in equal measure. For example, swimming baths were built near the factory, and employees were encouraged to use these; this both improved employee health and fitness, and improved cleanliness in the factory.

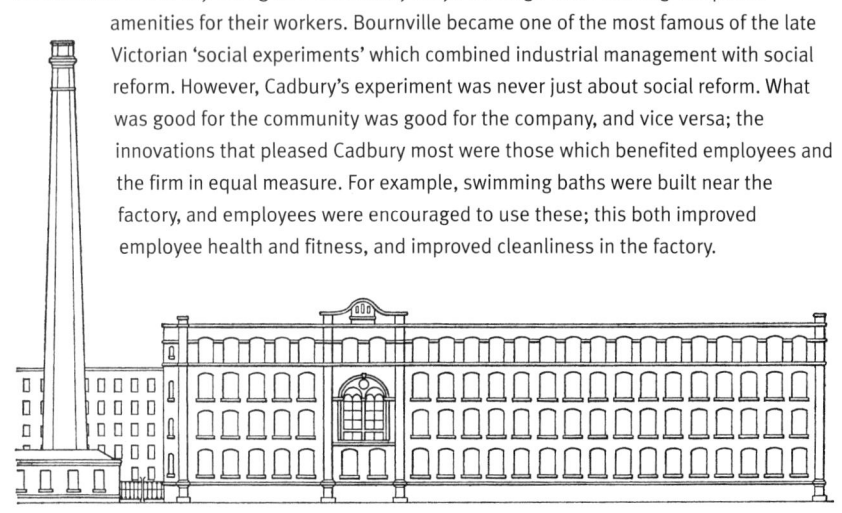

## OHARA MAGOSABURO

**OHARA WAS BORN IN KURASHIKI, JAPAN IN 1880**, the son of a cotton manufacturer who gradually built up a large business. Ohara succeeded his father as chairman of the firm in 1906, and grew it further through his career, turning the Kurashiki Spinning Company into one of Japan's largest textiles producers. In 1899, Ohara had converted to Christianity, and as chairman of Kurashiki developed what he called *rodo riso shugi* (labour idealism), a philosophy based on Christian values and Japanese culture in almost equal measure. The three principles of *rodo riso shugi* were seen as humanitarianism, the creation of harmony between capital and labour, and a view of labour which saw it not as a commodity but as a form of service. Ohara was strongly paternalistic, establishing a large education department and later an elementary school for the children of workers, and provided housing, food and other goods to employees either free or at cost. Many of his views were communicated to employees through the company newsletter, *Kurashiki Jiho*.[10]

Welfare schemes were also widespread in the USA. John Patterson, as noted, was an early exponent of welfare at NCR, and many of the major employers of the day, including Henry Heinz, W.K. Kellogg, Louis F. Swift and John Wanamaker to name just a few, had extensive employee welfare schemes. Employee welfare had notable benefits. Especially in the USA, where many workers were recent immigrants or the children of immigrants and lived in considerable poverty, poor health, housing and diet were endemic problems. Simple matters such as providing a hot meal each day could improve health and, therefore, an employee's ability to work; regular health checks by company doctors and nurses, either at the plant or at home, could improve matters still further. Another benefit to employee welfare programmes was discovered by the post-Second World War governor of Bank Melli in Persia (Iran), Abol Hassan Ebtehaj, who noted that the bank's security guards were looking flabby and installed a gymnasium which all employees were invited to use free of charge; but for security guards, use of the gym was compulsory. (The guards soon improved their muscle tone.)

But welfare also had its problems. An unlooked-for one in the early days was the general desire on the part of most people to avoid being seen to receive charity. Patterson, one of the first American businessmen to provide a restaurant for employees, initially offered meals free of charge, and was astonished to find no one was using it. He then began pricing meals at five cents, and thereafter the canteen was always full. Five cents was not the full cost of the meals, but it was enough to make the employees feel that they were paying for what they received. Honour was satisfied on both sides.

**Company welfare schemes in Europe and the USA began to be undermined as the state and other external providers began to provide education, health services, housing and so on for the poor**

More generally, company welfare schemes in Europe and the USA began to be undermined as the state and other external providers began to provide education, health services, housing and so on for the poor, and then also as general standards of living rose and the necessity for free provision became less. Japanese firms continue to offer high levels of employee benefits, and we noted earlier the Chinese example of the 'iron rice bowl', but these derive from a somewhat different tradition, that of the family-style of business where the employer has a duty to look after the employees. The ethically based philanthropy of Victorian business owners and managers seems largely to have had its day.

## Industrial democracy

This term seems to have originated after the First World War, though George Cadbury had introduced it in the 1870s and American businessmen like the department store owner Edward Filene had also created formal industrial democracy schemes. For those interested in industrial democracy, two routes were possible. The first was to grow one's own democracy, as George Cadbury and especially his son Edward did with great success. Under Edward Cadbury, the system of works committees laid down by his father was greatly expanded and, indeed, ran like a kind of parallel management structure throughout the firm. Two overall super-committees, one for male employees and one for female employees, met monthly, both chaired by Edward Cadbury himself, and these were empowered to comment on or offer advice on everything from working conditions to proposals for new plant and facilities to company strategy and policy. The views of these committees were not binding, but if Cadbury's own account is to be believed, they were often taken. The result was powerful; Cadbury had found a way not just of increasing worker involvement, but of tapping into the knowledge and creative ideas of his workforce and making this work for the company. As Herbert

Casson said approvingly of the Cadbury company, 'Everyone *thinks*.'

The other option was to encourage trades unions or labour unions or work with them on a cooperative basis, as the printer Sakuma Taiichi did in Japan and as the engineer Robert Bosch did in Germany. Bosch, a progressive employer nicknamed 'Red Bosch' by other German industrialists, paid high wages and encouraged a culture of commitment and enterprise in his firm in the 1920s, and regarded unions as a useful way of keeping in touch with employee concerns and problems; so long as he gave his workers nothing to complain about, the unions effectively handled personnel management for him. Industrial democracy sounds and looks like good practice. It has its risks; there is often a tension between the parties involved, and many industrial democracy schemes have been scuppered when one side or the other, usually the workers, decides that the other party's heart is not really in it. Nothing dooms an industrial democracy scheme faster than the perception by workers that management is only doing it for the PR; success requires a deep-rooted organizational culture of trust and commitment, as in the cases of Cadbury and Bosch.

## Cooperatives

The ultimate extension of profit-sharing, copartnership and industrial democracy is the cooperative, in which workers take a share in all aspects of the business including its management. Despite widespread and often justified cynicism about cooperatives, there have been some successful examples. However, Robert Owen, who did much to promote the cooperative moment in Britain, found that in order to succeed cooperatives had to have many of the same attributes as any other business; in particular, they had to have a clear and pragmatic purpose, and they had to have strong management. Owen, an idealist of considerable proportions, was dismayed by the utopian dreamers who ran most of the cooperatives with which he was associated. Though he remained a lifelong supporter of the cooperative movement, he continued to argue that bad management and lack of pragmatism were the cooperative's chief enemies.

## ROBERT OWEN

**BORN IN WALES IN 1771**, Owen left home at ten and moved to London, where he lived and worked with his elder brother. He later apprenticed as a draper, and at the age of sixteen moved to Manchester, then one of the centres of the Industrial Revolution. Investing his savings, Owen set up a small business making parts for spinning mules, and then set up a small spinning shop himself; by the age of 19 he was earning around £300 per year. A local millowner, Peter Drinkwater, was so impressed that he hired Owen as his works superintendent, in charge of more than 500 workers. This job came to an end when Samuel Oldknow bought out Drinkwater, and Owen set up his own company. In the 1790s he met and fell in love with Caroline Dale, daughter of David Dale, the owner of the New Lanark mill. Dale was a devout Christian and Owen was a convinced atheist; to gain his prospective father-in-law's goodwill, Owen offered to buy New Lanark for the colossal sum of £60,000.

Taking over New Lanark, Owen made the mill and community into a model of enlightened capitalism. The mill, which had been highly profitable under Dale, continued to be so under Owen; the patience, attention to detail and superb man-management that made him a success in Manchester continued to be exhibited here. But it was the model community he built up around New Lanark that attracted most attention. Owen had formed the belief that by improving the quality of life and the physical conditions of work for his workmen and their families, he would not only be contributing to the good of society; happier, healthier workers would also be more efficient and productivity and quality would improve. To this end, he provided education, accommodation, health care, and shops selling subsidized goods including, unusually, beer and whisky. Although a strong disciplinarian, Owen won a reputation for fairness and there were few labour problems.

His emphasis on education is perhaps the most striking feature of his time at New Lanark. Owen, like many later writers, believed that the workers were the most valuable feature of his company, and he argued that at least as much care and attention should be given to them as to the company's machines. He believed that education was an essential feature of human development, and encouraged learning and knowledge at all levels of the company. He was also a leading proponent of factory reform, and supported attempts at legislation to curb abusive employment practices. In later years he was a strong supporter of the cooperative movement and of trade unions, both of which he saw as devices for curbing the excessive power of his fellow mill owners.

Ironically, two of the most successful cooperatives of all time succeeded precisely because they had strong leadership. The Oneida community was a utopian socialist movement established by John Humphrey Noyes in the USA in 1848, based on communal living, free love and property held in common. The movement ended, as most such movements did, in tears, with the leader quarrelling with his followers and departing and then a short, swift slide into oblivion. In 1880 the elders of the community decided to end the experiment. Unusually, Oneida had been successful in terms of self-sufficiency, and its several businesses in fruit-canning, leather goods and making silver tableware were all turning a profit. Instead of sharing out property among the former members, the elders decided to convert the commune into Oneida Community Ltd and give each former member shares. However, none of the leaders had much commercial experience or acumen, and the business remained static into the 1890s.

In 1894 Pierrepont Noyes, son of the founder, returned to Oneida with the aim of modernizing the firm. Most of the directors were against him, but Noyes persuaded the individual shareholders to support him at a general meeting. As a result of this palace coup he took virtual control of the company, becoming general manager in 1899. Noyes decided to rationalize the business and focus on one product line, silver tableware, launching the hugely successful Community Plate brand a few years later. Though Oneida was not a cooperative in the strict sense of the word, in that the community members devolved most management responsibility to Noyes, they remained involved in its affairs through regular shareholder meetings; also, for several decades at least, the majority of employees were also shareholders. Noyes was the company's servant rather than its master, but it was his instinctive marketing skills and management talent that led Oneida to success.

**For several decades at least, the majority of employees were also shareholders**

The most astonishing cooperative story of all, however, must surely be that of Mondragón Cooperatives Corporation (MCC) in the Basque region of northern Spain. José Maria Arizmendiarrieta was a Catholic priest who had opposed Franco and was imprisoned and nearly shot in

1937. In 1941 he was released from prison and sent to the small town of Mondragón to replace a priest who had earlier been executed. Mondragón, like every town in the Basque region, was poor and backward, with high unemployment and few prospects. Arizmendiarrieta was strongly aware of the need for economic prosperity to combat the region's crippling poverty. In the mid-1940s he established a small technical college in the town, supported by donations from local people. The college, which survives today as the Mondragón Eskola Politeknikoa, provided technical and engineering education and helped graduates find jobs in factories.

In 1956, five graduates from the college, unable to raise capital to start their own business, decided instead to set up a cooperative to manufacture oil stoves and lamps. This business, called Ulgor (now Fagor), could not have been established without the support of Arizmendiarrieta, who helped the cooperators find members and premises. Ulgor flourished, and was soon joined by other cooperative businesses such as Arrasate and Eroski. In 1959 Arizmendiarrieta founded the Caja Laboral Popular, a cooperative savings bank which helped fund further cooperative ventures; in 1967 he led the founding of a cooperative social security department, and in 1967 he was the moving force behind the establishment of a research department, which in 1974 became Ikerlan, a cooperative in its own right.

Today, MCC contains around 120 cooperatives with operations in twenty-three countries and a combined annual turnover approaching $6 billion; it is the eighth-largest business entity in Spain. So effective has management been within the group that, throughout its history, only one of the cooperatives has gone bankrupt.

## Conclusions

Of all the advances in management thinking which transpired during the twentieth century, perhaps none has been so important as those that have occurred within the domain of what we now call human resource management. These advances have come in two basic forms. First, it has been learned that all business organizations (indeed, all organizations of any purpose) depend on their people for success. Second, it has been learned that by proper coordination, the people of an organization can achieve more by working together as a team than they can by working singly. The development of concepts such as the learning organization, human capital and knowledge capital are the building blocks of the new styles of organization now emerging.

To get the best from the people who make up an organization, it is first necessary to manage them in the most efficient and effective manner. Exactly what constitutes efficiency and effectiveness in this regard has been and continues to be a matter for debate. At one extreme, there is the view that employees are simply a resource, to be pressed for the maximum possible output. At the other end of the spectrum, the view is that employees are first and foremost human beings and that the employer has a duty to care for their human aspirations and needs. Pragmatically, of course, most employers fit somewhere between these two extremes; exactly where depends on their own outlook and inclination.

**Pragmatically, of course, most employers fit somewhere between these two extremes; exactly where depends on their own outlook and inclination**

The early twentieth century brought no consensus as to the best way of managing human capital, but all the movements that emerged in this period had a common dual aim: to raise industrial output while *simultaneously* improving the quality of life of the workers. Both these aims continue to be at the heart of most thinking in human resource management.

All the movements we have discussed here have been motivated by two principles: first, the abstract principle of social justice and a genuine belief that employers do have a responsibility to those who work for them, and second, an equal commitment to the view that by behaving fairly to their employees, firms would see a bottom-line result in terms of increased productivity and profitability. The discovery that men who worked an eight-hour day actually produced more in gross terms than those who worked a ten-hour day was a revelation at the time (and incidentally, a lesson that still might be learned by some of our leading consultancy firms, who routinely expect their employees to work twelve hours a day and more).

There is also the unavoidable conclusion that the commitment of an organization's leadership to effective human resource management is probably more important than the system used to implement that management. The industrial psychologists' view that people are more important than systems must apply here as well. In this as in so many other fields, with effective leadership, anything is possible; without it, even the best systems are doomed to failure.

*Notes to chapter 8*

1. The central section of this chapter is largely derived from an earlier work, my introduction to *Human Resource Management*, a collection of reprinted texts published by Thoemmes Press and Kyokuto Shoten in 2000. My thanks to Thoemmes Press for allowing me to re-use some elements of this work.
2. My thanks to Professor Sasaki Tsuneo for drawing my attention to this fascinating man and his career.
3. Gantt, H.L. (1905) 'The compensation of labour', *Engineering Magazine*, March, p. 883.
4. Watts, Frank (1921) *An Introduction to the Psychological Problems of Industry*, London: George Allen & Unwin, p. 118.
5. Emerson, Harrington (1913) *The Twelve Principles of Efficiency*, New York: The Engineering Magazine Co., p. 188.
6. Emerson, p. 197.
7. Redfield, William C. (1916) 'The employment problem in industry', *Annals of the American Academy of Political and Social Science*, May, p. 11.
8. Mayo, Elton (1930) 'The human effect of mechanization', *American Economic Review*, March, p. 156–76.
9. This and the above quote come from Watson, W.J. (1931) 'Scientific management and industrial psychology', *English Review*, April, pp. 444–55.
10. Many thanks to Professor Sasaki Jun for drawing my attention to Ohara and for providing the information about his career on which this passage is based.

# PART 3

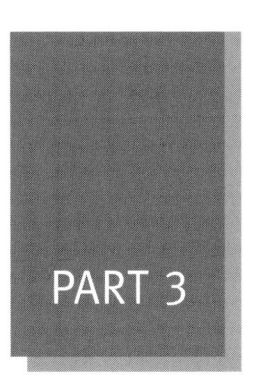

# THE PHILOSOPHY OF MANAGEMENT

# 9

# Ethics and identity

> The object of industry is not pure production of goods, but the production of those goods which, in the eyes of a part or the whole of the community, have some value
>
> *Oliver Sheldon*

The idea that management can be considered a philosophy was not an uncommon one in the nineteenth and early twentieth centuries. The founding decade of management philosophy can be said to be the 1830s, with the publication of *The Economy of Machinery and Manufactures* by the mathematician Charles Babbage and *The Philosophy of Manufactures* by the chemist and teacher Andrew Ure. The concept reached its apogee with the publication in 1924 of *The Philosophy of Management* by Oliver Sheldon, then an executive with the chocolate-makers Rowntree in York and a close friend and adviser to its head, Benjamin Seebohm Rowntree. Since then, though, the idea of a philosophy of management has gone somewhat out of fashion, and of today's management gurus, only Charles Handy speaks of management in philosophical terms.

This short Part III breaks away from the consideration of the practical disciplines of management discussed in Part II, and instead considers some of the 'big ideas' that lie at the heart of management. Attempts have been made, without much success, to describe concepts such as leadership, entrepreneurship and creativity as separate 'disciplines' or fields of study. As I noted in Chapter 1, these attempts seem somewhat absurd. Seeing leadership, entrepreneurship and creativity as merely separate concepts from management, or even as 'parts' or 'components' of management, is at best a sterile exercise. Management without leadership is like a Grand Prix racing car without an engine: expensive, elegantly built, and not going anywhere.

This first short chapter looks at another integral concept, ethics. Business ethics is often taught and studied as a separate subject in business schools, and indeed, a few companies even have 'ethics officers' (or some such; actual titles vary). This last seems particularly fantastical. Ethics officers are in effect glorified whipping boys, whom their colleagues bring out to be beaten when the company does something wrong. They are also sometimes used as compliance officers, to go around and make sure everyone else in the company behaves ethically.

Let us cut to the chase. Either a company behaves ethically or it does not. You cannot say that part of a company behaves ethically and part does not; that is like saying that your left foot behaves ethically because it does not kick the cat, while your right foot is unethical because it does.

**Either a company behaves ethically or it does not**

Okay, departments or subsidiaries of otherwise ethical companies go off the rails and do bad things, employing child labour, accidentally poisoning water supplies with toxic waste or similar. For head office to then devolve responsibility for this unethical behaviour onto the managers or subsidiaries concerned and pretend that otherwise all is well in the world is, in and of itself, unethical. First and foremost, practical business ethics is about taking responsibility.

Companies fall into ethical traps, as often as not, because they lose sight of the meaning of existence. That sounds extraordinarily deep, but actually is quite simple. What is a company *for*? Why does it exist? What purpose does it serve? For any company to behave ethically, its managers must be capable of answering those questions; for the answers are intimately connected to the nature of business ethics itself.

The history of business and management offers us four sets of answers to those questions, each of which deserves consideration. These are, briefly:

- the Aquinian view, derived from the philosophy of Thomas Aquinas, that being 'ethical' consists in working towards some previously determined end
- the Confucian view, that all relationships between individuals and groups are ethical constructs and must be governed by ethical norms
- the Friedman view, that organizations such as businesses are responsible to their owners, and that acknowledging any other responsibility is unethical
- the Davis view, that organizations such as businesses are formed as responses to social needs, and have no other function than to supply that need; thus they have an integral link with the societies that form them.

## Ethics is as ethics does

Writing in the thirteenth century, Thomas Aquinas has had a powerful and enduring impact on ethics in the West. Ethics, for Aquinas, is not a static concept. Each human being has an ultimate end towards which he or she is progressing. For medieval Christians, that 'ultimate end' was God, but Aquinas says that the ultimate end is also human happiness (which he equates with knowledge of God). Ethical behaviour, then, is that which promotes happiness and goodness. Likewise, deviation from that path is unethical; taking actions which detract from happiness and goodness is unethical.

Two points need to be noted. When we speak here of happiness, we do not mean the happiness of individuals; otherwise, it would be ethical for me to go out onto the highway and rob passers-by, provided I felt that this made me happy and brought me closer to God. It is the sum total of human happiness that is important. Second, it is not just deliberate action to do harm that is unethical. Failing to act, i.e. failing to progress down the road to ultimate happiness, can be considered unethical as well; neglect can be as harmful as deliberate action.

## The ethics of person and place

For Aquinas, then, ethics is a dynamic concept, moving forward towards a goal, and an action (or inaction) is judged as ethical or otherwise depending on whether it is oriented towards that goal. Ethics proceeds in a linear fashion. Seventeen hundred years earlier, Confucius had developed an ethical system which focused on the here and now. Behaving ethically, said Confucius, is a matter of doing right by those people around you, wherever you may be.

It is impossible to overestimate the importance of ethics to the Confucian way of thinking; one modern Chinese philosopher has called Confucianism nothing more than a series of guides to ethical behaviour. Confucian ethics is all about duties and responsibilities (and says absolutely nothing about rights, a term which only entered the Chinese language in modern times). It prescribes ethical behaviour in terms of relationships, such as 'filial piety', the duty to honour and obey one's parents (or teacher, or boss, or whoever is in authority over you). Much emphasis is placed on the correct form of behaviour, and rites and rituals were very important in the original Confucian system; ethics must not only be done, but must be seen to be done.

## Duty to one's self

The idea that the first and sole duty of a corporation's managers is to its owners and stockholders has a long history, but its most articulate expression came in the 1970s from the economist Milton Friedman. Against the background of a discussion of corporate social responsibility and pressure on large corporations to become more involved in charitable and community work, Friedman argued that such activity was itself unethical. Corporations, he said, do not have responsibilities; only individuals do. And for the managers of a large corporation, the first responsibility is to the shareholders, the owners of that corporation. Any profits made by the

> **For the managers of a large corporation, the first responsibility is to the shareholders, the owners of that corporation**

corporation are rightfully theirs; to spend those profits on schools, health care or social work is immoral.

As can be imagined, this view caused an outcry and Friedman found himself the target of abuse from many quarters. But note what Friedman is *not* saying. He is *not* saying that companies have *no* moral obligations; indeed, there is a very clear moral obligation to return a profit to shareholders. Nor is he saying that the shareholders cannot, if they so decide, instruct managers to spend money on providing social welfare and other public goods (although he was not generally in favour of this either, and believed that philanthropy should be a personal, not a corporate affair).

The Friedman affair evokes echoes of both Aquinian and Confucian thought. In terms of the latter, we have here repeated the concept of duty and responsibility as a core concept in business ethics. We also have the Aquinian idea of linear progress towards a greater good; a corporation's purpose is to make money for its shareholders.

## The social agent

This approach is found in several works of the early twentieth century, notably James Mooney's *Onward Industry!* (see Chapter 5) and Oliver Sheldon's *Philosophy of Management* (see above), but the earliest example I know of comes from John Davis's *Corporations* (1905).

Davis believes that corporations evolve as a societal response to social needs. For example, says Davis, a dominant social need in Europe in the Middle Ages was for religious belief; society's response was to provide structured groups capable of encouraging and developing religious faith, namely the Catholic church and, when this proved inadequate on its own, subordinate corporate bodies such as the monastic orders. In the turbulent political period following the Reformation, armed defence and security became a dominant need; the response was to create standing armies which, says Davis, adopted a corporate form.

And, he goes on to say, if corporations are social *forms*, then they must also have social *functions*. That is, whatever they do impacts on the societies which formed them and created them. To remain relevant, corporations must evolve to meet social needs. Those which do not, like the monastic orders over time, become redundant and are eventually destroyed by society which no longer has any use for them.

A lawyer by training, Davis does not go into detail on the ethical implications of this approach, but they are surely obvious. A corporation which is created by society has a duty to that society; unlike Friedman, he does not see corporations as being value-neutral, they have collective responsibilities and duties to those that created them. And, too, there is implicit the Aquinian notion of progress towards a goal. Corporations are created to satisfy certain needs on the part of society, and their function is to work to meet those needs.

## Asking the right questions

Ethics, said Aquinas, is about working towards a goal and not deviating from the path. Ethics, said Confucius, is about behaving correctly, acknowledging responsibility and doing one's duty towards others.

But what is the goal? And to whom are duties and responsibilities owed? Friedman and Davis give conflicting responses. The one argues that the corporation must serve the interests of its shareholders and the responsibilities of managers are to those shareholders. The other believes that the corporation should serve the interests of society, and its prime responsibilities are to society.

What is the right answer? One way of attacking the problem is to consider the following secondary problem: assume that you yourself are the owner and sole shareholder of the business. According to Friedman, your primary duty is to make money for yourself, and your only responsibility is to yourself. Then what? Have you, the individual, no further ethical duties, responsibilities or needs?

Yes, Milton Friedman would argue, you do; but that is not the same thing as a corporation's responsibility to its shareholders. Maybe, but this seems a very long way around in order to behave ethically. It should still be possible for corporations to behave ethically when dealing directly with the public, and cut out the middleman. Davis's argument that corporations have a duty to society seems to me unanswerable, on a pragmatic level if nothing else. When the monasteries ceased to serve society they were abolished. When the giant Morgan-backed trusts began to appear to act against the public interests, the US government responded with anti-trust legislation. Self-interest, if nothing else, would tend to suggest that companies should act ethically in their dealings with society.

**It should still be possible for corporations to behave ethically when dealing directly with the public, and cut out the middleman**

## Does it pay to be ethical?

There are plenty of examples of managers and business leaders behaving unethically, often quite openly, and flourishing. Cornelius Vanderbilt was one of the most ruthless entrepreneurs ever to enter a boardroom, and even the most sympathetic biographer is hard put to cast him in a favourable light; he drove competitors out of business (or took bribes from them to get out of the business himself), ran trains and ships that were dangerous to crew and passengers alike, and engaged in some share-dealing practices that, even by the standards of the time, were shady; he behaved abominably to almost everyone, including his son and heir William, and treated his customers like so many cattle.

Henry Ford started his career as an automobile manufacturer as a strongly paternalist employer who paid good wages and treated his workers well. By the end of his life, he was a suspicious, bitter man who treated his workers as potential enemies and encouraged his own force of internal security thugs, led by an ex-mafioso from Chicago, to spy on them and beat them up. Like Vanderbilt, his brutal behaviour towards his son Edsel, who died young of cancer, astonished even his closest supporters. (Ford's business success also waned as time went on; a friend of mine has suggested studying the early history of Ford by means of an 'Edsel index', correlating the progressive decline of Ford Motor Company with Ford's increasingly sadistic treatment of his son.)

Private morals do not seem to matter much either. Billy Butlin, founder of a British holiday camp empire and of modern mass tourism, insisted on correct behaviour between the sexes in his camps, but had a somewhat colourful private life which included leaving his second wife and moving in with her sister. Isaac Singer and Jack Daniels, founders of two of America's most enduring brands, were womanizers of a high order. William Whiteley, pioneer of the department store, came to a sticky end when he was murdered in his own office by his illegitimate son, whom he had refused to acknowledge.

Of all the tales of the wicked making good, that of Basil Zaharoff must surely top the list. Arms-dealer and bigamist, Zaharoff became an agent for several arms companies in Europe before the First World War. He developed what he called the 'Zaharoff system', which involved (1) selling a quantity of arms to one country, (2) informing that country's neighbours and enemies that the first country was now in possession of arms, and urging them to buy double the amount, and (3) repeating that process *ad infinitum*. Zaharoff's initial sale of a submarine to Greece led to orders for two more submarines from Greece's enemy, Turkey, and then five more from Turkey's enemy, Russia. To Zaharoff must go much credit for kicking off the European arms race and starting the First World War. Yet he received a knighthood, became fabulously wealthy, and married a duchess.

But, just because the wicked thrive, there seems no need to follow their example. For every corrupt manager who succeeds, there are others who fail. And there are many histories of men and women who succeeded and who also did have strong ethical principles. Sometimes they were less than perfect, like John Patterson who on the one hand ruthlessly drove his competitors out of business and on the other hand was passionate about caring for his employees and looking after their needs.

> **For every corrupt manager who succeeds, there are others who fail**

Perhaps Friedman had the wrong end of the stick; looking at business down through the ages, it is not organizations that are value-neutral, it is business itself, which can be either as ethical or unethical as the parties involved choose to make it. But for managers and their businesses, ethics is an ever-present part of our culture, our society, the world we live in. Some manage to ignore this and still succeed; but this surely is the more perilous path. It is, in the end, in our own best interests to be ethical.

# 10

# Leaders and servants

*A leader is someone chosen by the rest of the group to assist them in doing that which they already wish to do.*

*Thomas North Whitehead*

The idea that leadership is a consensual act – that is, the leaders lead only with the consent of those whom they govern – is a surprisingly old one. In antiquity, in both West and East, the idea that kings were chosen by heaven and ruled by divine right was a common one (the Tsars of Russia continued to hold to this view right down to the end in 1917). Many societies had close links between priesthoods or other religious orders and the crown, with the blessing of the former necessary to confer legitimacy on the latter; to this day, monarchs of England are crowned in Westminster Abbey by an archbishop, and presidents of the USA swear an oath to God with their hand on a bible.

Divine authority used to mean in theory that the ruler was chosen by God and was therefore untouchable by mortals. If the ruler went mad or proved impossibly corrupt or – worst sin of all – incompetent on the field of battle, there was in theory little one could do but pray to God or the gods to remove him. The more pragmatically minded sought methods that would remove the problem without compromising religious principles, of which hiring an assassin from a different and opposing religious faith was most common. The Byzantine Empire, which regarded its emperors as semi-divine beings, evolved a neat formula: if a coup or palace revolution failed, it signified that the emperor was indeed touched by God. If it succeeded, this proved that God's favour had been withdrawn and the emperor deserved to be overthrown. Chinese political thought offered a similar view on the withdrawal of divine favour, which, when signified, meant that the emperor deserved to be overthrown and replaced by one more worthy.

Thus, regardless of the theory of divine selection, in fact ancient rulers ruled with the consent of the governed. There were plenty of accepted mechanisms, of which assassination was one, for removing those who failed to live up to the mark. The same applied to self-selected leaders. Tribal leaders in many parts of the world, including Africa, North America and Asia, were often chosen by such means as ritual combat, in which a prospective leader would challenge and fight rivals and/or the incumbent for the position. This sometimes led to situations where an extraordinarily large, tough and stupid leader would emerge, but again there were always ways to get rid of him.

The democratic system, which began its long evolution in Athens around the sixth century BC, offered a simpler, more rational and less inherently violent way of replacing leaders who failed to meet the expectations of the governed. The Athenian philosophers, notably Plato and Aristotle, devoted much thought to the concepts of government, as did their Chinese near-contemporary Confucius. From all three, and from virtually every writer on politics and leadership since, comes a general consensus that is not far from the definition by Whitehead, quoted above: leadership, *to be effective*, requires that (a) those being led give the leader their consent, and (b) that leader and the led agree on a common aim. Whitehead, whose book *Leadership in a Free Society* in 1936 was derived in large part from his work as a researcher on the Hawthorne project (see Chapter 8), argued that anyone who attempted the role of leader *without* such consent was effectively forcing or driving employees. Not only was such behaviour unethical, he argued, it was also inefficient. Workers and leaders should always make common cause.

In order to be a good leader, find out what your organization wants to do, and then help it do it. It is a simplistic definition of leadership, but

I do not know of a better one. Over the past few years, I have researched and read the biographies of hundreds of successful business leaders down through history, and only in a tiny minority of cases did their style of leadership not conform to the above. Even in cases where the leaders did 'drive' their workers, some sort of consent could be detected. At Ford Motors in its most autocratic days in the 1930s, managers like Charles 'Cast Iron Charlie' Sorenson, a driver if there ever was one, commanded grudging respect from the workers and there was a commitment to a common goal: making and selling cars for profit. Leaders can and do use compulsion, as anyone who has studied military history will know: but the really great leaders, Frederick the Great, Napoleon, Alexander and the like, also used something more.

> In order to be a good leader, find out what your organization wants to do, and then help it do it

Over the past two decades, a number of books have been written attempting to analyze leadership and break it down into constituent parts. These books have come up with quite varied definitions, in which the issue of consent referred to above is one of the few constants. Illustrative in this context are the careers of notably successful business leaders of the past, who show a wide divergence of style and approaches. The following classification, with examples, gives some idea of the richness of variety available.

### THE PATERFAMILIAS

Just as many businesses are based on family models, so many leaders achieve success by taking on roles as surrogate father (or mother) figures to their employees. Matsushita Konosuke is one of the most famous of such in recent times. Although known in Japan as the 'God of Business Administration', Matsushita's style was human rather than divine. His powerful sense of mission, of bringing prosperity to the people through industrial progress, was shared with great passion by his workers, and was matched by his constant care for their welfare. His death in 1989 was accompanied by widespread mourning. George Cadbury was a highly protective employer deeply concerned for his people's welfare; like the Hong Kong department store owner Ma Ying-piao, who founded Sincere in 1900, he taught in the work's Sunday school every week. John Wanamaker, another department store entrepreneur, saw his employees' welfare as a paternal duty over and above making a profit. When he died in 1922, the city of Philadelphia closed for the day of his funeral and thousands lined the route of the funeral procession.

These leaders were all fine business brains and were highly successful as organizers and marketers. But their outstanding success was due to their personal style of leadership, which emphasized bonds of trust and obligation in very much a familial manner. They inspired loyalty through their apparent devotion to the well-being of their people. Their leadership style was founded on respect.

THE ENERGIZER

Some leaders are successful because they are able to instil in their organization a sense of energy, power and purpose, into which employees can buy. The most high-profile of these leaders are the great marketers and promoters, men like Samuel Colt and P.T. Barnum, or, in a less high-profile way, William Lever or the Chicago chewing-gum magnate William Wrigley. Others, like Robert Owen or Alfred Krupp (and how often do you see those two names in the same sentence?), channelled the bulk of their energies into organizing and leading the business, although Krupp turned away from this aspect of the business in later years. Energizers are often heroic figures, seemingly omni-present, and usually almost completely identified with the business itself in the public mind; their death or retirement is often seen as 'the end of an era', and one of the weaknesses of this style of leadership is that it can be difficult to find a successor suitable to fill the great man's shoes. Nonetheless, the energizers succeed because they are able to match their business ideas to a powerful energy and ability to get things done.

THE GUIDE

The opposite to the energizer, the guide is content to leave much of management in the hands of others, and to concentrate on planning and guiding the overall strategic course. John D. Rockefeller was a famous example of this style. At the head of the world's largest oil company, he seldom travelled or held meetings with any beyond his closest subordinates; his role, as he saw it, was to plan the company's direction and decide where it should go next. Once the decisions were taken, the implementation was handed over to subordinates. Cosimo dei Medici, after taking over the Medici Bank from his father, rarely left Florence and never visited any of the company's overseas branches; tours of inspection were left to others while Cosimo himself set the course by which the rest of the business would steer.

Guides sometimes have a problem in that their low profile can lead to weak relationships with employees. Successful guides are often those who also create a strong corporate culture in which employees know what is required of them and can use their initiative to a high extent. A good example here is Ernst Abbé, who created a culture of intense creativity at the Carl Zeiss works at Jena. Like some of the high-tech entrepreneurs of today, Abbé did not specify tasks for his workers; rather, he set them targets and then challenged them to meet or exceed these targets using whatever methods they deemed best. Guides succeed because they have a strong and powerful vision coupled to planning ability.

### THE INNOVATOR

The innovator or 'techno-entrepreneur' is someone who creates a vision of technological progress and encourages employees to work towards that. These men and women are not simply inventors; they are inventors with a vision. Abbé was one such; so too was Thomas Edison, who became an iconic figure even in his own lifetime. Edwin Land, the founder of Polaroid, was one of the great techno-entrepreneurs of twentieth-century America, who not only led much of the company's research but developed the overall corporate vision of the relationship between technology and progress. The scientists and engineers who made up Land's core staff forgave his frequent managerial failures because they shared his vision and believed he was leading them towards it.

Ultimately, Land failed because his directors and many of his employees no longer believed in his vision. More successful in this regard was Ibuka Masaru, who founded the Tokyo Communications Laboratory (later Sony Corporation) in a small office in a department store in the burned-out ruins of Tokyo in October 1945. Over the succeeding decades Ibuka, with colleagues such as Morita Akio, built up Sony into an international electronics goods giant. Ibuka's philosophy was to seek out and develop those products which no one else was willing to touch. When he was successful, others scrambled to imitate him; sometimes, as in the case of the VHS–Betamax conflict, he lost, but more often than not he kept his competitive advantage. Like Land, Ibuka generated a sense of excitement in pioneering new knowledge and new products. As with the guides, the innovators have vision, but theirs is based on scientific and technical knowledge and an understanding of the potential uses of that knowledge.

THE ORGANIZER

Superficially, the organizer appears to succeed by creating a first-class organization which is ideally suited to meet its goals. Yet, as noted in Chapter 5, the best organization in the world still requires to be led. One of the great organizers of modern times was Sir Eric Geddes. An executive at Great North-Eastern Railway, Geddes was seconded during the Second World War, first to the Ministry of Munitions where he greatly increased production; then to the British Expeditionary Force in France, where he reorganized railway transportation; and then to the Royal Navy, where he was made First Lord of the Admiralty and tasked with sorting out the administrative chaos that the Navy had got itself into. After a brief career in politics post-war, he became chairman simultaneously of Dunlop, one of the world's largest tyre manufacturers, and Imperial Airways, reorganizing and revamping both companies and greatly improving efficiency.

Geddes and other organizers like Inamori Kazuo, founder of Kyocera, succeed in part through their energy, but their most salient characteristic is their attention to detail. Geddes in particularly was famous for the quantities of research he undertook and his personal command of even the minutest details. A near contemporary in British management, Harry Pilkington, who built his family firm into the world's largest glass manufacturer, was also a tireless organizer with a superb command of detail, helped in his case by possession of a photographic memory.

THE CONTROLLER

Controllers are all-round leaders who insist on supervising every aspect of the business, from design through production to marketing. They are often autocrats: Henry Ford was a high-order controller who delegated reluctantly and then only to people whom he trusted implicitly. Less dictatorial but every bit as omnipresent was Henry J. Heinz, the processed-food manufacturer who set his own production standards, managed his own marketing and sales and took personal charge of employee relations. Controllers succeed because they animate the organization with their own sense of purpose. There is never any doubt as to who is the leader; but the vision is communicated so thoroughly and clearly that employees buy into it and make the organizational purpose their own.

THE SERVANT

The mirror image of the controller, the servant regards himself or herself as at the disposal of the organization. This is the truest and most exact parallel to the Whitehead definition; here, the leader seeks the explicit consent of the employees, unlike most of the models above where consent is implicit or assumed. True servants are rare. The twentieth century produced two well-known examples. Tomás Bat'a, the Czech shoe manufacturer who developed his own unique management style at his factory in Zlin, believed that the organization was much greater than he; his management philosophy involved the transfer of much responsibility to lower levels of the organization, while Bat'a reserved to himself the primary function of pulling the diverse elements together and coordinating their activities. In the 1990s Ricardo Semler, CEO of Semtech, took devolution of authority a step further and devolved virtually all authority to individual workers, noting cheerfully in the middle of the decade that he himself was now almost completely superfluous. In fact, both Bat'a and Semler provided a powerful focus for the reforms they instituted, and they continued to provide inspiration even after giving up much of their authority.

Respect, energy, vision, attention to detail, purpose and inspiration; these are the things a leader brings to the organization. Organizations can of course provide most of these things for themselves, but they require a focal point, a central reference from which all these virtues are seen to emanate. This last feature of leadership may be its most important. Truly great leaders, even the most autocratic, often surrender themselves to an extent to the organization and allow themselves to become part of it, to make its needs and goals their own. They do this not without cost to themselves. Shortly after retiring from Kodak, the business he had founded, George Eastman shot himself, believing that with his work finished his life was done as well. Edwin Gay, founding dean of Harvard Business School, died believing his career had been a failure. John Reith, founder of the BBC, and Montagu Norman, governor of the Bank of England who redefined central banking worldwide in the 1920s, both ended their days embittered and lonely, dwelling on their failures and unable or unwilling to remember their towering achievements. Leaders are well paid and compensated and receive honours and the respect of many. In return, they take on themselves the burden of organization and command. On good leaders, this burden leaves an indelible mark; it is only the bad leaders who come through the experience of command unchanged.

**Respect, energy, vision, attention to detail, purpose and inspiration; these are the things a leader brings to the organization**

# 11

# Risk and reward

> It would be far safer, sensible and more profitable to dismiss a do-nothing director and to put a bag of sand in his chair
>
> *Herbert N. Casson*

The term 'entrepreneur' was first popularized by the French economist and writer Jean-Baptiste Say sometime around 1800 (the term also appears in French economic writings around 1750). A supporter of the French Revolution and a follower of Mirabeau, Say worked as a journalist and frequently visited England, where he became familiar with the works of the economists Adam Smith and Thomas Malthus. Smith, in *The Wealth of Nations*, drew no formal distinction between the owner of capital and the manager or 'undertaker' who organized and ran the business. Say, however, noted that the role and functions of capitalist and undertaker are quite different, even when – as was often the case – those roles were combined in the same person. Dissatisfied with 'undertaker' or 'promoter', the previous words in use, he coined a new term, 'entrepreneur', which went on to enter the international management lexicon.

The nature and role of entrepreneurship were brought to their present state of the art largely thanks to the efforts of the Austrian economist Joseph Schumpeter in the early part of the twentieth century. Schumpeter's approach to entrepreneurship was primarily an economic one. It was entrepreneurs, Schumpeter said, who were the prime catalysts for innovation (see Chapter 12) and were thus responsible for all real economic growth. For Schumpeter, the creation of innovations is the primary function of entrepreneurs. They accept the costs and risks involved in innovation, and in return they capture the resulting rewards and profits.

Courage, says Schumpeter, is one of the chief virtues of the entrepreneur. Intelligence, in order to seek out new opportunities for innovation, is also important, but courage is required not only to take risks but also to challenge the establishment, to break through the instinctive resistance present in most societies most of the time to new ways of doing things. The combination of courage and intellect is rare, and entrepreneurs are consequently few in number.

> **The combination of courage and intellect is rare, and entrepreneurs are consequently few in number**

The limited number of entrepreneurs present in any society is borne out by modern research. In Britain, the Department of Trade and Industry reckons that only about 10 per cent of all businesses can be classified as 'growth firms'; that is, their top managers are willing to take the risks associated with growth and expansion and can be said to exhibit the combination of courage and intelligence that is required in an entrepreneur. Most of the remaining businesses in the country are in what the DTI calls a 'steady state'; that is, their owners and managers have reached a level of income and profitability which is sufficient to their needs, and are willing to limit growth in exchange for a lower level of risk. This category of managers are not necessarily lacking in either intelligence or courage; they simply see no need to run further risks. A third element in entrepreneurship, then, must be *motive*; one must not only have the necessary talents to be an entrepreneur, one must also have the driving will to become one.

Schumpeter also believed in a kind of 'wave theory' of entrepreneurship, and believed that entrepreneurs appear most frequently at certain moments in economic cycles. Historical analysis tends to bear this out. One great wave of entrepreneurship can be detected in northern Italy between about 1250 and 1500, when easy access to capital and an optimistic spirit accompanying the Italian Renaissance led men to gamble their livelihood and sometimes their lives on the chance to grow a great business. Remember how Iris Origo, commenting on the career of the merchant and cloth-maker Francesco Datini, remarked on how during the Renaissance, the real distinction between businessmen did not concern the size of the business or the products in which they dealt, but the attitude of mind which led some to stick to the safety of domestic markets and others to venture forth into the high-risk, high-return milieu of international markets. This was a great age of business adventure, when Marco Polo travelled the length of Asia and trade routes spanned the breadth of the planet from the Spice Islands to Iceland.

Another such wave occurred in the late eighteenth and early nineteenth centuries in the textile industry, possibly the greatest sustained wave of entrepreneurship of all time. Arkwright and his factory system were the touchstone on which further innovations were based, but many others followed. Samuel Oldknow took Arkwright's ideas on quality and ran with them, producing the highest quality yarn yet seen in his first factory and then risking all his success so far on a massive campaign of expansion that saw him running twenty mills in under ten years, before his supplies of capital failed and he was forced to retrench. After Oldknow came Robert Owen, son of a Welsh saddler, who by sixteen years of age was a partner in his own business and by nineteen was running a factory employing five hundred people. At twenty-four he bought his own mill; at twenty-nine, to secure the hand of the woman he loved, he mortaged his own future to buy New Lanark from David Dale, and, instead of cautiously settling for profits, used the opportunity to create one of the most ambitious experiments in workplace management ever seen.

**Courage, intelligence and motivation; three terms which could not better summarize the key features of the leaders of the Industrial Revolution**

Last on the roll of heroes of the Industrial Revolution must come the Yorkshireman Titus Salt. An innovator, Salt set up his first business with the purpose of making high-grade cloth from alpaca wool. Many had tried this before and all had failed, and it was widely believed that the task was impossible. Working in great secrecy, Salt and his partners quickly developed the technology for making alpaca cloth. Within a decade, he owned six mills, had become mayor of Bradford, had taken steps towards housing reform in the city, and had built his own giant factory and model village at Saltaire, north of the city, employing 4,500 people. Courage, intelligence and motivation; three terms which could not better summarize the key features of the leaders of the Industrial Revolution.

The same features were present in abundance during the period from 1890–1920 when the automobile industry grew from tinkerer's hobby to global giant. Henry Ford tried and failed three times before he managed to get Ford Motors off the ground. Ransom Olds founded one company, Oldsmobile, lost control of it to his financial backers, and immediately launched another, REO, both founded on the well-designed, low-cost cars that were his especial vision. Louis Renault, driven by what his friends referred to as a 'furious energy', launched his first car in 1899. Tough and stubborn, Renault pursued his own vision of engineering excellence right up until the day of his death in 1944, in a French prison on a trumped-up charge of collaboration with the Nazis. In Britain, Herbert Austin declared his life's work to be the bringing of motorized transport to the world, and pursued that vision with a single-mindedness and dedication matched only by his friend and rival William Morris (later Lord Nuffield). In Japan, Toyoda Kin'ichi and later Honda Soichiro showed the same dedication and drive in the development of a domestic auto industry that would first compete with foreign imports, then drive them out of the market, then invade the foreigners' own home markets in the USA and Europe.

Courage, intellect and motivation: let us have one more quick example. Though British industry in general has been rightly castigated for its rigidity and failure to adapt in the late nineteenth century, the shipbuilding industry was an honourable exception to the rule. In shipbuilding, Britain led the world; few other countries bothered to develop large-scale shipyards when Britain launched ships of a quality beyond imagination at affordable prices. Leading this movement was the Belfast-based firm of Harland & Wolff. Its co-founder and entrepreneurial genius was Edward Harland, born in Scarborough, the son of a doctor and amateur scientist who was a friend of George Stephenson, the developer of the first railway steam locomotive. Apprenticed at the Tyneside engineering works of Stephenson, Harland was educated at the cutting edge of engineering and shipbuilding technology, and by twenty-two had mastered both shipbuilding and management. Taking a job at Robert Hickson's yard in Belfast, then an insignificant port with just a few small shipyards, Harland suffered for five years under incompetent management, knowing all the while that he could do better.

In 1858 he got his chance. Hickson went bankrupt, and Harland, with capital provided by his friend G.C. Wolff, nephew of the Liverpool shipowner Gustavus Schwabe, bought the yard. Belfast, for Harland, was a *tabula rasa*. With no real history of shipbuilding, there were no entrenched practices and ways of doing work to be overcome; he could design his own systems with a free hand. Unskilled labour was cheap and plentiful; skilled hands could be recruited from yards on the mainland, using a combination of high wages and the chance to be part of something big and new. Schwabe, impressed by the young yardmaster's skills, began ordering ships from him almost immediately. For the next three decades, Harland & Wolff was at the forefront of innovation in ship construction and by the end of that time, when Harland handed over control to William Pirrie (see Chapter 4), it was the world's leader in shipbuilding. No better example of the three virtues of entrepreneurship can be found.

## A finite commodity

At times like those cited above, the supply of entrepreneurship seems almost limitless; there are more entrepreneurs than there is capital to support them. In the 1980s and 1990s there was another great Schumpeterian wave of entrepreneurship in the software industry, with plenty of men and women coming forward ready to run great risks in search of great profit. The dotcom collapse of early 2000 killed the dreams of most, with even giants like Son Masayoshi of Softbank in Japan teetering on their pedestals. Never has the need for courage and judgement been so well illustrated. Sadly, in any entrepreneurial boom, there always seems to be more of the former than there is of the latter.

This pattern of entrepreneurial boom and bust noted by Schumpeter is now a well-recognized phenomenon. One of the vexing problems, for economies and for companies alike, is how to iron out the peaks and troughs. It is better, surely, to have a little bit of entrepreneurship all of the time, rather than a glut at some points and none at others. This leads us to two further considerations. First, entrepreneurship seems to be in part inspired by conditions. The time has to be right for it. As in the gold rushes of the nineteenth century, there has to be gold in them thar hills to lure most of us out of our armchairs. There is no entrepreneurship without inspiration, and inspiration in turn must come either from particular circumstances, or from a very well-entrenched national or corporate culture which encourages risk and does not excessively penalize failure.

Second, we are not all entrepreneurs. As noted, the British government estimates that only about 10 per cent of British firms can be classed as 'entrepreneurial', in that they are willing to take risks to seek growth. The proportion may be higher in other regions, such as parts of East Asia or some regions of the USA; it may well be lower in others. Most of us, though, would prefer a quiet life and the certainty of a roof over our heads than the prospect of profits that might at the end of the day prove illusory.

**The British government estimates that only about 10 per cent of British firms can be classed as 'entrepreneurial', in that they are willing to take risks to seek growth**

Much the same is true of managers. Only a small proportion of managers truly want to lead; most prefer to delegate some other person or organization to provide leadership for them, as was described in the previous chapter. To understand this phenomenon, consider a well-known concept from psychology, Abraham Maslow's hierarchy of needs. Human beings, says Maslow, have a variety of different needs, but these needs have varying levels of importance at different times in our lives. At the most basic level there are fundamental physical needs, such as the need for food; when our bellies are empty, we have trouble considering anything else. Once we have enough to eat, we then seek to satisfy our need for personal security and ward off danger. Safe and satiated, we then seek to gratify our need to belong to a group, to receive the affection and respect of others. This achieved, we then seek to enhance our own self-esteem, to achieve reputation, prestige and honour in the eyes of our peers. Last of all, says Maslow, we may seek what he calls 'self-actualization', the desire for self-fulfilment, to become what we believe ourselves capable of being.

The hierarchy of needs is prepotent; that is, lower level needs, if unsatisfied, will always override higher level needs. The drive for entrepreneurship is part of the highest level of all, the need for self-actualization. People who become entrepreneurs do so because they are seeking fulfilment and realization of their own potential. Most of us never get that far; the needs for security, for belongingness and for esteem predominate. How many of us, offered a choice between a role which would give us the esteem and respect of our peers and one which would give us no esteem but a chance to fulfil our own inner dreams, would choose the latter? A lot of us would like to think we would; in practice, few do, especially when the former offers the chance to pay the mortage as well.

Entrepreneurship is a scarce commodity. Recently, some business schools have begun to try to teach entrepreneurship to their students. This concept is doomed to failure. Those students who have the gifts of entrepreneurial courage and intellect will become entrepreneurs if they choose to do so. For the rest, every so often, the teaching process will inculcate a series of actions and principles which, if followed slavishly, will lead to a positive business result that looks like entrepreneurial success. The law of averages says this must happen, just as if you teach enough monkeys to type, one of them will eventually bang out a quote from Shakespeare.

If history teaches anything about business, it is that entrepreneurship thrives in a supportive culture, but that true entrepreneurship is a combination of risk, motivation and intelligence that coincides in only one manager in ten, at best. Rather than teaching entrepreneurship to the masses, we should be looking at ways of identifying entrepreneurial potential and then encouraging and supporting that potential. In that process, all managers have a role to play; we should become capable of spotting entrepreneurs even if we do not have their attributes. Let us study history, not so that we can become entrepreneurs, but so that we can learn to recognize entrepreneurship when we see it.

# 12

# The quest for knowledge

> I have found that knowledge is infinite. The longer I live, the more I realize that what I know is only a very small thing. On every road I have travelled, I have found there is no end to it. Every man who wishes to live a worth-while life must keep on learning as long as he has breath. I dare say that when my doctor tells me I have only three more days to live, I shall begin to study coffins
>
> *Herbert N. Casson*

Knowledge, in business and management, is the new rock and roll. Practically every book on management these days has something to say about knowledge: what is it, where you get it, how you control it. Knowledge is capital, knowledge is power, knowledge is the new key to competitive advantage. Knowledge, one might be forgiven for thinking, is god.

The importance of knowledge cannot be denied, but anyone who has read the history of management, or indeed business history more generally, must surely feel compelled to take issue with the idea implicit, and sometimes explicit, in much modern writing on the subject, that all this is somehow new. Nowhere else is the passion on the part of theorists to reinvent the wheel so outstandingly clear. The latest fad is the 'knowledge organization', a term which clearly implies that there is some other kind. The 'stupid organization', perhaps? Well, my bank appears to be attempting to qualify for this status, but it has not quite got there yet. There is no such thing as an organization without knowledge. At the most primary level, everyone in the organization has to know *something*, such as what the organiza-

**There is no such thing as an organization without knowledge**

tion is, who at least some of the other members are, and what their own function is. The organization whose members lack even that level of knowledge exists only in the realm of Dilbert cartoons.

Starting from there, we go up a level. As discussed in Chapter 8, even the organization founded on the most intensive division of labour requires knowledge on the part of its members. The range of knowledge and skills required of each may be narrow, and there may be little or no requirement on the part of members to share their knowledge; but the sum total of knowledge in organizations like the Ford Motor Company before the First World War is awe-inspiring.

Knowledge is omnipresent. What changes is how we generate, organize, structure and use it. The new field of knowledge management has had at least this impact; it had made us all think in a new light about how we ourselves use and organize knowledge. If, as seems to be the case, we are all knowledge managers in some way, then another fact becomes clear: managers have always been knowledge managers. Since the dawn of organization, managers have functioned by using their knowledge – and often little else – to plan, guide, govern and coordinate the activities of members of organizations.

The uses of knowledge in management are many and various. Here I want to talk about just two, albeit two of considerable importance: innovation, in both products and processes, and more general management ideas of how knowledge can be employed to improve and enhance company effectiveness in broad terms.

## Product innovation: knowledge made tangible

The nineteenth century and early twentieth century was the great age of the Inventor as Hero. Edison, Samuel Morse, Alexander Graham Bell and the Wright brothers were folk heroes, with a status not so very different to magicians in earlier ages. Few really knew what they did in the solitude of their laboratories and test rooms; most people saw only the results, and marvelled.

In fact, the process of innovation, like war, consists of long periods of tedium punctuated by short bursts of intense excitement. Making a breakthrough discovery, the kind that results in shouts of Eureka! is an exciting time for all, particularly when someone gets out a notebook or a calculator and starts working out the potential profit to be made. But moments of these are the culmination of a process that can take years. Often, the original flash of inspiration comes when the inventor has neither the time nor the resources to make good on it, and more years must elapse until the invention can be tested and marketed.

Innovation is hard work and expensive, and yet everyone must do it. The company that cannot innovate even on an incremental basis, upgrading its products and services to keep ahead of, or at least up with, the competition will probably come to a messy end. But how is it to be done?

The key, as examples over the past couple of centuries show, would appear to lie in part in the creation of a managerial and corporate culture where innovation is not only possible, but expected. Ibuka Masaru, and after him Morita Akio, created a brilliant example of such a culture at Sony, with their philosophy of doing what others would not do; this approach gave Sony first-mover advantage on a number of occasions, and only once, with Betamax, was the company unable to translate this into enduring advantage. Other Japanese companies have shown equal ability in creating such a culture. Inamori Kazuo, the driven founder-manager of Kyocera, and Honda Soichiro, the technological genius behind Honda, provide examples of a type common in Japan in the first half of the twentieth century: restless dreamers, gnawed by an urge to create and to be their own masters, who went out into the wildnerness, made their inventions and built their organizations with that urge as the central guiding force.

America has plenty of examples as well. Thomas Edison, a restless dreamer if there ever was one, was not a spectacular success as a businessman, and much of the management of his most important company, the Edison Electric Illuminating Company, set up with backing from J.P. Morgan to bring electric lighting to New York, was delegated to others. But as one who knew him well commented, Edison did not bring the spirit of innovation to his own business, but to all of American society: he showed how scientific methods could be used in industry in a wide variety of ways, not just in technology and machinery. As this friend commented, 'he [Edison] is the founder of modern industry in this country. He has formed for us a new kind of declaration of independence…in the nature of a kit of tools, by the use of which each and every person among us has gained a larger measure of economic liberty than had ever previously been thought possible.'

> **Edison did not bring the spirit of innovation to his own business, but to all of American society**

The friend was Henry Ford.

That blend of technological idealism and practical tools for reaching it was repeated later in the twentieth century in the philosophy of Edwin Land. Another restless dreamer, a tall, romantic man who looked quite a lot like Cary Grant, 'Din' Land saw the ideal business of the future as being what he called a 'science-based corporation', in which the core of the corporation was a team of researchers whose sole function was to generate knowledge and potential new products. The exploitation of these products would then be carried out by management teams centred around each product line. Polaroid itself was structured along these lines, and it is possible that this model was the partial inspiration for Ken Olsen's 'matrix organization' model which he developed at Digital Equipment Corporation in the 1950s and which has been widely analyzed and commented on since.

The great European inventors of the day were less flamboyant and less intense, but they too understood the importance of a culture of innovation. William Lever, soap-maker and master of the art of branding, was a prosaic innovator who believed that his products were helping to improve people's lives but also saw them, quite pragmatically, as a means of besting his opposition. His culture of innovation was based firmly in marketing, as he encouraged his firm to develop new products in line with the needs of the market. The Cadburys, George and Edward, were more idealistic, as might be expected, and believed strongly in the social value of their products, but their approach to innovation was practical and methodical. Under Edward Cadbury's leadership there existed a kind of parallel organization, based on devices such as works committees and suggestions schemes, which brought virtually every worker in the company into the innovation process.

Engineering in Victorian Britain was practised as a science but often treated as art by its practitioners who, after the example of Isambard Kingdom Brunel, saw beauty and poetry in not only their creations but in the art of creating. Charles Parsons, son of an earl and the inventor of the turbines that powered virtually every ship and power station in the world for decades, created a centre of excellence at his factory at Heaton, near Newcastle. Parsons had a high regard for his workers and their technical skills, and preferred to refer to them as artisans rather than workmen. He paid very high wages for the time, hoping to attract the most skilled and most creative engineers, and by and large he succeeded; a number of engineers who rose to later prominence in other fields passed through the ranks at Parsons between 1890 and 1930. In 1919 Parsons, who had long been concerned that the country lacked sufficient numbers of engineers for its needs, set up an apprentice school at Heaton. His efforts created a technological advantage that lasted for four decades. During that period, Parsons's firm had probably the largest skills base of any engineering firm in the world; it was also one of the most profitable.

Ernst Abbé created a very similar culture at the optical equipment-maker Carl Zeiss Jena which lasted until it was snuffed out by the Nazis and then the communist government of East Germany. Abbé, a former university professor, regarded creation as a thing to be done for its own sake, and the profits made thereby (which were vast) were incidental. Few went as far as Hans Renold, the Swiss-born chain-maker whose company, based near Manchester, could have had a world monopoly of drive chains for automobiles, based on his patents. In fact, Renold was quite content with his share of the British market and simply gave away the US patent rights to the bush roller chain, going so far as to encourage and provide technical support to the American firm which went on to make and sell it there. Renold's son, who took over the business in the 1930s, remarked of his father that:

> ... the keynote of his whole life was a passion for good work. He

enjoyed money when it came, but commercial success was of quite secondary interest. What drove him on was the joy of creation – of doing something just as well as he knew how. 'Good enough' was a sentiment that was quite unknown to him.

## Process innovation: knowledge in action

Innovation, of course, is not just about making new things but about making the same thing better. One of the great process innovators of all time must surely be Richard Arkwright. Enough has been said by now in this book about Arkwright, in Chapter 2 and *passim*, but it is worth repeating the salient point about his career. With the spinning frame and his later developments of the factory system, Arkwright did not just invent a way to spin yarn faster; he also invented a way to spin it *better*, producing a good of higher quality. The best process innovations see quality of product and efficiency of product go hand in hand. That too was the philosophy of the great Toyoda Kin'ichi, the leader who brought Toyota into the automobile age, and his managers, notably the Japanese quality guru Ishikawa Kaoru. For Ishikawa, perfect efficiency in production meant nothing unless perfect quality was achieved as well.

**The best process innovations see quality of product and efficiency of product go hand in hand**

It is time we talked about Ford. Leaving aside the paranoid old man who drove his company to the brink of ruin in the 1930s, the Ford of the period 1900–1915 was not only a first-class designer but a brilliant process engineer, who was able for a decade to command the services of some of America's best managerial talent: James Couzens, William Knudsen, Charlie Sorenson among them. Ford is chiefly famous for the Model T, but to my mind his finest achievement was the assembly plant at Highland Park, Illinois.

Designed by architect Albert Kahn and purpose-built for the production of the Model T, the Highland Park plant covered sixty-two acres. It featured the largest assembly line yet seen in the world, and had been carefully engineered to increase car production to speeds beyond anything yet attempted. Instead of 12–14 hours to assemble a finished car, the previous norm, Model Ts could now be assembled from stocks of finished parts in an hour and a half. The opening of Highland Park sent a shock through the US business world. Visitors from other companies and even other countries flocked to see it; among those who learned from Ford's production methods was the Czech shoemaker Tomas Bat'a, who would later establish his own revolutionary approach to management in Europe. Ford won plaudits not only for his mechanical engineering but for his attention to detail and carefully engineered production system, which was based in large part on the methods of scientific management then in vogue, but also owed much to earlier mass production systems such as that developed by Cyrus Hall McCormick at International Harvester. In terms of worker relations, too, Ford was seen as a visionary. In 1914 he cut the working day to eight hours, believing this to be the optimum working day for worker efficiency, and also initiated the famous $5 daily wage, nearly double the going rate in the industry. When Highland Park began recruiting workers, it received something like a hundred applications for every job going, meaning Knudsen and Sorenson, the production supremos, could take the cream in terms of skilled workers. Highland Park itself became a legend around the world. Twenty years later, touring a truck factory in the Soviet Union, Sorenson walked down the assembly line and was greeted with shouts of 'Hi, Charlie!' It transpired that some of the men had worked at Highland Park, and its fame and that of Sorenson had spread to the rest of the crew.

River Rouge, the vast Ford plant which opened in 1927 to produce the Model A, dwarfed Highland Park in scale and was lauded by engineers, but it lacked the beautiful simplicity of Highland Park; over-complex and dogged with problems, it never really worked as it should have. But for the Model T and Highland Park, two innovations perfectly designed for their time, Henry Ford deserves his immortality.

## A philosophy of learning

Many of the innovators mentioned put learning and knowledge generation as a core value of their corporation: Land, Honda, Inamori and Edison all saw learning in these terms. But there are other examples of managers and leaders who saw knowledge not as necessarily leading directly to product and process innovations but as an important grounding function, a necessary foundation for a strong and vigorous organization. Sir Eric Geddes, mentioned in Chapter 10, put the collection and analysis of knowledge as among his first management principles, and in every organization he ran, established permanent systems for collecting and monitoring information. A Briton, Geddes was thus part of a tradition of information collection and analysis that stretched back to the twelfth century and the great administrators Richard Fitz Neal and Hubert Walter.

> There are other examples of managers and leaders who saw knowledge not as necessarily leading directly to product and process innovations but as an important grounding function

The great Japanese educator and polymath Fukuzawa Yukichi, founder of Keio University, played a pivotal role in transforming Japanese business culture after the Meiji Restoration of 1868 by constantly emphasizing the role of and need for education. Almost single-handedly, Fukuzawa instilled a culture of learning and knowledge-gathering into Japanese business, a culture which survives to this day; even now, Japanese companies and managers are superior to almost all others in the world in terms of environmental scanning and the storage and use of acquired knowledge. Fukuzawa seldom discriminated between 'useful' and 'not useful' knowledge; everything from management methods and new technology to law, politics, economics and psychology was gathered into his net and turned into practical knowledge for businesses.

In the final analysis, two features have distinguished the innovative business through history. One has been this philosophy of learning, usually accompanied by a belief in the intrinsic value of learning and a refusal to discriminate between categories of knowledge; *all* knowledge is valuable, in the end. The second has been the role of the leader as innovator or, at least, catalyst for innovation. Though there are exceptions, most of the great innovative firms of the past, whether the innovation be in product, process, or even forms of organization as described in Chapter 8, have been firms where the leader has driven the innovative process forward.

To manage, I argued at the start of this chapter, is to manage knowledge. Does it follow that to manage is to innovate? Not all managers are innovators; some pass through their entire working careers without a single original idea (admittedly, most of these do seem to work for my bank). But management should not be about doing the ordinary, the humdrum, the daily routine, purely for its own sake. Routine there must be, alas, or things would fall apart. But long-term success in management surely must be about creating innovation, not so much in great inventions that change the world, but in developing a culture of progressive thinking and learning. In that, surely, we all have our own part to play.

# 13

# Personal postscript

> There are nearly as many myths and delusions in business as there were in ancient philosophies and religion. I have seen many an industrial process that was as absurd as a ceremonial in a temple in Thibet
>
> Herbert N. Casson
>
> History is not what you think. It is what you remember
>
> Sellars and Yeatman, 1066 And All That

This book is by no means complete. Management has a history of at least four millennia, spanning the globe; its full history would – and should – fill a library. Even as a superficial sketch, there are many topics that have had to be left out lest this book become an encyclopedia. I have, for example, said very little about quality. It would have been fascinating to add a chapter to describe the history of the quality movement, from Arkwright and Babbage in the Industrial Revolution to W. Edwards Deming and Kaoru Ishikawa in the twentieth century. I would have liked to have taken the time to examine the origins and ideas behind the quality movement in Japan and to tell stories such as the marvellous account of an American computer-maker which contracted with a Japanese firm to supply a hundred thousand microchips. In the grip of quality fever, the American buyers firmly instructed the Japanese supplier that the acceptable defect rate was one in 10,000. When the order arrived, there was included a small box containing ten chips over and above the order. Puzzled, the Americans contacted the supplier in Japan and asked about the box. 'Oh', came the reply. 'Sorry, we forgot to label it. Those are the ten defects you asked for.'

I would have liked, too, to devote a chapter to management education, to talk about Edwin Gay and the founding of Harvard Business School, Fukuzawa and the birth of management education in Japan, and further back, Thomas Malthus and the founding of Haleybury College, the East India Company's management training college that is arguably the first business school in the world. I would have liked to have devoted a chapter to women in management, and to have said more about some of the great female pioneers like Florence Nightingale, who brought professional management to health care for the first time. I should have liked to have had a chapter on culture and its role and impact on management through the ages, and another on globalization, showing how Marco Polo and his contemporaries developed a global view of business long before Ohmae Kenichi and James Burnham put the idea into our heads in the twentieth century.

> **I would have liked to have devoted a chapter to women in management**

But these ideas remain ready to be discussed, and as for the ideas that I *have* so cursorily covered, there is much, much more to be said. If this book inspires even a few readers to go out and conduct their own investigations into the history of management, asking their own questions and drawing their own lessons from its study, then it will have succeeded in its purpose. Which brings me to my final point.

There is always a temptation when writing a book to add a concluding chapter which asks the question, 'So what have we learned from all this?' and then goes on to answer it. But history is not like that. I do not believe that it is possible, from the vantage point of the present, to turn to history and ask questions about the meaning of our time, or of the future, and receive firm, clear-cut answers.

History's value is more subtle. The past, a wise man once said, is a mirror we can hold up to examine ourselves. The value of business history and management history is not in any ability to offer concrete practices or sets of guidance for management now and in the future. We cannot say that, because Cosimo dei Medici or Richard Arkwright or Henry Ford responded to a particular challenge in a particular way, we in our own time should necessarily respond to the same kinds of challenges in the same ways. Those methods might indeed work; then again, they might not. Ultimately, the response is down to our own judgement.

But we can use history for many things. One of the chief of these, I believe, is inspiration. In Chapter 1, I argued that management needs to study its heroes. In the discipline of history, proper, the 'great man' theory is now out of fashion, and the study of the lives of individuals is decried by neo-Marxist historians, who prefer history as dialectic, and neo-Braudellian historians, who favour history as process. Maybe the study of the lives and careers of people like Matsushita and Heinz and Lever and Eric Geddes and Ernst Abbé would offend the purist among historians; but for managers in companies racked by change and threatened by competitive forces from all sides, seeking inspiration and reassurance, these stories and others like them can offer a power of comfort in the still watches of the night.

History can also serve as a useful filter through which to examine new management trends and fads. As Casson remarked, for all its supposed rationality, management is extraordinarily full of odd and superstitious beliefs. (There are still, for heaven's sake, companies using graphology (the study of handwriting) as a means of analyzing suitable candidates for employment, and doubtless these companies are convinced that this is a really new and up-to-date technique.) It is always interesting to see just how many 'new' ideas turn out to be old ideas dressed up in new clothes. Having recognized the imposters for what they are, it is then possible to look at what happened to these concepts in their earlier form and how and why they succeeded or failed. My own personal favourite is the mail-order marketing industry in the late nineteenth century, when genuine pioneers like Aaron Montgomery Ward and Richard Sears used new methods of communication and transportation to develop a new method of marketing based on a complex and sophisticated distribution model. A hundred years on, the dotcom retailers, in the grip of a massive delusion that they were doing something 'new', tackled the same problem but forgot to develop the distribution model. Their failure caused more than one wry smile in the ranks of the business history community. It would all be quite funny, if it had not cost so much.

**History can also serve as a useful filter through which to examine new management trends and fads**

I will not belabour the point further. The beauty of history is its endless flexibility. It offers no hard and fast certainties; what it offers instead is a fertile ground for examining and testing ideas and concepts and analyzing information. Everything in business is new, and yet everything in business is as old as the hills. Accept and understand that paradox, and you will have added a powerful new weapon to the armoury of your business skills.

# Index

| | |
|---|---|
| Abbe, Ernest, | 238 |
| Adamieki, Karel, | 72 |
| administration, art of, | 116 |
| advertising and publicity, | 106–108 |
| Aquinas, Thomas, | 81–82, 253 |
|    writings of, | 80 |
| Arkwright, Richard, | 45, 89 |
| | |
| Babbage, Charles, | 47 |
| Bedaux, Charles, | 66 |
| brands, | |
|    early history of, | 109–110 |
|    living the, | 90–92 |
| Buddhist strategy, | 188–189 |
| bureaucracy, | |
|    2000 years of, | 34–35 |
|    China, in, | 126–127 |
|    excessive, | 144 |
|    middle ages, in, | 128–129 |
|    modern image of, | 125–126 |

business,
   corporate hybrid form, 143–145
   emerging new models of, 7
businesses, state of, 5
businessleaders, plight of, 3

Cadbury, George, 240
Carnot, Lazare, 141–142
Casson, Herbert, 57–58
Cherington, Paul, 84
Clausewitz, Karl Von, 197–199
Colt, Samuel, 92–93
cooperatives, 243
Coutts, Thomas, 164–165

Daoist strategy, 188–189
Datani, Francesco, 123
Deloitte, William, 172–173
direct sales management, 94–95
distribution,
   challenge and risk, 105–106
Dutton, Henry Post, 233–234

early traders, 30–34
efficiency,
   principles of, 53–57
   scientific management, versus, 67
Emerson, Harrington, 53
employers, relationship with workers, 61
ethics,
   business and, 257
   duty to one's self, 254–255
   identity and, 251–259
   person and place, 254
   private morals, 258

| | |
|---|---|
| questions and, | 256 |
| social agent, | 255–256 |
| everything is new, | 11–12 |
| explorers, status of, | 4 |
| | |
| factory system, | |
| reaction to, | 11 |
| faith, organization and, | 129–135 |
| families and partners, | 118 |
| finance, | |
| accounting and control, | 169–174 |
| auditors, appointment of, | 173–174 |
| banking, | 162–163, 165–167 |
| commercial paper, | 158–160 |
| credit, rise of, | 157–158 |
| evolution of, | 153–156 |
| futures, | 161–162 |
| professional, rise of the, | 174–176 |
| role of, | 152 |
| financial markets, | |
| bubbles, bursting of, | 15–16 |
| déjà vu and, | 176–177 |
| focus, narrowness of, | 19 |
| Frederick the Great, | 139–141 |
| freewill, impact of, | 14 |
| Fugger, | |
| Hans Jakob, | 121 |
| Jakob, | 121, 160–161 |
| fundamentals, deviation from, | 19–20 |
| future, understanding the, | 14 |
| | |
| Gilbreth, Frank and Lillian, | 65 |
| Gresham, Sir Thomas, | 162 |
| Guggenheim, Daniel, | 218–219 |

| | |
|---|---|
| Haney, | 84–86 |
| Heinz, Henry J, | 108–109 |
| history, | |
|     ignoring, consequences of, | 18–22 |
|     place of, | 5–6 |
|     prediction and, | 13–16 |
|     views of, | 10 |
| Hongzhang, Li, | 127–128 |
| human resources management, | 211 |
|     capitalism, spirit of, | 215–216 |
|     face-to-face contact, | 212–220 |
|     growing people, | 230–232 |
|     Hawthorne studies, | 232–233 |
|     personnel management, | 228–230 |
|     places or work and, | 234–235 |
|     profit-sharing and, | 236–239 |
|     spirit of, | 235–236 |
|     welfare schemes, | 239–242 |
| humility, | 21 |
| | |
| industrial democracy, | 242–243 |
| isolation, | 21–22 |
| | |
| Jomimi, Antoine-Henri, | 196 |
| | |
| Kautilya, | 126 |
| Knowledge, | |
|     philosophy of learning, | 283–284 |
|     process innovation, | 281–282 |
|     product innovation and, | 277–281 |
|     quest for, | 276–284 |
| Kotler, Philip, | 81 |
| Krupp, Alfred, | 89, 90 |
| Kwok, Robert, | 119 |

## INDEX

| | |
|---|---|
| lawyers, common heritage of, | 5 |
| leadership, | |
|    consent and, | 260–262 |
|    energizing, | 263 |
|    guiding, | 263–264 |
|    innovation and, | 264–265 |
|    organizer and, | 265–266 |
|    paternalism and, | 262–263 |
|    servant and, | 266–267 |
| Lever, William Hesketh, | 96–99 |
| Lewis, John, | 236–237 |
| Liang, Zhuge, | 187 |
| | |
| Machiavelli, Niccolo, | 191–199 |
| Magosaburo, Ohara, | 240–241 |
| management, | |
|    faces of, | 25–27 |
|    fields of, relationship between, | 6–7 |
|    industrial revolution, after the, | 44–48 |
|    middle ages, in, | 36–40 |
|    professionalism and, | 73–74 |
|    revolution, | 50–75 |
|      goals of, | 70 |
|    scientific, | 60–66 |
|      failings of, | 72–73 |
| managers, | |
|    ethical view of, | 16–17 |
|    history, view of, | 9–10 |
| marketing, | |
|    brand, living the, | 90–92 |
|    discipline, as a, | 113–114 |
|    history, in, | 99–100 |
|    marketers before, | 86–87 |
|    modern age, in, | 111–113 |

|  |  |
|---|---:|
| showmanship and, | 92–93 |
| three ages of, | 82–84 |
| marriage and business, | 122 |
| Martin, Thomas, | 163–164 |
| Matsushita, Konosuke, | 98–99 |
| McCormick, Cyrus Hall, | 94 |
| Medici, The, | 41 |
| Militarism, |  |
|    Carnot, Lazare, | 141–142 |
|    Frederick the Great, | 139–141 |
|    middle ages, in, | 137 |
|    organization and, | 136–142 |
| Moltke, | 199–200 |
| monastic trading, | 36–40, 129–135 |
|    Cistercian order, | 132–135 |
|    Clairvaux, Bernard of, | 133 |
| Mooney, James D, | 145–146 |
| Morgan, J.P., | 167–168 |
| Musashi, Miyamoto, | 190 |
|  |  |
| organizations, |  |
|    administrative approach, | 146–147 |
|    behaviour of, | 115 |
|    biological approach, | 148–150 |
|    psychological approach, | 147–148 |
|    status of, | 116–117 |
| output, crisis of, | 220–222 |
| Owen, Robert, | 244–246 |
|  |  |
| Partnership, | 124 |
| Patterson, John, | 95 |
| personnel management, *See* human resource management | |
| philosophy of learning, | 283–284 |
| piecework, | 62 |
| Pirrie, William, | 87–88 |

| | |
|---|---|
| Political science, | 70 |
| price, | |
|    regulation and value, | 102–105 |
|    single-pricing, | 104–105 |
| process innovation, | 281–282 |
| products, | |
|    innovation, | 277–281 |
|    specialization and quality, | 100–101 |
| profit sharing, | 61–62, 236–239 |
| promotion, *See* advertising and publicity | |
| Prussian Army, | |
|    success of, | 50–52 |
| psychology, | 69, 111–1112 |
| pyramid power, | 27–30 |
| quality, | 100–102 |
| re-engineering, | 74–75 |
| risk and reward, | 268–275 |
|    entrepreneurship, | 272–275 |
| rootlessness, | 20 |
| Samurai, | 42–43 |
| Sanji, Muto, | 231 |
| scientific management, | 60–66 |
|    disadvantages of, | 72–73 |
|    efficiency versus, | 67 |
|    Japan, in, | 69 |
|    labour and, | 222–226 |
| scientific marketing, | 112–113 |
| selling concept, | 79 |
| Shogun, | 191 |
| Simonsen, Roberto, | 72 |
| social justice, concern for, | 226–228 |
| social responsibility, | 58–59 |

| | |
|---|---:|
| societal marketing, | 79–80 |
| strategy, | |
|    classical world, in, | 182–183 |
|    Eastern approaches, | 184–191 |
|    strategic principles reviewed, | 201 |
|       enemy, knowledge of the, | 204–205 |
|       environment, knowledge of the, | 204 |
|       flexibility, | 206 |
|       focus and purpose, | 201 |
|       leadership, | 201–202 |
|       preparation, | 205 |
|       requisite organization, | 202 |
|       resources, deployment of, | 203 |
|       self-knowledge, | 203–204 |
|       speed and surprise, | 207–208 |
|       stratagem and deception, | 207 |
|       virtue, | 205–206 |
|       will, imposition of, | 206–207 |
|    strategic thinking, late arrival of, | 179–182 |
| Sunlight, | 97–98 |
| Sunzi, | 186–187 |
| Takatoshi, Mitsui, | 104 |
| Taylor, Frederick Winslow, | 63–64 |
|    system, of, | 63–65 |
| Teiici, Sakuma, | 212–213 |
| time and resources, | 17 |
| Toichiro, Araki | 71 |
| tradition, | 6 |
| Tucker, Josiah, | 216–217 |
| Urwick, Lyndall Fownes, | 59 |
| Von Bulow, Heinrich, | 195 |

| | |
|---|---|
| Walter, Hubert, | 129 |
| Weber, Max, | 215–216 |
| wheel, re-invention of, | 18–19 |
| Willys, John North, | 96 |

# More power to your
# [ business-mind ]

Even at the end there's more we can learn. More that *we* can learn from your experience of this book, and more ways to add to *your* learning experience.

For who to read, what to know and where to go in the world of business, visit us at **business-minds.com**.

Here you can find out more about the people and ideas that can make you and your business more innovative and productive. Each month our e-newsletter, *Business-minds Express*, delivers an infusion of thought leadership, guru interviews, new business practice and reviews of key business resources directly to you. Subscribe for free at

- **www.business-minds.com/goto/newsletters**

Here you can also connect with ways of putting these ideas to work. Spreading knowledge is a great way to improve performance and enhance business relationships. If you found this book useful, then so might your colleagues or customers. If you would like to explore corporate purchases or custom editions personalised with your brand or message, then just get in touch at

- **www.business-minds.com/corporatesales**

We're also keen to learn from your experience of our business books – so tell us what you think of this book and what's on *your* business mind with an online reader report at business-minds.com. Together with our authors, we'd like to hear more from you and explore new ways to help make these ideas work at

- **www.business-minds.com/goto/feedback**

[ www.business-minds.com
www.financialminds.com ]